CHALLENGE

Upper Intermediate Students' Book

SIMON HAINES and SIMON BREWSTER

CONTENTS

CONTENTS

◆ What do these photos and illustrations suggest to you? How usual or unusual are these situations in your country?

Compare ideas with a partner.

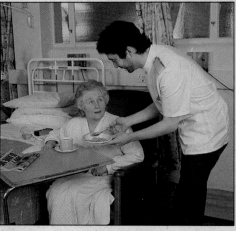

◆ What sort of work do you do, or would you like to do? What is the most interesting thing about this work?

◆ Now ask other students questions about their ideal jobs. What sort of jobs seem to be the most popular?

◆ In your country, are any of these jobs more commonly associated with either men or women?

> vet • sports commentator • chef • fashion designer • secretary
> pilot • gardener • nursery school teacher • porter

Men, Women and Society

1 Reading

As you read these texts, match them with the appropriate photographs opposite.

1

Mark Styles has a very unusual job – a very unusual job for a man, that is: he is secretary to the Accounts Director of Randolph Advertising Ltd.

Mark feels that the prejudice against women in many male-dominated fields is reversed in his case. 'People often say that women in industry have to work twice as hard as the men to prove that they're good enough. Well, that's exactly the same for me, though it rarely causes me any problems. The sound of a male secretary on the phone still causes some confusion, and occasionally people are shocked, but I like my job and I do it well. It was a bit difficult at first, but now I'm really enjoying the work. Anyway, things are changing these days; men are doing many jobs that were previously done only by women, and vice versa.'

Mark took a secretarial course at college and did very well in his exams. He now finds that people are usually very impressed with his abilities. His boss at Randolph – a woman, by the way – says that although Mark is their first male secretary, they wouldn't hesitate to employ another man as a secretary now.

2

Alana MacFarlane is a 20-year-old from San Rafael, California. She's one of our first women telephone installers. She won't be the last. We want more men and women to do what they want to do, and what they do best.

Women like her are moving into new areas of work. For example, Alana likes working outdoors. 'I don't go for office routine,' she said, 'but as a telephone installer, I get plenty of variety and a good chance to move around. And I always get a kick out of working 20 feet up in the air.'

3

Hunting is no more natural to men than housework is to women. In one study of 224 traditional cultures there were 13 where women hunted, and 60 where they fished. House-building was an exclusively female occupation in 36 cultures, while there were five where men did all the cooking, and 38 where cooking was routinely shared. In parts of Indonesia and Zaire the mother almost never takes care of infant children: it is the father who usually has to look after them.

4

According to studies in the US and UK, it was found that in the 1920s women in the US spent an average of 60 hours a week doing housework. By the 1970s housework was taking up even more time: an average of 70 hours a week. In 1925, when most clothes were washed by hand, women spent 5.5 hours a week doing the laundry. After the invention of the washing-machine, the time had gone up to 6.25 hours. By 1982, 80 per cent of UK households owned a washing-machine and 95 per cent had a vacuum-cleaner, but even so, women are doing more housework than ever nowadays. This is because families change their clothes more often and expect a cleaner house and a more varied diet – and because today's mother does not often get any help from the rest of the household.

● Reading for detail

1 Match these summaries with the correct texts:

   a Women can do physical jobs as well as men can.
   b Women still spend a lot of time on housework.
   c In many societies it is women who provide the food.
   d Secretaries don't have to be female.

2 Answer these questions:

   a What evidence is there that Mark Styles is a successful secretary? (*Text 1*)
   b Why did Alana choose her job? (2)
   c In how many cultures is all the cooking done by men? (3)
   d What is interesting about mothers' roles in parts of Indonesia and Zaire? (3)
   e In the US in the 1970s how many hours a week did women spend on housework? (4)
   f In 1982 what percentage of homes in Britain had a washing-machine? (4)
   g Why are women doing more housework than ever nowadays? (4)

2 Vocabulary

Match these words and phrases from the texts with their meanings:

1	prejudice (*Text 1*)	a	normally
2	prove (*1*)	b	use, fill
3	go for (*2*)	c	at the present time
4	get a kick out of (*2*)	d	show, demonstrate
5	culture (*3*)	e	unreasonable dislike of or preference for something
6	routinely (*3*)		
7	take up (*4*)	f	feel a thrill
8	household (*4*)	g	be attracted to
9	laundry (*4*)	h	the washing of clothes, towels, etc.
10	nowadays (*4*)	i	society or civilisation
		j	group of people living in a home

3 Talking about the present (1)
(Language review A1, page 12)

Read these Present Simple sentences from the texts in Exercise 1:

1 *I like my job and I do it well. (Text 1)*
2 *I always get a kick out of working 20 feet up in the air. (2)*
3 *Alana likes working outdoors. (2)*
4 *Today's mother does not often get any help from the rest of the household. (4)*

Match them with one of these uses:

a a regular action or habit
b something which is true at the present time

Now find more examples of these two uses of the Present Simple in the texts.

4 Frequency adverbs
(Language review A2, page 12)

● In some sentences in Exercise 3, the frequency adverbs *always* and *often* are used. Look through the texts in Exercise 1 again and make a list of all the frequency adverbs used. Add any more you know to your list, and then put them into order of frequency:

always —————————————————————— **never**
100%   0%

● Frequency adverbs can go in several different positions in sentences.

Look at the examples in the texts and answer these questions:

1 What is the most common position for frequency adverbs?
2 Where does the frequency adverb go in sentences with the verb *to be*?
3 What other positions do frequency adverbs appear in?

5 Practice

Add frequency adverbs to these sentences to make them true statements about your country. Use negatives if necessary.

EXAMPLE:

Married women have jobs.
*In Britain married women **often** have jobs.*

1 Men are secretaries or nurses.
2 Women do the cooking and housework.
3 Families have a lot of children.
4 People get married very young.
5 Girls and women go to bars and pubs on their own.
6 Men have a better education than women.
7 Young people live with their parents till they get married.
8 Men earn less than women.

6 Talking about the present (2)
(Language review A3, page 12)

Read these Present Continuous sentences from the texts in Exercise 1:

1 *It was difficult at first, but now I'm really enjoying the work. (Text 1)*
2 *Things are changing these days. (1)*
3 *Men are doing many jobs that were previously done only by women. (1)*
4 *Women like her (Alana) are moving into new areas of work. (2)*
5 *Women are doing more housework than ever nowadays. (4)*

Match them with one of these uses:

a a temporary activity which is happening around the time of speaking
b a present trend

7 Discussion

Work in small groups.

Think about how these aspects of life are currently changing in your country:

> marriage • education
> bringing up children • travel
> jobs and work • leisure time
> home life / housework

EXAMPLE:

health *People are eating healthier food.*

These photographs of life in Britain in the 1940s and the 1990s may give you some ideas.

Compare ideas in pairs or groups.

8 Writing

You are going to write about the changes that are currently taking place in your country. Plan your composition like this:

- Make notes about three of the aspects of life you talked about in Exercise 7.

- These are going to be the subjects of the three main paragraphs of your composition, so decide on their order of importance.

- Start your composition like this:

  There have been a lot of changes in my country over the last fifty years, and things are still changing very fast, especially in the areas of ...

- The rest of your composition should follow this plan:

  Paragraph 2: subject 1
  Paragraph 3: subject 2
  Paragraph 4: subject 3
  Paragraph 5: conclusion – Give your own opinion of these changes.

9 Listening 🔲

You are going to listen to someone talking about being a 'househusband'.

What household jobs do you think he will mention? Write a list.

Now listen to the recording and tick the jobs on your list that he mentions.

● **Understanding**

Listen to the recording again. Say whether these statements are true or false. Correct the false statements.

1 The speaker's wife doesn't enjoy housework.	T/F
2 He taught his wife how to cook.	T/F
3 She occasionally cooks a meal at weekends.	T/F
4 He thinks many men would like to stay at home.	T/F
5 He says his wife would find it difficult to look after the children.	T/F
6 He is always very calm with the children.	T/F

10 Talking about the present (3)
(Language review A4, page 12)

In the recording the 'househusband' says:

I'm always losing my temper with the kids.

How do you think this is different in meaning from this sentence?

I always lose my temper with the kids.

Compare ideas with a partner.

Now think about your own behaviour and then finish this sentence in five different ways:

I'm always ...

S*tage two*

Children and Families

1 Pre-listening

Do you think it is better to be the youngest or the eldest child in a family?

Compare ideas with a partner.

2 Listening 🔲

You are going to hear three sisters talking about growing up together. As you listen, identify the girls in the photographs.

Do you think Emma, Sara and Alison are happy about their particular positions in the family?

○ **Listening for detail**

Listen to the recording again and make a note of the characteristics of the three sisters. Notice that they talk about each other as well as themselves. The first few have been done for you.

Name	Characteristics
Emma:	*quiet, shy*
Sara:	*responsible*
Alison:	*outgoing*

3 Vocabulary

● Look at these extracts from the recording and choose the best meaning for each of the phrases in italics:

1 My sisters used to *boss me around.* a show me how to do things b give me orders c shout at me

2 She's *got a mind of her own.* a intelligent b unusual c independent

3 I always *hung around with* friends of my own age. a worked with b spent time with c lived near

4 *I'm more outgoing* than my younger sister. a I go out more b I'm more extrovert c I'm more energetic

5 We've always had our *ups and downs.* a enjoyable moments b good and bad times c lots of changes

6 They used to have a lot of *rows.* a arguments b chats c discussions

● **Idioms**
(Language review B1, page 13)

In the recording Sara says that Alison is:

… tied to my mother's apron strings.

This means that Alison is not very independent, she is controlled by her mother.

Here are some more idioms to do with family relationships. Use the context of each sentence to work out their meanings.

1 He's *the black sheep of the family.* He decided to be a rock singer while the rest of us became lawyers.
2 Both Nigel and his brother have fair hair – *it runs in the family.*
3 Maggie is *the apple of her father's eye:* he won't hear anything negative about her.
4 Chris is *a real chip off the old block.* He's as stubborn as his father.

Compare ideas with a partner.

4 Pronunciation 🔊

The stresses in English sentences are on words which give new or important information.

Listen to the recording and repeat these five sentences:

1 *Everyone says I'm quiet and shy.*
2 *I'm sure she'll do well at university.*
3 *Her flight leaves on Friday actually.*
4 *They used to have a lot of rows.*
5 *Term starts in October and I know I'll enjoy being independent.*

Listen again and mark the stresses.

EXAMPLE:

■   ■   ■
Everyone says I'm quiet and shy.

---

5 Talking about the future
(Language review A5, page 13)

● Look at these sentences from the recording and match them with one of these uses:

> a prediction • an arrangement • an intention • a timetable

Write **P**, **A**, **I** or **T** in the boxes.

1 *I'm not going to make the same mistakes (as my sisters).* ☐
2 *She's starting a course at university this autumn.* ☐
3 *I'm sure I won't mind being on my own.* ☐
4 *I'm sure she'll do well at university.* ☐
5 *Her flight leaves on Friday.* ☐
6 *I know she'll get really good results at school.* ☐
7 *I'm certainly not going to get married for some time.* ☐
8 *I don't think I'll settle down as quickly as she has.* ☐
9 *Term starts in October.* ☐
10 *I know I'll enjoy being independent.* ☐

Which form of the future expresses each of the four uses?

Compare answers with a partner.

● Now look at these two sentences from the recording. Which sentence expresses **a prediction** and which expresses **an intention**?

1 *I'll definitely have more than one child.*
2 *I'm going to miss them when I'm away, I'm sure.*

Compare ideas with a partner.

---

6 Personalised practice

● Write five answers to each of these questions. In each set of five answers, four should be true and one should be false.

> What are your arrangements for the next few weeks?

> What do you intend to do over the next six months?

> Can you predict some of the things that will happen in the next year of your life?

● Now work in pairs. Ask and answer questions about each other's arrangements, intentions and predictions.

Try to guess your partner's false answers.

7 Writing

You are going to write a letter to an ex-classmate who recently left your school and went to live in another country.

Tell your ex-classmate about your future using the different forms from Exercise 5.

EXAMPLES:

I'm starting an English course in London next spring.

Term starts in June.

I think I'll have a great time.

I'm going to travel all round Britain.

8 Reading

What do you think are the advantages and disadvantages of being an only child? Compare ideas in groups of three or four and make lists.

Now read what different people have said about being only children. How many of the points you discussed are mentioned?

What other advantages and disadvantages are mentioned? Add these to your lists.

Only Children

A 'I did invent playmates for myself. I invented games for my toy soldiers too. I was never very spoilt, but the attention was all mine.'

Frederick Forsyth (novelist)

B 'I arrived when my mother was already forty and consequently I was the apple of her eye. I think I was probably rather spoilt.'

Leslie Crowther (television presenter)

C 'It's tough being an only child. You tend to be under the illusion the world revolves around you. It might have been nice to have a sister or brother to take the attention away from me. I used to be an isolated kid, just writing poetry and imagining things a lot.'

Annie Lennox (pop singer)

D 'It's an advantage. You get undivided attention from your mother. Being alone made me closer to animals, but it also made me quite demanding. But I want lots of children myself.'

Matthew Rice (designer)

E 'I was a clever, pompous, precocious girl. But if you don't have sisters or brothers, you need friends, and so I tried hard to make them. I am good at making them still.'

Andrea Newman (novelist)

F 'I felt lucky, and my friends were jealous because of my single state, particularly because I didn't have to share a bedroom. I think as a child I was materially spoilt. The greatest luxury for me now is my own company.'

Julie Burchill (journalist and novelist)

G 'You get the best of both worlds. There was a children's gang in the village so I was never lonely, but then I returned to my own room and my own books. At home I never had to share.'

Terry Pratchitt (sci-fi author)

H 'It may be true that an only child is spoilt, but, believe me, there are occasions on which you wish there was a brother or sister to share problems. You tend to become self-centred, which is the outward form of self-sufficiency. You spend more time alone, and in the company of adults.'

Peter Ustinov (actor, dramatist, writer)

I 'I enjoyed my isolation. During my childhood I had an imaginary friend called Fisher who travelled a lot. Whenever I went out I imagined I was retracing his footsteps.'

Patrick Garland (film and TV director)

● Understanding

Which two people made the same points about these subjects?

1 inventing characters
2 being particularly close to a parent
3 not having to share things
4 needing a brother or sister
5 being given too many things
6 having other children to play with

9 Self-

(Language review B2, page 13)

In Text H in Exercise 8, Peter Ustinov says:

You tend to become **self-centred**.

What does *self-centred* mean? Can you rephrase the sentence without changing its meaning?

Guess the meanings of these *self-* adjectives:

self-confident
self-conscious
self-employed
self-satisfied
self-sufficient

Compare ideas with a partner, and then look each word up in a dictionary to check your guesses.

Finally, write sentences using each *self-* word.

10 Discussion

Work in small groups.

Discuss these questions, using your own experience and ideas:

1 How can parents make sure that:

a) they do not spoil only children?
b) only children do not feel lonely?

2 Do children need brothers and sisters? What do you think is the ideal number of children in a family?

Extension

Habits

1 Reading

Read about one family's annoying habits. Make a list of the habits mentioned.

Do (or did) any of the members of your family have these or similar habits?

One thing I really dislike is having to share a room with my older sister, Paula. She doesn't snore or have any unpleasant habits like that, it's just the lack of space and, you know, not having much privacy. Another thing about being in a large family is the problem of the bathroom — someone always seems to get in there first. It's the same with the phone. Sam spends hours chatting to his friends, especially Jane, his current girlfriend. Oh, yes, and of course I have to wear Paula's old clothes, which is a real drag. And Paula bosses me around — she's always telling me what to do. It's hard being the youngest in the family.

2 Discussion

Look at this list of habits. Add any other personal habits that you find annoying in other people, and then put them in order, starting with the most annoying.

- spending hours in the bathroom • talking for hours on the telephone
- leaving the top off the toothpaste • always getting to places late
- smoking without asking other people's permission • snoring
- drumming their fingers on the table • chewing gum
- borrowing things and not giving them back • nail-biting

Compare ideas in groups. Do you agree on which are the two most annoying habits?

What habits do you have that other people find annoying?

3 Writing

Write a paragraph describing the good and annoying habits of your friends or of people in your family. Use the text in Exercise 1 as a model.

Language review

A Grammar and Use

Some of the grammar points in the first few units of Challenge Upper Intermediate will be familiar to you. They are included here as revision.

I The Present Simple

The Present Simple is used to talk about:

1 a regular action or habit:

Families change their clothes more often.

2 something which is true at the present time:

I like my job and I do it well.

3 facts or things that are always true:

The sun rises in the east.

2 Frequency adverbs

● **Meaning**

Frequency adverbs tell us how often something happens.

Here is a list of the commonest adverbs in order of frequency:

100% *always*
      almost always / nearly always
      usually / normally / regularly / generally
      often / frequently
      sometimes / occasionally
      almost never / hardly ever / scarcely ever /rarely /
      seldom
0%   *never*

● **Position**

1 Before the main verb:

People often say that women have to work twice as hard as men.

2 After the verb *to be*:

People are usually very impressed with his abilities.

3 Between the auxiliary verb and the main verb:

I can never find my keys when I need them.

4 These adverbs can be used at the beginning of a sentence or clause:

usually, normally, generally, frequently, sometimes, occasionally

Occasionally people are shocked.

5 Most 'positive' frequency adverbs can also come at the end of a sentence:

People are shocked sometimes.

Notes

1 When *often* comes at the end of a sentence, it is usually with *very*:

I don't see you very often.

2 *Rarely* and *seldom* can come at the end of sentences when they are used with *only* and *very*:

People get shocked very rarely.

3 *Always* and *never* are not usually used at the end of sentences.

3 The Present Continuous

The Present Continuous is used to talk about:

1 an action that is happening at the moment of speaking:

Just a minute. I'm talking to someone on the phone.

2 a temporary activity which is happening around the time of speaking:

It was difficult at first, but now I'm really enjoying the work.

3 a present trend:

Women like her are moving into new areas of work.

4 continually repeated actions (See Section 4):

He's always complaining about his job.

4 Talking about habits: Present Simple or Present Continuous?

Both the Present Simple and the Present Continuous can be used to talk about habits or repeated actions.

The Present Simple emphasises the regularity of an activity:

I lose my temper with the kids.

The Present Continuous with *always* emphasises the fact that the action is continually repeated:

I'm always losing my temper with the kids.

In the third person, this use of the Present Continuous with *always* is used to express annoyance or a complaint:

> *My older sister is always telling me what to do.*

5 Talking about the future

● The *will* future is used:

1 to talk about things that (you think) are certain to happen:

> *It's my birthday next week. I'll be seventeen.*

2 to express predictions or expectations based on your opinions:

> *I know she'll get really good results at school.*

3 to talk about something decided on at the moment of speaking:

> *I think I'll phone my sister.*

4 to express strong intentions:

> *I'll definitely have more than one child.*

● The *going to* future is used:

1 to talk about intentions and plans:

> *I'm not going to make the same mistakes as my sister.*

2 to make predictions about the immediate future, or when there is present evidence that a prediction will come true:

> *I'm going to miss my sisters when I'm away, I'm sure.*

● The Present Continuous is used to talk about fixed future arrangements:

> *She's starting a course at university this autumn.*

● The Present Simple is used to refer to timetabled events:

> *Her flight leaves on Friday.*

B Vocabulary

1 Idioms

The following idioms are commonly used to describe relationships between people:

*They **get on like a house on fire**.*
= like each other's company a lot

*I forgot my mother's birthday, so I'm not **in her good books** at the moment.* = in favour

*There's **no love lost** between the two of us.*
= we don't like each other at all

*We used to be close, but we're **poles apart** now.*
= very different in opinions and attitudes

*She can **twist him around her little finger**.*
= has him in her power

*Their relationship seems to be **on the rocks**.*
= in danger of breaking up

*They don't **see eye-to-eye** on anything.* = agree

*When I was younger, my brother and I were always **at each other's throats**.* = arguing

*He's the manager's **blue-eyed boy** – I'm sure he'll be promoted soon.* = favourite

2 Expressions with *self-*

● *Self-* can be used to form compound adjectives:

> *Only children can sometimes be very **self-centred**.*
> (concerned with personal wants and needs)

> *He's a **self-made** millionaire.*
> (successful through personal efforts)

> *Mr Smith is really **self-opinionated**.*
> (believing your own opinions are the only right ones)

> *He's a **self-taught** pianist.*
> (having learnt something by yourself, not by formal teaching)

● *Self-* can also be used to form compound nouns:

> *He was so upset that he lost his **self-control** and started shouting.*
> (ability to control feelings and emotions)

> *Mixing with other people at an early age helps children to develop **self-confidence**.*
> (feeling sure of your own abilities or value)

> *I shot him in **self-defence**. He had a knife in his hand.*
> (something you do to defend yourself from attack)

> *Van Gogh painted several fascinating **self-portraits**.*
> (drawing or picture you do of yourself)

UNIT 2

first impressions

◆ Look at the photographs and discuss with a partner why the English language is important in these situations.

◆ Read these facts about English and try to guess the correct number to fill the gaps. Compare answers with a partner.

- Of all the world's ___(1)___ languages, English is the richest in vocabulary.
  1 a 2700   b 1000   c 500

- The Oxford English Dictionary lists about ___(2)___ words.
  2 a 1,000,000   b 750,000   c 500,000

- About ___(3)___ million people speak English as a first language – that is about ___(4)___ of the world's population.
  3 a 500   b 350   c 100
  4 a ⅙   b ⅛   c ⅒

- ___(5)___ of the world's mail, faxes and cables are in English, and more than ___(6)___ of the world's technical and scientific periodicals.
  5 a ½   b ⅔   c ⅒
  6 a ½   b ⅓   c ¼

- English is the medium for ___(7)___ per cent of the information stored in the world's computers.
  7 a 95   b 80   c 65

◆ Talking points
Work in pairs or small groups.

How did you first come into contact with English?

Where do you use your English now?

In what situations do you think you'll need to use English in the future?

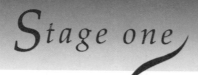
The Story of English

1 Pre-reading
Work in pairs.

Look at the map and the photograph. What historical event is being illustrated?

• Can you think of any reasons why this event might have occurred?

• Think of the effects this had on the United States.

• Which countries or languages do you think these American English words came from?

> ranch • delicatessen
> pizza • tomahawk

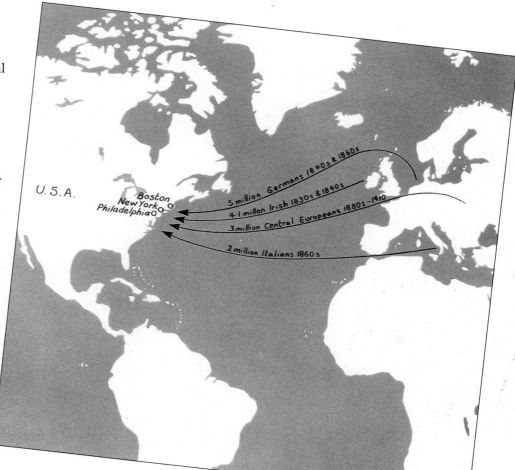

U.S.A.

Boston
New York
Philadelphia

5 million Germans 1840s & 1860s

4·1 million Irish 1830s & 1840s

3 million Central Europeans 1880s - 1910

2 million Italians 1860s

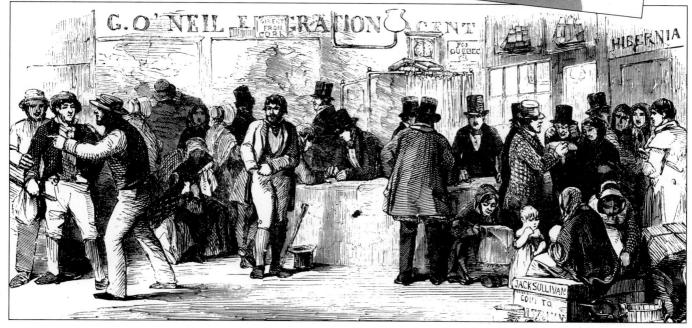

G. O'NEIL EMIGRATION AGENT

DIRECT FROM CORK

FOR QUEBEC

HIBERNIA

JACK SULLIVAN

2 Reading

Read the text quickly and check your answers to the questions in Exercise 1.

THE 'HUDDLED MASSES'

1 In the 19th century the port of New York became the entry point for one of the greatest migrations in history. Over fifteen million immigrants arrived in the United States during this period.

2 In 1790 a large number of Irish were already living in the US (perhaps as many as 400,000) but during the course of the 19th century this number increased dramatically as a total of 4.1 million Irish arrived. They were fleeing from the potato famine of 1848 and other catastrophes which made life impossible in their native Ireland. As they already spoke English it is difficult to analyse the effect of this group on American English.

3 The other large group of immigrants was the Germans. Many were escaping from the 1848 revolutions in Europe. They established themselves quickly: by 1860 there were twenty-eight daily German newspapers in fifteen cities. It is probably for this reason – the formation of a large, successful, literate culture – that American English acquired German words like *delicatessen* and *kindergarten*.

4 The Italians, who followed the Germans, were of a different social class and status. They emigrated mainly because of the poverty in southern Italy. Between 1865 and 1920, as the age of the steamship brought cheap travel to more and more Europeans, over two million Italians came to the US. Before long, there were so many of them living in the north-east that every major city had its 'Little Italy'. The influence of Italian was mainly found in food words like *pizza, spaghetti, espresso, pasta, broccoli,* etc.

5 While the Italians were settling in cities like Chicago, Philadelphia and New York, the final wave of immigration started. The immigrants were the three million East and Central European Jews who were fleeing from the persecutions of the 1880s.

6 But even before the 19th century, words from other languages had become part of American English. The first English settlers, who arrived in the early 17th century, had to communicate with the American Indians. As a result of this contact, Indian words like *wigwam, moose, moccasin, tomahawk* and *papoose* were quickly adopted. Contact between cowboys in the west and Spanish speakers brought a number of new words into American English: *rodeo, stampede, lasso, mustang, ranch* and *bronco*.

7 This large-scale immigration into the US is one of the reasons for many of the differences between American and British English: *elevator* (lift), *garbage* (rubbish), *mail* (post), *pants* (trousers), *sidewalk* (pavement), *vacation* (holiday) and *zero* (nought).

● Understanding

Complete the sentence beginnings in column A with the appropriate endings in column B. Some of the beginnings have more than one correct ending.

A
1 Over 15 million immigrants…
2 A large number of Irish…
3 The German immigrants…
4 The immigrants from Italy…
5 The Jews from East and Central Europe…
6 The American Indians…
7 The Irish immigrants…

B
a were escaping from revolutions.
b gave some of the earliest foreign words to American English.
c arrived in the USA during the 19th century.
d were fleeing from poverty.
e became part of US business life.
f were fleeing from persecution.
g contributed a lot of 'food' words.
h were living in the US at the end of the 18th century.
i were fleeing from the potato famine.

3 Vocabulary

Match these words from the text with their correct meanings:

1 migration (*Para. 1*)
2 to flee (2)
3 catastrophe (2)
4 to analyse (2)
5 to establish yourself (3)
6 literate (3)
7 to acquire (3)
8 major (4)

a to get, obtain
b able to read and write
c important
d disaster
e movement of people into or out of a country
f to settle
g to run away from, escape
h to study and understand

4 American English
(Language review BI, page 23)

● **Spelling**

The following words are written using American English spelling. Can you rewrite them using British English spelling?

    1 color   2 center   3 tire (of a car)
    4 traveler   5 offense

● **Vocabulary**

Do you know the British English equivalents of these words?

    1 apartment   2 drugstore   3 freeway
    4 garbage-can   5 subway train

5 Pronunciation

- When you listen to the recording, you will hear five pairs of sentences.

Decide in each case which sentence of the pair has American English pronunciation and which one has British English pronunciation. Put A (American) or B (British) in the appropriate box.

	1	2
a		
b		
c		
d		
e		

Compare answers with a partner.

- Listen again and make a note of the main differences between the American and the British pronunciation.

---

6 Talking about the past (1)
(Language review AI and A2, page 22)

● Read these sentences from the text in Exercise 2:

1 *Over 15 million immigrants arrived in the United States during the 19th century.* A
2 *In 1790 a large number of Irish were already living in the US.* D
3 *The Irish were fleeing from the potato famine of 1848.* D
4 *They already spoke English.* A
5 *Many Germans were escaping from the 1848 revolutions.* D
6 *They established themselves quickly in America.* A
7 *The Italians followed the Germans.* A
8 *Between 1865 and 1920 over 2 million Italians came to the US.* A

● Which sentences are concerned with the duration of events or actions?

Which verb tense is used in these sentences?

● Which sentences describe:

    a a situation or state that was true in the past? 4
    b a completed past action? 1
    c a habit or repeated past action? 8
    d a situation existing at a particular point of time in the past? 2
    e an action in progress at a particular point of time in the past? 3

Compare ideas with a partner.

7 Practice

Use the verbs below to fill the gaps. Use either the Past Simple or the Past Continuous.

> **be   change   continue   influence   enter   have
>   speak (×2)   contribute (×2)**

1 The Irish immigrants (not) _contribute_ to the language very much because they already _spoke_ English.
2 By the early 20th century the German population in the US _had_ a positive effect on American business.
3 Many Germans in the US _changed_ their names after the War.
4 By the late 19th century the German language _influenced_ the American language in many ways. However, the Italian language _contributed_ only food words.
5 Between 1880 and 1910 the Jews from East and Central Europe _entered_ the US at a rate of up to 15,000 a day.
6 By the early 20th century, the children of the immigrants _were_ almost bilingual: they _spoke_ English at school but _continued_ to speak their own language at home.

8 Listening

Work in pairs

● Listen to someone describing their arrival in a foreign country.

Who interrupted the speaker's conversation with one of the staff at the tourist information desk?

● Now interview your partner to find out about an occasion when they arrived in a strange place. (The strange place needn't be a foreign country.) Find out answers to these questions:

> Where? • When? • Who with?
> What did your partner do?
> What was happening when they arrived?
> What happened after they arrived?
> How did they feel?

Make written notes about your partner's arrival.

9 Writing

You are going to write about your partner's arrival, but before you do, check with your partner that the notes you wrote in Exercise 8 are correct. Don't forget to include:

1 Background information: scene setting
2 The main events or storyline: what your partner and other people did
3 Your partner's feelings

Stage two

Learning a Language

1 Pre-listening

What do you think are the most important aspects of learning a foreign language? Put these seven skills or abilities into order of importance.

- learning new vocabulary
- translating into your language
- being able to use the language in the country where it is spoken
- listening
- writing essays
- reading
- understanding the grammar system

Compare ideas in groups.

2 Listening

Listen to two people talking about their experiences of learning a foreign language. Which of the skills in Exercise 1 are mentioned by the speakers?

● **Listening for detail**

Each of the sentences below contains a factual error. Listen to the speakers again and correct the sentences.

1 The man learnt to speak French at school.
2 In his school all aspects of the language were studied.
3 The exams consisted of grammar, translation and listening.
4 The first time he went to France he communicated very well.
5 The girl didn't study languages at school.
6 She did an Italian course with Italian teachers in England.
7 She didn't get much practice when she was in Italy.
8 The girl wanted some soap in the chemist's.
9 She thinks it's bad to make mistakes when you use a language.

3 Talking points

Work in pairs or small groups.

1 Have you ever had an amusing experience when you were trying to communicate in a foreign language?

2 Have you ever had an amusing experience when a foreigner was trying to use your language?

3 What do foreigners find difficult to understand or learn in your language?

4 Pre-reading

What do you think are the advantages and disadvantages, for a child, of being brought up in a bilingual family?

Compare ideas with a partner and make lists.

5 Reading

Now read the text and check how many of your points are mentioned.

IT'S TUESDAY SUPPERTIME, SO IT MUST BE SWEDISH.

1 When Edith Harding married an Englishman, she was perfectly prepared to leave her native France behind. But she drew the line at losing her mother tongue. 'I felt this was part of my culture and identity. When we had the children, I didn't want them just to speak English, but French as well. After all, being fluent in two languages will always help them.'

2 Edith and her husband Ted decided it was sensible to speak French at home and English elsewhere. This has been working quite well, as the children have turned out to be completely bilingual.

3 Most experts now agree it is more natural for parents of different nationalities each to speak their native language to the children. However, it is difficult to achieve a balance. Steve, who is English, has been married to Concepcion, a Chilean, for ten years.

4 'We decided from the start each to use our own language', says Steve, 'but we've been living in Chile since 1988 and the kids use Spanish nearly all the time. They've been going to a bilingual school, but even there they use Spanish with the other children. At the moment they can read in English and understand nearly everything I say but they usually answer me in Spanish, unless I insist on English. Their English really picks up only when we go to England on holiday and they're with their grandparents, who don't speak any Spanish at all.'

5 Concepcion adds, 'This suits us as we tend to mix languages anyway, switching from one to the other. The only rule is that when we have an argument we both use our own language!'

6 The Rileys are a triangular household: English father, Swedish mother, and living in France, with their three children switching between French, English and Swedish. The children obviously spend a lot of time with native speakers of French but are happy with all three languages. For parents worried that bringing up the children bilingually might be harmful, the Rileys' advice is clear: *Don't worry.* Children adapt to all sorts of arrangements – one language at home, another outside, a different language with each parent, a weekday language and a Sunday one.

7 Some become receptive bilinguals, understanding but not speaking the second language. One toddler, Patrick, even briefly developed a sex-based theory of language – you spoke English with men and French with women – a view which collapsed when he heard his grandfather speaking French.

● **Understanding**

Complete the sentence beginnings in column A with the appropriate endings in column B.

A

1 Edith Harding didn't mind leaving France but …
2 Edith and her husband spoke French …
3 Experts now think it's better if …
4 Steve's children speak better Spanish than English …
5 Steve's children understand English but …
6 From their experience the Rileys think that …
7 Being bilingual doesn't necessarily mean …
8 Patrick believed for some time that …

B

a each parent uses their own language with the children.
b children can adjust to most language situations.
c men and women spoke different languages.
d speaking both languages.
e as they use it most of the time.
f all the time at home.
g was reluctant to lose her language.
h usually speak Spanish.

---

6 Vocabulary

● Discuss the differences in meaning between these pairs of words, and then write sentences to illustrate their meanings correctly. (The first word of each pair is from the text in Exercise 5.)

EXAMPLE: **bring / take**

bring *Come and see me this evening. **Bring** your sister with you.*

take *Shall I **take** you to the station to catch your train?*

1 to lose / to miss
2 sensible / sensitive
3 at the moment / actually
4 to suit / to fit
5 argument / discussion
6 to bring up / to educate

● **Phrasal verbs with *turn***
(Language review B2, page 23)

*The children have **turned out** to be completely bilingual.*
= The children have **become** completely bilingual.

Work out the meanings of the *turn* verbs in these sentences. Then rewrite the sentences replacing the verbs.

1 John's friends suddenly stopped talking to him. He couldn't understand why they had *turned against* him.
2 Whenever she couldn't think of what to do, she *turned to* her mother for advice.
3 I thought I'd lost my address book, but eventually it *turned up* in my coat pocket.
4 She's very talented – she can *turn her hand to* anything.
5 Can you believe it? His own father *turned* him *over* to the police!

7 Talking about the past (2)
(Language review A3, page 22)

● Read these sentences from the recording in Exercise 2 and the text in Exercise 5:

1 *I learnt French at school.*
2 *I've never been much good at languages.*
3 *I bought a lot of language books.*
4 *This (arrangement) has been working quite well.*
5 *Steve has been married to Concepcion for ten years.*
6 *We've been living in Chile since 1988.*
7 *The children have been going to a bilingual school.*

● Which sentences describe:

a an event or action which happened in the past and is now finished?
b a situation or an action which started in the past and is still continuing (or is still true) in the present?

● Which two expressions are used in the sentences to say how long a situation or an action has lasted?

● What are the differences in meaning between these pairs of sentences?

a 1 I learnt French for three years.
  2 I've been learning French for three years.

b 1 Steve was married to Concepcion for ten years.
  2 Steve has been married to Concepcion for ten years.

c 1 We've lived in Chile.
  2 We've lived in Chile for three years.

d 1 I've worked hard (all my life).
  2 I've been working hard (all week).

Compare ideas with a partner.

8 Practice

Some of these sentences contain grammatical errors. Find the errors, say what is wrong and why, then correct the sentence.

1 I've learnt two languages when I was at school.
2 She's been studying Russian since three years.
3 We lived in this country for ten years and we still like living here.
4 I've never been able to understand people who don't want to learn a foreign language.
5 I've started studying Spanish three weeks ago.
6 I learnt German for three years ago.

9 Class survey

Think about your own experience of learning languages. Make notes under these headings:

- Languages you know (speak), and how well you know (speak) them
- When you started learning
- How long you have been learning
- Where you learnt, and teaching methods
- Main difficulties in learning another language
- Experiences of using languages abroad or with native speakers in your country

Now interview other students in your class to find out how common your own experience has been. Ask questions like this:

> What was the first language you studied?
> Have you ever used a language abroad?

10 Writing

A large educational organisation has invited students to write to them about their language learning experiences. Use your notes from Exercise 9 to help you write the report.

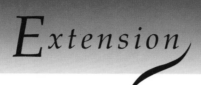

*E*xtension

Word Games

1 The correct meaning

You are going to play a team game which involves guessing the meanings of English idioms. Before you form teams, guess the correct meaning of the idiom *to split hairs*:

Meaning 1: 'If you split hairs, it means that you get very impatient with people who do things slowly.'

Meaning 2: 'To split hairs means always to look neat and tidy.'

Meaning 3: 'To split hairs means to argue about trivial matters or unimportant differences of opinion.'

Now work in groups of six – two teams of three.

In this game, members of the two teams have to try to mislead or trick each other with their meanings. Here are the rules:

1 Team A thinks of or finds an unusual idiom. Then each member prepares a meaning for it which they will read out to Team B. Of course, only one of the meanings is correct – the other two are deliberately misleading. You may need a dictionary to help you.

2 The members of Team A read out their meanings to Team B, each person trying to make their definition sound like the correct one.

3 The members of Team B try to guess which of the three meanings is correct.
If they choose the correct meaning, they get a point.

4 Team B now reads out their meanings, and Team A guesses.

Here are a few more idioms to practise with:

- *to get out of bed the wrong side*
- *to kill two birds with one stone*
- *to put your foot in it*
- *to keep your head above water*

2 Tennis–Elbow–Foot

Play in pairs.

This is a game of word associations, which is played like tennis. Here are the rules:

1 Player A says a word to Player B.

2 Player B says a word which is connected with player A's word.

3 Player A says a word which is connected with player B's word, and so on.

EXAMPLE:

A: *glass*   B: *window*   A: *curtain*   B: *dark*

If one of the players takes too long (more than five seconds) to say a word, or if they say a word which has no connection with the previous word, that player loses a point. You can score like tennis: 15-love, 15-all... 40-30, deuce, advantage, etc.

3 First letters

Play in teams of three.

1 Team A thinks of a subject and writes a list of 10 examples of this subject, like this:

Cold drinks: 1 orange juice 2 milk 3 water 4 lemonade ... etc.

Red things: 1 lipstick 2 roses 3 blood 4 fire-engines ... etc.

2 Team A then tells Team B the subject, and Team B has to guess as many things as they can on Team A's list. Team B gets a point every time they mention something that is on A's list.

3 Team B then tells Team A their subject, and so on.

It is important to set a deadline of 1–2 minutes for the guessing stage of each round.

---

*L*anguage review

A Grammar and Use

1 The Past Simple

● **Form**

Regular Past Simple verbs end in *-ed*. Many important verbs are irregular. (There is a list of irregular verbs on page 173.)

● **Use**

1 completed past actions:

> *I bought a lot of language books.*

2 situations or states that were true in the past:

> *They already spoke English.*

3 habitual or repeated past actions:

> *Over 15 million immigrants arrived in the United States during the 19th century.*

2 The Past Continuous

● **Form**

was / were + -ing form

● **Use**

1 actions or situations which were already in progress at a particular moment in the past, or for a temporary period in the past:

> *It was just getting light when my plane touched down at Rio airport.*
> *The Irish were fleeing from the potato famine.*

2 a longer action which is interrupted by a shorter action:

> *The receptionist was telling me where to find a taxi, when a short man grabbed my suitcase.*
> *While the Italians were settling in cities like Chicago, the final wave of immigration started.*

3 two actions that were in progress simultaneously:

> *While I was waiting for my case, people were rushing here and there.*

3 The Present Perfect Simple and Continuous

● In general, the Present Perfect tenses are used when we want to draw attention to a connection between the past and the present.

This connection is often highlighted in Present Perfect sentences by the inclusion of *since* and *for* phrases. *Since* is followed by a point in time, and *for* is followed by a period of time:

> Steve and Concepcion have been married for ten years.
> We've been living in Chile since 1988.

● **The Present Perfect Simple form**

have/has + past participle

● **Use**

1 past experiences (what you have done in your life up to now):

> I've visited Rio de Janeiro.

2 actions, events or situations that began in the past and are still continuing (or are still true) now:

> I've never been much good at languages.
> Steve has been married to Concepcion for ten years.

3 past events whose results are still noticeable or important in the present:

> He's cut down that lovely tree!
> I've lost my car keys.

● **The Present Perfect Continuous form**

have/has been + past participle

● **Use**

1 to emphasise the duration of actions or events that began in the past and are still continuing (or are still true) now:

> We've been living in Chile since 1988.
> The children have been going to a bilingual school.

2 to emphasise the duration of past actions or events whose results are still noticeable or important in the present:

> The arrangement has been working quite well, as the children are now bilingual.

B Vocabulary

1 American English

● **Spelling**

Here are some points of difference between British and American English:

American English rule	American example	British example
1 The final *-l* in an unstressed syllable is not usually doubled.	traveler quarreling	traveller quarrelling
2 Nouns end in *-og*, not *-ogue*.	dialog catalog	dialogue catalogue
3 Nouns end in *-or*, not *-our*.	color flavor	colour flavour
4 Nouns end in *-ter*, not *-tre*.	center theater	centre theatre
5 Nouns end in *-se*, not *-ce*.	defense license	defence licence

● **Vocabulary**

Here are some examples of differences between British and American English words with the same meaning:

British	American	British	American
autumn	fall	lorry	truck
film	movie	biscuit	cookie
lift	elevator	petrol	gas
main road	highway	shop	store
rubbish	garbage	holiday	vacation
bill	check	pavement	sidewalk
garden	yard	sweets	candy

2 Phrasal verbs with *turn*

Here are some more *turn* verbs in addition to those on page 20. In these examples, the *turn* verb in the first sentence in each pair has a literal meaning. The *turn* verb in the second sentence in each pair has a non-literal meaning.

- 1 *He turned the car around.*
     = faced in the opposite direction
  2 *The property market turned around completely.*
     = showed an opposite trend
- 1 *He turned away in horror at the sight of the accident.*
     = stopped looking at something unpleasant
  2 *We were turned away from the concert as all tickets had been sold.* = refused entry
- 1 *Please turn down the TV. I'm trying to sleep.*
     = make less bright or loud
  2 *The insurance company turned down my claim.*
     = rejected.

first impressions

◆ What do you know about dinosaurs? Write a list of facts you know. Compare lists of facts with one or more partners.

◆ What else would you like to know about dinosaurs? Write a few questions. Now turn to page 156 and read the text.

◆ Were any of your facts confirmed by the text? Were any of your questions answered?

◆ Although there are many theories, no one is quite sure about why dinosaurs became extinct. Which of these explanations for their disappearance do you think is the most probable? Put them into order of probability.

1 A rise in sea level flooded the earth.
2 A meteorite hit the earth and dust from the collision blocked out the sunlight.
3 The dinosaurs ate poisonous plants.
4 Mammals stole the dinosaur eggs.
5 Dinosaurs became bored.
6 Dinosaurs suffered from cancer.

◆ Discuss your ideas with a partner and add ideas of your own to the list.

Stage one

How Did It Happen?

1 Reading

Match three of these headlines with the newspaper stories.

Judge sheds light on cottage phenomenon

SOVIET COUPLE SAW SPACE SHIPWRECK

FOUR MONTHS ON UPTURNED WRECK

Pin-headed aliens invade Russia

1

Experts in New Zealand have called the voyage of the *Rose-Noelle* one of the most remarkable stories ever told of survival at sea. Four men have claimed that they spent 118 days on the hull of their boat after a huge wave had overturned it.

The 41-foot trimaran had left New Zealand for Tonga on 1 June and had capsized in a storm about 125 miles off North Island on 4 June. The boat had then drifted in a semi-circle for 1000 nautical miles, before it hit Great Barrier Island, north of Auckland, on 30 September. The crew said they had survived on the upturned hull by sleeping huddled together in a compartment the size of a double bed. They had found crates of soft drinks and rice floating in the sea, and had rigged up a system to collect rainwater. They had also caught and grilled fish, using wood from the boat.

But doubts remain about the truth of the story. Scepticism began after the first television interview with the men, who did not seem to fit the popular image of castaways. Investigators too were puzzled by a number of details; for example, this was the second shipwreck the craft's owner had survived.

Despite these doubts, there was no proof that the crew had made the story up.

2

A couple who maintain that they left their home in terror because of strange happenings after a power supply cable had been attached to their cottage, have lost their claim for damages against their local Electricity Board.

Mr Joseph Orchard and his wife June claimed that they fled next door after metal objects, including a cooker door and a bath tap, had flown around their cottage. The cottage had also become flooded and the ceiling had fallen down. The couple blamed a phenomenon known as electro-osmosis, resulting from the Electricity Board's cable.

The judge rejected their claim, commenting that, in his opinion, a member of the Orchard family must have caused the events. The phenomenon could not be blamed on the Electricity Board, said the judge, because electricity had been supplied to the house for more than 65 years and there had been no previous damage.

3

Last week a Moscow news agency reported that the town of Voronezh in the Russian heartlands had allegedly been terrorised by 'at least three' visitors from outer space. According to the report, a large shining ball or disc had hovered over the park. It had then landed, a hatch had opened, and three creatures similar to humans, and a small robot had come out. The agency report continued:

'The aliens were, apparently, two or three metres tall, but with very small heads. They walked near the ball, or disc, and then disappeared inside. Witnesses were overwhelmed by a fear which lasted for several days.' Many claimed that they had seen a banana-shaped object in the sky.

● Understanding

Are these statements about the news stories true or false? Write T or F in the boxes.

1 Four men spent 118 days in a shipwrecked boat. ☐

2 The trimaran was 41 feet long. ☐

3 When the crew of the boat were interviewed on TV, not everyone believed their story. ☐

4 Mr and Mrs Orchard proved in court that electricity was responsible for the damage to their home. ☐

5 The High Court judge thought that Mr and Mrs Orchard or one of their children had caused the damage themselves. ☐

6 According to the Moscow report, the aliens who landed in Voronezh looked rather like people. ☐

7 The report claims that people who saw the spaceship land were not at all frightened. ☐

2 Talking points

Discuss these points with a partner:

1 What reason could the crew of the trimaran have had for making up the story of their shipwreck?
2 What reason might the Orchard family have had for damaging their own house?
3 Why do you think the normally serious Moscow news agency reported this 'aliens from outer space' story?

3 Vocabulary

● Ships and the sea (Story 1)

1 Find three words in the text which are used instead of *ship*.

2 Which word in the text tells us that the boat turned over?

3 Which words in the text mean:
   a the group of people on a ship
   b a journey by sea
   c to be carried along by water currents, without direction
   d the bottom of a ship
   e a person who reaches land after surviving a shipwreck

● Verbs (Story 2)

1 What are the infinitive forms of these irregular verbs?
   a left   b lost   c fled   d flown   e fallen

2 What is the difference in meaning between *left* and *fled*?

3 Which four reporting verbs are used in this story?

● Nouns (Story 3)

1 Which three nouns are used to refer to the 'beings' who landed in Voronezh?

2 Guess the meanings of these words from the story:
   a heartlands   b a hatch   c witnesses

● The prefix over-
(Language review B1, page 33)

The prefix *over-* can add two different meanings to a verb.

EXAMPLES:

A *A huge wave overturned the Rose-Noelle.*
   (*over* has a physical meaning)

B *He looks very fat. I think he's been overeating since he lost his job.*
   (*over* means 'too much')

Which of the two meanings does the prefix *over-* have in these sentences? Write A or B in the boxes.

1 She looks tired. I think she's been overworking. ☐

2 When it rains heavily, rivers sometimes overflow their banks. ☐

3 I was walking by the river when I overbalanced and fell in. ☐

4 That was a very expensive meal. Perhaps the waiter overcharged us. ☐

4 Sequencing past events
(Language review A1, page 32)

Which of these past events from the first two stories happened first in each case? Write 1 or 2 in the boxes.

1 a The boat's crew spent 118 days on the hull of their ship. ☐
   b A huge wave overturned the trimaran. ☐

2 a The boat drifted for 1000 nautical miles. ☐
   b The boat hit Great Barrier Island. ☐

3 a Investigators were puzzled. ☐
   b The ship's owner survived two shipwrecks. ☐

4 a An electricity supply cable was attached to the cottage. ☐
   b The couple left their home in terror. ☐

5 a Mr and Mrs Orchard fled next door. ☐
   b Metal objects flew around their cottage. ☐

Compare answers with a partner.

Look back at the texts in Exercise 1. For each pair of sentences above, find the verbs in the texts and underline the exact form of each verb.

Now make two lists of verbs, as in the example.

First event	Second event
1 had overturned	spent

What do you notice about the verbs in each list?

5 Practice

Read these short news reports and work out two different explanations for what happened in each case.

EXAMPLE:

Children sent home early

Over three hundred children were evacuated from their school in Leeds yesterday.

a *A man-eating tiger had escaped from a nearby zoo.*

b *Someone had phoned the school to say there was a bomb in the playground.*

1

Man bites dog

Robert Hanshaw bit off a dog's ear last week.
'I was so angry that I just bit the first thing I could find,' he said.

3

Earthquake shooting

In the early hours of Friday morning, a San Francisco man woke up, leapt out of bed, got his gun out of a cupboard and shot himself in the foot.

5

Young Dentist

7-year-old Jonathan Roehorn pulled out five of his own teeth with his Dad's pliers.

2

Taking it lying down

Student Joanne Lowther nearly fell asleep during an important school exam. One of the girl's teachers explained. 'She was lying on her stomach at the time.'

4

Early Christmas presents

Christmas came early to 300 customers of a London bank, when they each received unexpected cheques for £500 in the post.

Now compare explanations with a partner. Which do you think is the most probable in each case?

---

6 Relating past events
(Language review A2, page 32)

For each of the stories in Exercise 5, make two compound sentences using your explanations. In each sentence, use a Past Simple verb, a Past Perfect verb and one of these words: *after, because, when.*

EXAMPLE:

Children sent home early

Three hundred school children were sent home early after/because a tiger had escaped from a nearby zoo.

7 Listening 📼

Before you listen to the recording, re-read Story 1 on page 25. Now listen to George, one of the trimaran's crew, talking about his experiences. Make a note of any factual differences between the two versions of the story.

Compare lists of differences with a partner.

8 Writing
(Language review A4, page 32)

Write a newspaper story reporting what George said. You may use only two direct speech quotations. The rest of the story should be in reported speech. Start like this:

Rose-Noelle Crew Member Speaks Out

George, one of the crew of the Rose-Noelle, said that five men had set sail on 21st June.

9 Personalised practice
Work in pairs.

Student A:
Write notes about an unusual or newsworthy event that has happened to you or that you have heard about recently.

Student B:
Write notes about something funny that has happened to you.

Ask questions to find out about your partner's story.

Now write your partner's story using reported speech.

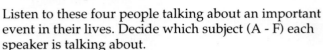

Stage two

Explanations

I Listening

Listen to these four people talking about an important event in their lives. Decide which subject (A - F) each speaker is talking about.

A the break-up of a relationship
B finding out about a serious illness
C remembering a holiday romance
D winning a large sum of money
E the decision to get married
F remembering a serious accident

> I couldn't believe it ...

> Of course I never really thought it'd happen to me ...

> She'd been staying with a friend ...

> I'll never forget that day ...

● Listening for detail

Do you and your partner agree about the subjects of the four conversations? When you have reached agreement, listen to the recordings again and write down the clues which helped you to match the speakers with the subjects. The first one has been done for you.

Speaker	Subject	Clues/Evidence
I	E	Something surprising / they were still getting to know each other / going out together / he felt he'd always known her / he asked her something
2		

---

2 Predicting

Listen to the four speakers again. How do you think each speaker continued? Here are the unfinished endings:

1 *In the end I surprised myself by saying* …
2 *She told me she'd been* …
3 *Apparently, the man I'd been sitting next to* …
4 *I'd even planned what I was going to say* …

Make notes, and then compare ideas with a partner.

3 Vocabulary

● Phrasal verbs
(Language review B2, page 33)

Choose the best replacement for these phrasal verbs from the recording in Exercise 1.

1 *I thought he was **having** me **on**.* (Speaker 1)
a laughing at me   b joking
c inviting me out

2 *I **made out** that everything was normal.* (2)
a pretended   b thought   c said

3 *… she just **came out with it**.* (2)
a returned   b gave me a present
c told the truth

4 *… was **coming round** in hospital.* (3)
a arriving   b waking up
c getting up

5 *… if my number **came up**.* (4)
a won   b was called
c appeared

6 *… **giving up** work* (4)
a leaving my job   b finding a new job   c working harder

● **Idioms: parts of the body**
(Language review B3, page 33)

In the recording in Exercise 1 the second speaker says:

> *... she seemed different. I couldn't quite*
> ***put my finger on it.***

This means that she couldn't work out how or why she was different.

Here are some more examples of body idioms. Use the context of each sentence to work out their meanings.

1 I haven't really got time for a cup of coffee, but if you *twist my arm* I might have one.
2 I never have any spare time these days. I'm *up to my ears* in work.
3 Good luck at your interview. I'll *keep my fingers crossed* for you.
4 I was going to ask him to go out with me, but at the last moment I *got cold feet*.
5 I was only *pulling your leg* when I said I couldn't come to your party. Of course I'll be there.
6 I can't stand the way he always talks about himself. He's a real *pain in the neck*.

Compare ideas with a partner.

4 Pronunciation 🔲

● Listen to the recording and repeat these three sentences:

1 *I thought he was having me on.*
2 *I didn't have time to open the post.*
3 *Last year I went to Canada and the USA.*

Now listen to the three sentences again, What sound can you hear between these pairs of words?

   1 **me on**   2 **to open**   3 **Canada and**

● Work with a partner.

Take it in turns to read these phrases aloud. Think carefully about the sound between the pairs of words in bold type.

a **me and** you
b **No I** don't
c in **the end**
d It's an **idea of** his
e **So is** she

f He's in **Australia or** New Zealand
g easy **to understand**
h **He isn't** late
i a **law of** nature

Now listen to the recording and check your pronunciation.

---

5 Feelings
(Language review A5, page 32)

Here are two sentences used by the first speaker in Exercise 1:

A *He felt as if he'd always known me.* (This means 'He had the feeling or impression that he had always known me.')
B *I felt like laughing.* (This means 'I wanted to laugh / I had a desire to laugh.')

Rephrase these sentences using a sentence like A above:

1 I had the feeling that I'd been there before.
2 He had the impression that he had met me before.
3 I have the feeling that I'm losing my memory.

Now finish these sentences using a sentence like B above:

4 The film was so sad that I ...
5 It was such a cold night that I didn't ...
6 The service in the restaurant was so bad that we ...

6 Past activities
(Language review A3, page 32)

What is the difference in meaning between these pairs of sentences? Discuss ideas with a partner.

1 a She's been going out with someone else.
  b She'd been going out with someone else.

2 a The evening before she'd thought about what she'd do with the money.
  b The evening before she'd been thinking about what she'd do with the money.

Now answer these questions about what the four speakers in Exercise 1 said. (Look at the tapescript on page 162 if you wish.) In your answers, use the words in brackets.

1 Why did the first speaker think her friend was joking? (three months)
2 What didn't the second speaker really believe? (stay with a friend)
3 How do we know the train journey didn't last long? (twenty minutes)
4 What was funny about the evening before the phone call? (if her number came up)

7 Practice

While you were away on a business trip last month, your friend Sam stayed in your apartment.

The picture opposite shows what it looked like when you got back home last week.

Make a list of all the things that were wrong.

EXAMPLE:

There was a hole in one of the pillows.

Now think up explanations for all the things that were wrong.

EXAMPLE:

Sam had been smoking in bed.

Now compare ideas with a partner.

8 Writing: mini-autobiography

Write a list of five important events in your life.

EXAMPLE:
When I was eleven I failed a very important examination.

These five events are going to form the subject of five short chapters in your mini-autobiography. Write what you remember about the background to these events.

EXAMPLE:

> Chapter 1   My First Big Failure
>
> I remember that morning very well: I couldn't wait for the postman. When he arrived, he brought a letter which was addressed to my father. Slowly he opened the envelope and took out the letter. I couldn't believe it – I'd failed.
>
> I'd been at Grange Hill Junior School for three years. Everybody had always said that I was very intelligent and that I would easily pass the exam. For the previous six months I'd been working very hard. My parents had helped me with my homework …

9 Explaining moods and expressions

How many explanations can you give for these people's expressions?

Think of what had happened/what had been happening immediately before these scenes were painted.

Compare ideas with a partner.

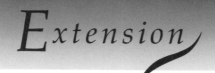

Problem Solving

1 Lateral thinking

This is a dictionary definition of the term 'lateral thinking':

Thinking sideways, not in a straight line. Using the imagination, not logical sequences, to solve problems.

Read this 'lateral thinking' problem and try to answer the question at the end of the story.

Discuss this question with a partner. (Think laterally!)

Do you know any stories like these? Write or tell one and see if other students in your class can work out the answer.

'Here's a mystery,' said Dr Gregory to his friend. 'It happened last Tuesday afternoon. There had been a heavy fall of snow that morning. There was a knock at my door; it was Paul Austin, who lives with his wife on a small farm nearby. I walked down to the farm with Paul, and as we got to his farm gate, I noticed his footprints clearly marked in the snow from when he had left the farm earlier. There were no other footprints anywhere around the farm, so obviously Paul had been the only person to enter or leave since the snowfall. When we got to the cottage, however, there was a stranger with Paul's wife.'

Dr Gregory's friend looked puzzled. 'Paul had never seen him before and he was absolutely sure that his wife had been the only person in the house when he left?' he asked.

'Without doubt,' replied Dr Gregory.

'And what was Paul's reaction?' asked the friend.

'Surprised, but pleased as well,' said Dr Gregory, smiling.

Who was the stranger with Paul's wife?

2 A real mystery

How do you explain this newspaper story? Discuss ideas with a partner.

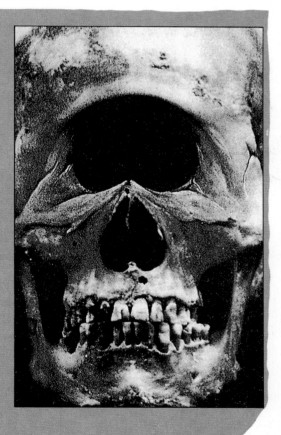

CYCLOPS SKULL FOUND IN SHEFFIELD

STUNNED steelworker **Fred Maddox told last night how his pet dog dug up the skull of a monstrous one-eyed Cyclops ... in his local park.**

Experts were baffled when they heard of Fred's freak find, which is believed to be the remains of a creature thought to be a myth until now. Fred confessed he was mystified when he saw his dog digging on a small patch of open ground in the Sheffield park.

'He had dug down about two feet when he started barking really excitedly. Then he pulled out this round thing about the size of a football.' It was then that Fred realised it was a SKULL – with only ONE eye socket.

Language review

A Grammar and Use

1 The Past Perfect

● **Form**

had ('d) + past participle

● **Use**

We use this tense to talk about a past action or event that happened before a particular time in the past:

This was the second shipwreck the craft's owner had survived.
We'd never spent more than an hour together before the day of the trip to London.

2 The Past Simple and the Past Perfect

We often relate two actions or events in the past by using the Past Perfect for the first action and the Past Simple for the second:

The children went home early because a tiger had escaped from the zoo.
The man bit the dog after it had attacked him.

3 The Past Perfect Continuous

● **Form**

had ('d) been + -ing form

● **Use**

We use this tense when we want to stress that an action took place over a period of time, before a particular time in the past:

We'd only been travelling for about twenty minutes when it happened.
The evening before the phone call, I'd been thinking about what I'd do.

4 The Past Perfect in reported speech

One of the common uses of the Past Perfect is in reported speech.

1 A verb in the Present Perfect Simple or Continuous in direct speech changes to the Past Perfect Simple or Continuous in reported speech:

'We've seen a banana-shaped object in the sky.' (direct)
Witnesses claimed they'd seen a banana-shaped object in the sky. (reported)

'I've been staying with a friend.' (direct)
She said she'd been staying with a friend. (reported)

2 A verb in the Past Simple or Continuous changes to the Past Perfect Simple or Continuous in reported speech:

'You were very lucky.' (direct)
She said I'd been very lucky. (reported)

Note

It is not necessary to make this change if the context makes it clear that the action referred to took place in the past:

'We lived in France in 1986.' (direct)
They said they lived in France in 1986. (reported)

However, without the time reference *in 1986* the Past Perfect would be necessary in reported speech:

They said they had lived in France.

5 To feel

● **Summary of uses**

The main meaning of *to feel* is 'to experience a sensation'. This verb is used in several different ways:

1 *to feel* + adjective or noun:

I feel hungry.
Do you feel tired?
He felt a pain in his right shoulder.

2 *to feel as if / though* + clause:

I felt as if I was going to collapse.
We felt as though we hadn't slept for days.

3 *to feel like* + -ing form:

When I heard the news, I felt like crying.
I've got a terrible headache. I feel like going straight to bed.

B Vocabulary

1 The prefix over-

The prefix *over-* can add a literal, physical meaning to verbs:

to overturn = to turn over / upside down
  The huge wave overturned the boat.

to overflow = to flow over the top of
  After three nights of heavy rain, the river overflowed its banks.

Over- can also add the meaning of too much or more than is advisable:

  He's put on a lot of weight. He must have been overeating recently.
  Yesterday I overslept and was late for work again.

2 Phrasal verbs

Here are some more phrasal verbs to learn:

● *Have*

to have someone back = to let your partner (boyfriend, girlfriend, husband or wife) return to you after an argument:

  I know I've been stupid, but I hope my wife will have me back.

to have (it) out with someone = to discuss something that has been causing unpleasantness between two people:

  If he goes on being rude to you, you should have it out with him.

● *Make*

to make up for = to compensate for something that is damaged, lost or missing:

  He's working really hard today to make up for the time he wasted yesterday.

to make up = to invent (a story or excuse):

  He said he'd met Michael Jackson, but I think he was making it up.

● *Come*

to come in for = to receive or attract (criticism):

  The new TV quiz show has come in for some very bad reviews.

to come out with = to say something (surprising):

  I'd no idea James was getting married. He just came out with it at the party.

● *Give*

to give in (to) = to surrender or submit (to):

  The President is giving in to public opinion. He's resigning next year.

to give (someone/something) away = to betray / to reveal a secret:

  I'm hiding from the police. Please don't give me away.

3 Body idioms

Can you remember what these 'relationships' idioms from Unit 1 mean? They all contain vocabulary to do with the body:

  to twist someone around your little finger
  to see eye-to-eye on something
  to be the blue-eyed boy

Look back to page 13 to check whether you were right.

Here are some more 'body' idioms, in addition to those you learnt on page 29.

to cost an arm and a leg = to be very expensive
to put your back into something = to work or try very hard at something
to get something off your chest = to say something that has been worrying you for a long time
to be all ears = to listen with great interest
to turn a blind eye to something = to ignore something / pretend it isn't there
to have egg on your face = to be seen to be foolish
to put your foot down = to be assertive / to insist on something
to let your hair down = to relax and enjoy yourself in a carefree way
to have your head in the clouds = to be a dreamer
to keep your nose clean = to stay out of trouble by behaving well

◆ What were you frightened of when you were a child? These illustrations may help you to remember.

Compare your memories with a partner.

◆ Why are so many children and even adults afraid of the dark? Discuss this question in groups. Think of as many explanations as you can.

◆ One of the main fears associated with night-time is a fear of bad dreams or nightmares. Do you think dreams and nightmares mean something? Discuss with a partner what dreams about these subjects might mean.

> a snake • falling into a deep hole • a knife • death • a tunnel
> something burning • a ghost • a shipwreck

Now find the interpretation below of dreams about these subjects and check if any of your guesses were 'correct'.

1 Seeing a deep hole – or worse still, falling into one – is a sign of great danger. Take great care in your life and keep your eyes open.

2 Any kind of fire in a dream has a positive significance. Burning oil or petrol is a warning to be careful, but a burning house means that relief is on the way from problems or an illness that has been troubling you.

3 Death often occurs in dreams and is rarely a bad sign: it simply means that you are in a nervous state of mind and that maybe you are very pessimistic. Dreaming that you are about to die shows that your health may be at risk in a small way.

4 Ghosts indicate coming problems or financial worries. If the ghost is wearing white, you will have good health, but if it is dressed in black, there will be a disagreement caused by a friend's selfishness.

5 An ordinary table knife is a favourable sign in a dream, indicating new successes. But other dreams about knives, for example a kitchen knife, or one being sharpened, indicate possible danger.

6 If you are involved in a shipwreck, it is a sign that things are going to go badly. You can expect difficulties following a break with someone close to you. It also suggests that your health is not as good as it could be, probably because you have been working too hard.

7 If you see a snake in a dream it means either that an enemy is trying to harm you financially, or that a rival in love is trying to destroy your happiness. If you manage to kill the snake, you will be able to prevent this person from harming you.

8 Going through a tunnel in a dream means that you can expect a period of happiness, both with your family and at work.

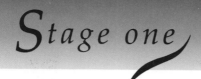

Stage one

Phobias

1 Listening

Listen to some people talking about their phobias. While you listen, tick the subject you think they are referring to.

Heights ☐   Snakes ☐

Enclosed spaces ☐   Dolls ☐

Flying ☐   Dogs ☐

Open spaces ☐   Large shops ☐

● **Listening for detail**

Listen to the four speakers again and then fill in the chart.

	1 – John	2 – Sue	3 – Nigel	4 – Maureen
1 Phobia?	Dogs	Dolls	Enclosed spaces Underground	Large shops
2 How long has it lasted? / When did it start?	long time father	After 5 7– –	16 lift of people	
3 Describe the person's behaviour or reaction.	Attack Park long roads	Aunt Pulled doll to pieces nightmares Sick/dizzy	Travel weak/pass out trapped	panicky agoraphobia

2 Vocabulary

● Look at the tapescript for Exercise 1 on page 163. Find words or phrases which mean:

1 to move or shake something from side to side *(John)*
2 a place I didn't dare to go *(John)*
3 it affected me gradually *(Sue)*
4 to overcome, to beat *(Sue)*
5 to become unconscious, to faint *(Nigel)*
6 to hang in mid air without moving *(Nigel)*
7 to tear with your fingernails *(Nigel)*

● **Idiomatic uses of *go***
(Language review B1, page 43)

Sue says: *I went absolutely crazy.*

This means she lost her self-control.

Guess the meaning of the phrases with *go* in these sentences:

1 Whenever my teacher spoke to me I went red.
2 There's a lot of noise outside. I wonder what's going on.
3 My car won't go. I'll have to take it to the garage.
4 Ten goes into a hundred ten times.
5 I like your pink T-shirt. It goes well with your black jeans.

3 Talking points
Work in pairs.

How would you define a phobia?

Guess what the people who suffer from these phobias are afraid of:

> chromatophobia • doraphobia
> erythrophobia • gamophobia
> gatophobia • haematophobia
> mysophobia • necrophobia
> nyctophobia • phagophobia

How do you think people develop these phobias?

4 Expressing opinions (Making deductions)
(Language review A1, page 42)

Read these extracts from the recording in Exercise 1:

1 *My father was scared of dogs, so that must be where I got my phobia from.*
2 *My mother says I loved dolls until I was about five, so it can't be something I was born with.*
3 *I hate feeling trapped so I suppose that must be why I'm phobic about lifts, too.*
4 *… a trip to the supermarket can become a nightmare. That's why I think I might be suffering from a kind of agoraphobia.*

For each of these extracts decide what is 'fact' and what is 'opinion'.

How do the speakers express their opinions? How sure are they about their opinions? Which words tell you this?

5 Practice

Work in pairs.

Use the facts in the following illustrations to express an opinion about what the people are doing. Then turn to page 156 to find further clues.

Use *may* or *might* to talk about possibilities, and *must* or *can't* if you are sure.

The first one has been done for you.

EXAMPLE:

Student A: It's nine o'clock … Mike is washing his face and cleaning his teeth.

He might be going to bed or he might be getting up …

Student B: *He must be going to bed. There's a street light on outside, so it can't be nine o'clock in the morning.*

---

6 Pre-listening

You are going to hear some people talking about their fear of flying. Before you listen, predict some of the things they are going to say. Make notes under these headings:

Possible reasons for fear of flying	Possible symptoms of these fears
fear of crashing	dizziness

7 Listening

Listen to the recording and check which of your predictions are mentioned.

● Understanding

Listen again and answer these questions:

1 Why was the first speaker particularly aware of the possibility of two planes crashing?
2 Why, according to the second speaker, is it normal for people to be worried about flying?
3 According to the third speaker, how is flying different from other kinds of travel?
4 What worries the fourth speaker about air turbulence?
5 Why is the fifth speaker particularly concerned about not being able to see the pilot of an aeroplane he is travelling on?
6 What did the sixth speaker do to try and calm herself down when she was flying?
7 What were the symptoms of the seventh speaker's fear of flying?
8 What was the original cause of the eighth speaker's fear of flying?

8 Vocabulary

● **Air travel**

Look through the tapescript for Exercise 7 on page 163 and find air travel words or phrases which mean:

1 a crash between two planes in the sky
2 to leave the ground (planes)
3 violent movement of air which causes an uncomfortable flight
4 the part of a plane where the pilots sit during a flight

Now make a list of the words or phrases the speakers use to mean 'plane'.

---

9 Pronunciation

Listen to the recording and repeat the phrases you hear.

Now look at the extracts and listen again. What do you notice about the words in bold type?

1 *I organised my **whole life** around this fear.*
2 *My mother says I **loved dolls**.*
3 *My **aunt tried** to help me …*
4 *I hear my **voice saying** …*
5 *… **from my** bedroom window …*
6 *… I wonder how on **earth they** miss each other.*
7 *… a little bit **of fear** …*
8 *… go to the airport **and drop** somebody off.*

Working in pairs, take it in turns to read these sentences to each other. Pay particular attention to the words in bold type.

1 You may **experience symptoms** of your fear anywhere.
2 Many **people learn** to tackle the problem themselves.
3 If you go to a psychotherapist, you'll be **taught techniques** to use.
4 These techniques are helpful if you feel an **attack coming** on.
5 The **best treatment** for you depends on your symptoms.
6 Most sufferers **make complete** recoveries.

Now listen to the recording to check your pronunciation.

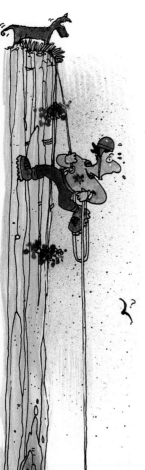

10 Modal verbs
(Language review A2, page 42)

Read these extracts from the recordings and say whether they express ability, possibility or necessity. Write **A**, **P** or **N** in the boxes.

1 *I could never walk along roads …* ☐
2 *I just have to get away from it.* ☐
3 *I had to travel on the underground.* ☐
4 *I couldn't handle it.* ☐
5 *I must get out!* ☐
6 *… to see if anything's near that we might collide with.* ☐
7 *You have to have a little bit of fear.* ☐
8 *All other modes of transport you can stop and get out.* ☐
9 *As far as we know there may be no one there at all.* ☐
10 *I couldn't breathe.* ☐

Read through the tapescript for Exercise 7 on page 163 and find five more sentences like these.

11 Talking about possibilities

● *May, might* and *could*

Think of some of the problems people might have in these stressful situations. Make a note of your ideas.

EXAMPLE: 'I'm starting a new job next week.'

> *She might not get on with her new colleagues.*
> *She may have to work longer hours.*
> *She could find her new job less interesting than her old one.*

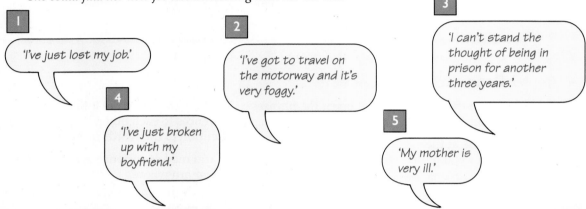

1 'I've just lost my job.'

4 'I've just broken up with my boyfriend.'

2 'I've got to travel on the motorway and it's very foggy.'

5 'My mother is very ill.'

3 'I can't stand the thought of being in prison for another three years.'

---

12 Necessity: *have to* and *must*
(Language Review A2, page 43)

In which of these statements are the speakers

1 expressing personal opinions or obligations?

2 referring to a fact or an external situation of some kind?

Write 1 or 2 in the boxes.

1 I'm really tired. I must go to bed early tonight. ☐
2 My train leaves at seven o'clock tomorrow morning, so I'll have to get up at half past five. ☐
3 I'm sorry I have to leave so early, but my parents told me to be home before midnight. ☐
4 You must see that film. It's brilliant! ☐

How are sentences 1 and 4 different from 2 and 3? Think particularly about the verb forms.

Compare ideas with a partner.

13 Survey

You are going to carry out a survey to find out some of the things other students have to do at home, at school or at work.

Make a list of some of the things you have to do – include things that you really dislike, and things that you don't mind doing.

EXAMPLES: *I have to work three evenings a week.*
I have to look after my little brother when my parents go out.

Now find out whether other students in your class have to do the same things as you. Ask questions like this:

> *Do you ever have to work in the evenings?*
> *Do you ever have to babysit for your parents when they go out?*

Make notes about what each student has to do in a table like this.

You	Partners				
	1	2	3	4	5
1 Work three evenings a week					
2 Babysit					

Finally write a short report summarising the results of your survey.

EXAMPLE: *In all I interviewed ten other students in my class. Only two students have to work in the evenings …*

Use some of these phrases in your report:

> *most (of the)   the majority of the   all (of) the   none of the*

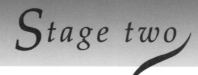

Accidents and Dangers

1 Pre-reading

Before you read the text, look at the photograph and discuss this question with a partner:

What do you think happened immediately after the photograph was taken?

Now check your ideas by reading quickly through the text.

2 Reading

Now read the text more carefully and try and decide what kind of writing this is:

a a newspaper story
b a personal letter
c an advertisement
d a police accident report

Compare ideas with a partner, and try to explain the reasons for your answer.

Mrs Sharpdent drove her Golf to a public car park overlooking the sea in North Devon. With her were her seven-year-old daughter and her daughter's eight-year-old friend.

They went for a walk. The weather was bitterly cold. The two girls, keen to get back to the car, ran on ahead. 'Let's sit in the car till Mummy arrives,' said the daughter.

No, her daughter shouldn't have released the handbrake.

No, her daughter's friend should not have pushed the car.

And no, there should not have been a post missing in the protective barrier. The Golf started rolling across fifty yards of field. Mercifully the daughter jumped clear.

Launching itself off the cliff, the car landed feet first on the pavement below. Actually it started first time and was capable of making its own way to the local Volkswagen garage.

The damage? A cracked radiator, two broken headlights and the odd bump here and there.

And the repair bill was a drop in the ocean.

● Understanding

1 How were the three people in the car related?
2 Why did the two girls get back to the car before the woman?
3 Why did the car start moving?
4 Why did it continue moving?
5 Why did it roll right over the cliff?
6 Why weren't the two girls injured in the accident?
7 How did the car land?
8 How do you know that the engine was not damaged?

3 Vocabulary

● Which word or phrase in the text:

1 tells you that you could see the sea from the car park?
2 describes the weather?
3 tells you that part of the car park barrier was not there?
4 describes the movement of the car towards the edge of the cliff?
5 tells you that the damage was not expensive to repair?

● Adjectives describing damage or injury

(Language review B2, page 43)

What is the difference in meaning between these adjectives?

cracked (a cracked radiator)
broken (two broken headlights)

Work with a partner; make a list of adjectives you know which have similar meanings to these.

4 Something wrong
(Language review A3, page 43)

Find the sentences in the text which tell you …

1 … that the daughter caused the car to start moving.
2 … that the friend helped the car to continue moving.
3 … that the car park barrier was broken.

Which verb form is used in all three sentences?

What is the difference in meaning between these sentences?

The daughter shouldn't have released the handbrake.
The daughter couldn't have released the handbrake.

Compare ideas with a partner.

5 Practice

● Read these news stories and then choose the best headline for each one.

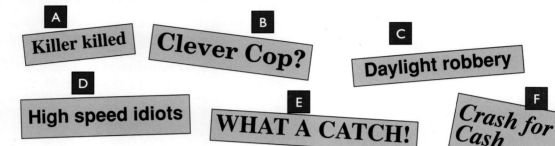

A **Killer killed**

B **Clever Cop?**

C **Daylight robbery**

D **High speed idiots**

E **WHAT A CATCH!**

F **Crash for Cash**

1 A lorry driver got his revenge on a bank which refused to cash his cheque. He drove a 40-ton lorry through the town and smashed down the bank's doors. Revenge is sweet, but it cost him nine months in jail.

2 Robbers escaped from the police after a high-speed car chase. They crashed their car and climbed over a wall – straight into a police station.

3 A policeman gave his watch, wallet and notebook to a colleague, before diving into a river to help two women to safety. His colleague put the things into his own pocket and then dived into the river himself.

4 A hunter was killed by a snake in Cyprus last week. Ali Asghar Ahani tried to catch the snake alive by pressing the wooden end of his shotgun against its head. But the snake coiled itself around the end of the gun and hit the trigger with its tail, firing the gun and shooting Ahani in the head.

5 An Australian fisherman got into trouble when he caught a giant fish. The six-foot monster fish dragged the fisherman a mile out to sea before the line broke.

6 Bank robber Frank Colella didn't get very far after escaping with £1300 – he was attacked and robbed outside the bank! When Colella reported the attack to the police, he was promptly arrested.

● Fill in a chart like this with answers to these questions. The first one has been done for you.

1 What mistakes did the main characters (people) in these stories make?
2 What could they have done to avoid their mistakes? (Make several suggestions.)
3 What should/shouldn't they have done? (Express a personal opinion.)

Compare ideas with a partner. Decide on the best suggestions for each story.

story	mistakes	could have	should have	shouldn't have
1	smashed down the doors of the bank	a) written a letter to the manager b) complained	complained to the manager	got angry
2				

6 Writing

Look at these pictures from a strip cartoon and put them into the right order.

Now write the story in the past. Start like this:

Jack was on a strict diet. His wife, Gladys, wanted him to be slim and healthy for their summer holiday in Tenerife. One night, when Gladys

was asleep, Jack went down to the kitchen…

End your story with a moral:

Jack should/shouldn't have …

*E*xtension

Advertising

● Look back at the photograph and car advertisement on page 39.

Do you think it is an effective advertisement?

Discuss your reasons.

● Look at these two advertisements, and discuss these questions:

1 What products are they advertising?

2 How effective are the advertisements? What makes them effective (or not)?

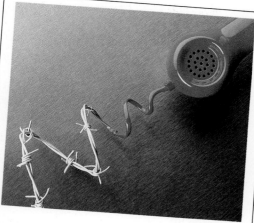

You are going to write advertising copy for one of these recent inventions.

- First decide what each thing is and what it can do.
- Decide as a group on a suitable name for the invention you have chosen.
- Individually, write sentences or phrases to accompany the photograph.
- Discuss each student's advertisement in turn and suggest improvements.
- Write the final improved advertising copy.

*L*anguage review

A Grammar and Use

1 Making deductions

A deduction is a belief or opinion based on factual evidence. If you are certain about a belief, use *must* or *can't*:

It must be raining. Everyone's got their umbrellas up.
I hate feeling trapped. That must be why I'm phobic about lifts.
He can't be coming. He's never as late as this.
My mother says I loved dolls until I was about five, so my phobia can't be something I was born with.

If you are not certain that your belief is true, use *may* or *might*:

That's why I think I might be suffering from a kind of agoraphobia.
He looks quite ill. He may just be overtired.

There is little difference in meaning between *may* and *might*, but if we think something is quite possible, we tend to use *may*; if we think that something is less possible, we use *might*.

2 Expressing ability, possibility and necessity

● Ability

Use *can* for present abilities and *could* for past abilities:

From my bedroom window I can see all the planes landing.

My father's 45 and he still can't swim.
By the age of four I could ride a bicycle.
I couldn't breathe and I couldn't swallow on planes.

Remember that *can* has no infinitive or participle forms; you have to use *be able to* instead:

I'd love to be able to swim. (Infinitive)
He hasn't been able to speak since his operation. (Present Perfect)

● Possibility

For present possibilities, use *can, may, might* or *could*:

A trip to the supermarket can become a nightmare.
As far as I know, there may be no one there at all.
I might be suffering from a kind of agoraphobia.
It could just be nerves …

For future possibilities, use *may, might* or *could*:

I look out of the window to see if there's anything we might collide with.
I suppose I could go and see my doctor.
The weather may be bad tomorrow.

For past possibilities, use *could have* + past participle:

Did you really walk all the way home? You could have caught a taxi.
We could have gone to the theatre instead of watching TV.

Note

Remember that *can* and *could* are also used to express permission:

Could I open the window, please? It's really hot in here.

● **Necessity**

Use *must* or *have to* to talk about necessities or obligations:

I hear my own voice saying: 'I must get out!'
You must read that book. It's fantastic!
I mustn't forget my father's birthday next week.
My phobia was so bad, I had to take valium.
Sorry, I can't come out. I have to work this evening.

The differences between *must* and *have to*:

- *Must* is used to refer to the opinions or feelings of the speaker, that is, when the speaker has decided that something is necessary:

  I'm really tired. I must go to bed.

- *Have to* is used to refer to facts, rather than matters of opinion, that is, when there is an external necessity or obligation:

  When I was six, I had to spend three weeks in hospital.

Must has no past tense and no *-ing* form or infinitive. If you need these forms, use the verb *have to* instead:

I've just had to buy a new TV licence. (Present Perfect)
I'm sorry, I'm going to have to phone the police.
(Infinitive)

3 Expressing opinions about past behaviour

Use *should/shouldn't have* + past participle to criticise someone's past behaviour or to give advice after the event. (It is also possible to use *ought to have* instead of *should have*):

You should have telephoned to say you were going to be late.
The girl shouldn't have released the handbrake of her mother's car.

Use *could have* + past participle to talk about past possibilities or to make suggestions after the event:

Did you really walk home? You could have caught a taxi, you know.
We could have gone to the theatre instead of watching television.

B Vocabulary

1 Idiomatic uses of *go*

● *Go + adjective*

Go is a process verb which can be followed by an adjective. It is used to describe changes.
In these examples *go = turn/become*:

Children's hair often goes blond in the sun.
My tea's gone cold.
My mother's going deaf.

● **Other uses of *go***

My car won't go. = move, function
I wonder what's going on. = happening
Six goes into thirty five times. = $30 \div 6 = 5$
Your pink T-shirt goes well with your black jeans.
= matches
The plates go in this cupboard. = belong

2 Adjectives to describe damage or injury

bent: not straight, out of shape
*The only damage to my car was a **bent** aerial.*

broken: 1 in more than one piece
*My glasses are **broken**.*

2 not working
*The TV's **broken**.*

burst: broken open, letting something out
*I've got a **burst** tyre.*

chipped: with a small piece broken off
*After my grandmother has washed up, there are often a few **chipped** cups.*

cracked: broken, but still in one piece, covered with lines
*I'm not drinking out of this glass - it's **cracked**.*

fractured: broken or cracked, especially of bones
*After the accident, doctors found that he had a **fractured** skull.*

shattered: broken into a lot of small pieces
*The car had a **shattered** windscreen.*

smashed: completely broken
*After their argument, there were **smashed** plates all over the floor.*

UNIT 5

first impressions

◆ Look at the cartoon and read the description of one of the 'homes' it is advertising. How would you change it to make it absolutely accurate?

This charming property is spacious and well-ventilated – ideal for hotter weather.

The interior is in need of some attention, but there is plenty of storage space and potential for building extra rooms. For a family, it is solid and resistant to any of the damage children can do.

The property is secluded and situated in a peaceful pollution-free area. There are magnificent views of the surrounding countryside.

◆ Work with a partner. Look at the advertisement and an artist's impression of The Old Swan Inn. How honest is the advertisement?

The Old Swan Inn

The Old Swan Inn is a very special kind of hotel. It has something for everyone, and a tradition of hospitality that dates back to the 16th century. We have a reputation for first class service and comfort. Nothing is too much trouble for us to give our guests a memorable stay.

☆ delicious five-star cuisine
☆ lush, attractive garden
☆ delightful, safe children's play area
☆ scenic surroundings, views
☆ excellent tennis facilities
☆ superior accommodation

What would you do if you read the advertisement, then went to stay in the hotel and found the reality so different from the publicity?

◆ Have you ever been misled by an advertisement or a salesperson?

◆ 'Honesty is always the best policy.' Do you agree?

Honesty

1 Listening

Part 1

Listen to the first part of the conversation. What question is being discussed?
What would you do in the same situation? Compare ideas with a partner.

Part 2

Listen to the second part. What is the next question the man asks?

● Listening for detail

Complete these sentences with information from Part 2:

1 The woman would try to find the person who'd dropped the money if she thought

_____
_____.

2 She would feel awful if she thought the money belonged to

_____
_____.

3 She thinks it would be difficult not to hand over money to someone, even if you believed it wasn't theirs, because

_____
_____.

4 The second woman didn't believe that the money belonged to the man who claimed it because

_____
_____.

5 This woman felt that she couldn't keep the money because

_____
_____.

What would you have done in this situation? Compare ideas with a partner.

Part 3

Listen to the third part and note down the examples of dishonesty mentioned by the three speakers.

● Understanding

Read these questions and try to answer them. Then listen to Part 3 of the recording again to check your answers.

1 Why does the man think he is honest?
2 When does he make international telephone calls?
3 In what circumstances does the first woman think being dishonest is not so serious?

2 Talking points
Work in pairs.

• How honest do you think the speakers in the third extract are?

• Give an example of a white lie. Are they always justifiable?

• Why do people take things from offices, restaurants and hotels?

3 Vocabulary

● *Steal* or *rob*
(Language review B1, page 53)

Read these sentences containing the verbs *steal* and *rob* and think about the difference in meaning between them.

> *I've never robbed anybody.*
> *The ashtrays said 'stolen from Brendan's Bar'.*

After they'd robbed the bank, the gang broke into the corner shop and robbed the shopkeeper of £20.
They stole a ridiculous £20 from the shopkeeper after stealing more than £12,000 from the bank.

Now fill the gaps in these sentences with these words:
people   places   things

1 You steal _____ from _____ or _____.

2 You rob _____ or _____ of _____.

● Opposites
(Language review B2, page 53)

Here are some adjectives from the recording. Fill in the gaps with adjectives which have the opposite meaning. The first one has been done for you.

1	sufficient	*insufficient*
2	_____	dishonest
3	able	_____
4	true	_____
5	_____	illegal
6	_____	unpleasant
7	_____	immoral
8	sensitive	_____

4 Pronunciation

Listen to these sentences from the recording in
Exercise 1. What do you notice about the words in bold
type? Listen again and repeat each example.

> If somebody **dropped a** ten-pound note on the floor...
> I've never found a **lot of** money **at any** one time.
> I **picked it up** immediately.
> He immediately took some money **out of his** pocket.

In the following sentences, mark which words run into
each other when you say them.

1 Is there any salt and pepper?
2 He's an American.
3 The plane's arriving at 1 p.m.
4 She never asked anyone to help her.
5 Take it off at once!
6 If you call us tonight, we'll be in.

Work with a partner. Take it in turns to read these
phrases aloud. Listen to the recording and check your
answers.

5 Conditional sentences
(Language review A1-3, page 52)

● Look at these six extracts from the recording in
Exercise 1 and try to fill in the gaps.

1 *If it _____ a corporation, I usually _____ no qualms
   about doing something illegal or dishonest.*
2 *If somebody _____ a ten-pound note on the floor,
   _____ you tell them?*
3 *If I _____ quick, nobody _____ notice on the phone
   bill.*
4 *If I _____ in somebody's house and they _____ not
   there, I _____ long-distance telephone calls.*
5 *If I _____ the person was in the same room as me, I
   _____ try and find who the person was who'd
   dropped it.*
6 *If I _____ not straight with this person, I _____ feel
   bad.*

Now listen to the extracts and check your answers.

● There are three different types of conditional
sentence here. What are these three types, and what
verb tenses are used in them?

● Which extracts express:

   a a general rule / something that always happens?

   b a likely situation?

   c an imaginary situation?

Compare ideas with a partner.

6 Practice

Decide whether each of these sentences should be Zero,
First or Second Conditional and complete the gaps with
verbs in the correct tense.

1 I've never stolen anything. I think if I _____
   something now, if it _____ necessary for some
   reason, I _____ from a large department store.
2 I don't believe in being dishonest. I find that if you
   _____ straight with other people, then they
   always _____ you well.
3 I know that a good friend has been in trouble
   recently. If she _____ to tell me about it, I
   _____ very understanding.

4 He's not very fair. If a shopkeeper _____ him too
   much change, he always _____ it, but if he
   _____ too little change, he always _____ to the
   shopkeeper.

5 My parents are extremely strict. If they _____ I
   was dishonest in any way, they _____ me
   severely.

7 Questionnaire

How honest are you? The questionnaire opposite will help you to find out.

Work in groups of four: **A, B, C** and **D**.

Students A and B: Turn to page 156.

Students C and D: Read questions 1 – 4 and make sure you understand them. Answer the questions for yourselves.

When you have finished, work in different pairs: **A** with **C**, and **B** with **D**. Ask each other the questions you have read and note your partner's answers. Then check your scores on page 158.

Finally, write two more questions of a similar nature to ask your groups.

Questionnaire

1 What would you do if you found a wallet full of money, with the owner's name, phone number and address in it? Would you:
a hand it in at the nearest police station?
b contact the owner and give it back – he may give you a reward?
c put it in your pocket before anyone saw you?

2 If you crashed into a parked car and the owner wasn't there, would you:
a wait for a few minutes in case the owner arrived, then leave?
b drive away as fast as you could?
c leave a note with your phone number on the windscreen?

3 If you were paying for something in a department store and the assistant undercharged you by a large amount, would you:
a calculate how much you'd saved?
b do nothing, but feel guilty?
c point it out immediately?

4 If a good friend of yours with very little money gave you an expensive present which you really didn't like, would you:
a pretend to be very grateful?
b tell her that you'd already got one and suggest that she kept it?
c tell her that you didn't like it, and anyway, she shouldn't buy you presents because she's so poor?

---

8 Discussion and reading

Work in pairs.

- Discuss these points:

1 What do you do to make sure your home is safe from burglars?

2 What would you do if you were in bed at night and you heard a window being broken downstairs?

- Now read the text. Are any of your safety ideas mentioned?

- Read the text again and rank the list of **don'ts** in order of importance. Add any more points you can think of to this list.

SECURITY IN THE HOME

Every sixty seconds thieves break into a house. Make sure the next one isn't yours. Some 'dos' and 'don'ts':

Do – make sure you have secure locks on all your doors and windows
– install a burglar alarm if you can afford it
– fit a security light outside if you have a dark garden
– leave a light on when you go out, or use a timer to operate a table-lamp

Don't – leave ladders in the garden
– leave windows open when you go out
– leave your keys in visible places, inside or outside
– attach your address to any keys
– open your door if you don't know who is there
– allow strangers into your house without proof of identity.
– give your address to strangers over the phone.

If you think there might be a burglar in your home:

Don't go inside. (If you are inside, try to get out.)

Don't shout or confront the burglar.

Phone the police immediately from a neighbour's home.

Stage two

Famous Errors

1 Pre-reading

Look at the photo, the map and the other pieces of information. Make a list of all the facts you have about Amy Johnson.

Compare lists with a partner.

The Times
6 January 1941

Air Ace in fatal crash

London-Melbourne (May 1930)

2 Reading

As you read the text about Amy Johnson, look for the answers to these two questions:

1 What was the reason for Amy Johnson's last flight?

2 Why did she originally take up flying?

Amy Johnson's last flight

1 AIR ACE AMY JOHNSON became a legend in her own lifetime, hailed around the world for her brave pioneering flight from Britain to Australia when she was 26. A heroine's welcome awaited her in Melbourne when she landed there after the epic 19-day flight in her single-engined, secondhand Tiger Moth.

2 Yet this intrepid pilot, whose courage and determination were legendary, inexplicably ran out of fuel on a short flight from one British airfield to another. The mistake led to her death as she plunged into the icy waters of the Thames estuary on 5th January 1941. No one could understand how a pilot as skilled and experienced as Amy Johnson could have made such a basic, fatal error.

3 She had taken off from an airfield near Blackpool earlier that day to deliver a twin-engined aircraft to RAF Kidlington in Oxfordshire, 175 miles to the south.

4 The next news of Amy Johnson came when rescuers fished her body out of the river Thames. She had baled out, but instead of parachuting safely to the ground, she had plummeted into freezing water, which was too shallow to allow rescuers to pick her up by boat. Valiant efforts were made to reach her; one man died in the attempt. She might have landed safely if she had baled out a few moments later.

5 The fuel gauge in her aircraft showed empty, which explained why she had had to bale out. She had run out of fuel because she had been flying for four and a half hours – the maximum range of her aircraft.

6 She had probably got lost in poor visibility and had been too proud or stubborn to turn back. There is no record that she made any attempt to land and refuel.

7 Experts later pieced together the likely sequence of events leading up to her fatal accident.

8 The weather on that day in midwinter was not ideal for flying, with a dangerous inversion of warm air above cold air. They think that she probably had to fly at a higher altitude than normal to prevent her aircraft icing up, and that this probably affected her ability to see clearly. She knew from experience that there were hills and radio-masts in Oxfordshire which posed a hazard to low-flying aircraft. If there had not been so much cloud cover, she could have dropped down lower and found her position visually. There is little doubt that her best bet would have been to turn east and head for her normal base at Hatfield. If she had done this, she would have been able to drop safely under the clouds in a flat part of the country and find her course to Hatfield.

9 Amy Johnson suffered most of her life from depression over unsuccessful love affairs. She met a Swiss businessman when she was 18 and fell in love with him. If that relationship had gone well, she would not have started flying in the first place. But he had married someone else, and, feeling rejected, she decided to take up flying.

● **Reading for detail**

Read the text again and complete the chart with information about the flight.

LAST FLIGHT: THE FACTS

1 Pilot:	
2 Date:	
3 Aircraft:	
4 Departure from:	
5 Destination:	
6 Weather:	
7 Visibility:	
8 Cause of accident:	

---

3 Vocabulary

● **'Aircraft' words**

Read the text again quickly and make a list of all the words associated with aircraft or flying. Use some of these words to fill the gaps in these sentences. (You may have to change the word from its original form.)

1 The oil and fuel level on a plane is checked by looking at the _____ _____.

2 Most modern jets fly at a very high _____.

3 In an emergency, a pilot has to _____ _____ of the plane using a _____.

4 Pilots have to use instruments when _____ is bad.

5 Taking off and _____ are the most dangerous times for an _____.

6 Nowadays aircraft have a _____ of several hundred miles.

7 Amy Johnson's most famous _____ was from Britain to Australia.

8 On very long journeys, planes have to stop to _____.

● **'Descending' words**
(Language review B3, page 53)

The text about Amy Johnson's flight contains several words which mean to 'descend' or 'come down'. Read through the text again and make a list of these verbs.

Can you explain the differences in meaning between them?

Check your guesses by looking the words up in a dictionary.

4 Conditional sentences (2)
(Language review A4, page 52)

Look at these examples of conditional sentences from the text in Exercise 2:

1 *If there had not been so much cloud cover, she could have dropped down lower. (Para.8)*
2 *If she had done this (turned east), she would have been able to drop safely under the clouds. (8)*
3 *She might have landed safely if she had baled out a few moments later. (4)*
4 *If that relationship had gone well, she would not have started flying in the first place. (9)*

Now answer these questions with a partner:

a) In the first sentence, was there a lot of cloud? Did Amy Johnson drop down?
b) In the second sentence, did she drop safely under the clouds?
c) In the third sentence, did she land safely? How do you know?
d) In the fourth sentence, did the relationship go well?
e) Which tense is used in the *if* clause in these sentences?
f) Which tenses or verb forms are used in the main clause?
g) How are these three sentences different in meaning:
　　1 If I'm quick, nobody will notice.
　　2 If I was quick, nobody would notice.
　　3 If I'd been quick, nobody would have noticed.

---

5 Practice

For each of the following situations taken from the text, talk or write about what *would, could* or *might have happened* to Amy under different circumstances.

EXAMPLE:

She made the journey because she had to deliver an aircraft.
If she hadn't had to deliver an aircraft, she wouldn't have made the journey/ she might not have flown that day.

1 The weather was not good for flying that day.
2 She ran out of fuel and baled out.
3 She baled out a few moments too early.
4 The water was too shallow for a rescue by boat.
5 She got lost because of poor visibility.
6 She was too proud or stubborn to turn back.
7 She took up flying after her relationship with a Swiss businessman had gone wrong.

---

6 Reading and writing

Read these texts and write down what *might, could,* or *would (not) have happened* in each case.

EXAMPLES:

1 *If Mr Basil had been more careful, he wouldn't have hit the other car.*
2 *The French doctor could have gone to look for his wife if he had noticed she wasn't in the car.*

3 *Mr Latham might have avoided problems if he had left the car with a mechanic.*

Compare answers with a partner.

1

Helpful pensioner Thomas Basil lived to regret his good deed when he took his wife shopping. First he drove into the back of a stationary car. He immediately pulled over to apologise – and hit another vehicle. His wife, greatly distressed, jumped out of the car. She was run over by her husband. The shopping trip ended with Mrs Basil in hospital and Thomas heading home. He was so worried that on the way he drove into an office block.

2

A French doctor driving home to Paris heard an SOS on his car radio – and realised he had left his wife at a garage 200 miles back. He hadn't realised she had gone to the toilet when he stopped three hours earlier.
  'I didn't miss her because we don't talk much while travelling,' he said.

3

Marine engineer Peter Latham thought fixing his Mini's starting trouble would be child's play. Three months later he was about to admit defeat. He had spent a fortune on new parts. He then discovered that instead of operating the choke, he had been pulling out the heater control.

---

7 Personalised practice

Write three or four sentences about important decisions you have made in your life.

EXAMPLES:
I changed schools last year.
I decided not to take my English exam last term.

Give the sentences to your partner, and then ask your partner questions about their sentences.

EXAMPLES:
Why did you change schools last year?
Why didn't you take your English exam last term?

Answer your partner's questions, like this:

If I'd stayed at my last school, I would have had too far to travel.
Because I would have failed it if I'd taken it.

Now write a paragraph about something funny, strange or unusual which happened to you or someone you know.

Show your paragraph to your partner, who should then make comments about how you would, could or might have avoided the situation. Use the texts and example sentences in Exercise 6 as models.

Extension

Frauds

1 Pre-reading

Look at the photo and headline. Can you predict what you are going to read in the article?

Discuss ideas with a partner.

$35,000 FRAUD – CONMAN JAILED

2 Reading

Read the article and note down the 'cons' which are mentioned. Were any of your predictions correct?

JUST after the Second World War, a conman named Stanley Lowe offered to sell the Eiffel Tower as scrap to an unsuspecting Canadian. The wealthy Canadian was on a visit to Paris when Lowe managed to convince him that the Tower – one of the most famous monuments in the world – had been so badly damaged during the war that the city's officials had decided to sell it off as scrap metal. According to Lowe, the historic monument was up for sale at its scrap value – $35,000. The gullible tourist fell for the story.

Luckily for the tourist – and for Paris – Lowe's con was discovered and he was sentenced to six months in jail – an experience not entirely new to him. In fact, until his 'retirement' at the age of 50, he had spent more than 18 years in prison for a variety of frauds and cons. One was a spending spree in America, where he spent no less than $3000 of phoney currency. For that little adventure, he was deported.

Then there was the time he persuaded a Japanese tourist to part with $10,000 to help restore London's Westminster Abbey. He had worn one of the clerical gowns in his collection for the occasion, just to add authenticity to the appeal.

Stanley Lowe eventually ended his life living in an old-people's home. Gone were the days of handmade shirts and shoes; the times when life revolved around magnums of champagne, weekends at hotels in Paris and luxury holidays in Bermuda – all paid for by clever cons involving the rich and gullible.

3 Listening

You are going to listen to a radio programme about Stanley Lowe. You will notice that there are certain factual differences between the text you have just read and the information you hear. As you listen, underline the 'errors' in the reading text.

Now listen a second time, and write down the correct information.

4 Talking points
Work in pairs.

- What do you think about the sentences Stanley Lowe received for the crimes he committed?

- Do you know of any other famous cons?

- Do you agree with the saying 'Crime never pays'? Can you think of any real-life examples where this saying has been true, or where the opposite has been true?

Language review

A Grammar and Use

1 Zero Conditional

● Form

if + Present Simple; Present Simple

● Use

We use the Zero Conditional to talk about general rules, and about situations that are frequently or always true:

If it's a corporation, I usually have no qualms about doing something illegal or dishonest.
If you always tell the truth, sooner or later you end up hurting someone's feelings.

Note

In Zero Conditional sentences, *if* can usually be replaced by *when*.

2 First Conditional

● Form

if + Present Simple; *will (can* or *might)* + infinitive

● Use

We use First Conditional sentences to talk about likely situations and results in the future (if the conditions are fulfilled):

If you tell them the truth, it will hurt them a lot.
I might go if I'm invited.

Note

Will in the main clause suggests a more definite possibility than *can*. *Might* suggests that the possibility is even less likely.

3 Second Conditional

● Form

if + Past Simple; *would (could* or *might)* + infinitive

● Use

We use the Second Conditional when we imagine the future or the present to be different – when we are talking about something unlikely or untrue:

If somebody dropped a £10 note on the floor, I would tell them.
(If I found it ...,) I would always try to give money back!
I might not give money to someone if I thought it wasn't theirs.
If I had the chance to steal something, I couldn't do it.

4 Third Conditional

● Form

if + Past Perfect; *would have (could have* or *might have)* + past participle.

● Use

The Third Conditional is used to talk about unreal situations in the past, i.e. the opposite of what really happened:

She might have landed safely if she had baled out a few moments later.
(But she didn't bale out, so she didn't land safely.)
If there had not been so much cloud cover, she could have dropped down lower.
(But there was a lot of cloud cover, so she couldn't drop down lower.)
She would have been able to find her course to Hatfield if she had done this.
(But she didn't do this, so she wasn't able to find her course to Hatfield.)

Conditional sentences contain a main clause and an *if* clause. Either clause can come first. When the *if* clause comes first, it is separated from the main clause by a comma.

B Vocabulary

1 Crime verbs

Here is a list of crime-related verbs with similar meanings:

steal: things are stolen
He stole her bag.

rob: people and places are robbed of things
They've robbed me of my wallet.
The Midland Bank was robbed of £20,000 last night.

burgle: to break into a building and steal from it

nick (slang): to steal

pinch (informal): to steal

kidnap, abduct: to take someone away illegally, by force

shoplift: to steal from a shop

2 Adjective opposites

The opposites of many adjectives can be formed by the addition of a negative prefix. Here are some examples:

- *un-* is the most common negative prefix:

    unhappy   unusual   unattractive   unpleasant

- *in-* is also very common:

    inexpensive   incorrect   inconsiderate   invisible

- *il-* is added to some adjectives starting with *l*:

    illegal   illogical   illiterate

- *im-* is added to some adjectives starting with *m* or *p*:

    immoral   immovable   impossible   improbable

- *ir-* is added to some adjectives starting with *r*:

    irresponsible   irregular

- *dis-*

    dishonest   discontented

- *non-*

    non-violent   non-human

3 'Descending' words

The following verbs all mean 'to move from a higher position to a lower one':

drop	=	to fall or let fall, to manoeuvre into a lower position, for example in a plane
fall	=	to come down from a position by losing one's balance, or as a result of gravity
plummet	=	to fall suddenly from a great height
plunge	=	to move or be thrown suddenly downwards and/or forwards
land	=	to come down to the ground after a jump or flight

UNIT 6

first impressions

◆ Look at the photographs. Can you identify the countries, and the customs or traditions shown in each case?

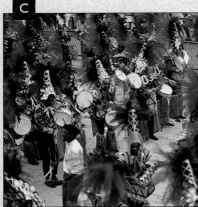

◆ Discuss the following points with a partner:
1 Do you think these traditions will continue in the future?
2 Are there any customs or traditions in your country that are similar to any of these?
3 Do you think any of these customs could offend people? Do you personally find any of them offensive? Why?

◆ Read the text, and then discuss these questions with a partner:
1 What other fighting sports are still popular today?
Why do you think people like them?
2 Have you ever participated in any of these? What was it like?

Ouch! There are many different fighting sports which are enjoyed by people all over the world. One of the simplest is shin-kicking, which was practised in England until the seventeenth century. Single contestants fought each other, wearing iron-tipped boots. The rules were quite straightforward – each kicked at the shins of the other until he either gave up in agony, or was unable to stand. Even players who were quite expert in this sport limped heavily after a contest.

Customs and Superstitions

1 Reading

Read these three texts about customs in different countries and match each text with one of the photos.

Which text describes these three types of event? Write the numbers in the boxes.

a) a competition ☐
b) a 'beginning' ☐
c) a religious event ☐

1 The most popular festival in Japan takes place from 1st–3rd January, and is called *Ganjitsu*, which means 'the beginning of the year'. People believe that good or bad luck in the first few days of the year represents the luck you will have for the rest of the year. *Ganjitsu* is celebrated by ceremonial housecleaning, feasting and by the exchanging of visits and presents. Most people put up special decorations at the entrance to their houses to keep out evil spirits. The main decoration is a sacred rope decorated with ferns, oranges and lobster. All of these things are thought to bring good fortune, prosperity and long life. Finally, no celebration is complete without *mochi* cake and *zoni* soup. Both the cake and the soup are made from traditional recipes.

2 The Mexican Day of the Dead is celebrated on 2nd November. On this day, or the evening before, many people visit cemeteries to leave presents and flowers at the graves of relatives. You can even buy skeletons in different costumes or skulls made of either sugar or chocolate, and inscribed with people's names. *Pan de muerto*, a special kind of bread with 'bones' on top, is baked and eaten during the festival. In country areas some families spend whole nights in the cemetery with candles, flowers and gifts. Offerings, such as the favourite food, drink or cigarettes of departed relatives, are also placed on a kind of altar in people's homes. But none of these objects compares with the elaborate paper skeletons used to decorate houses and churches. As far as Mexicans are concerned, the celebrations associated with the Day of the Dead show a positive attitude towards death, and neither the food nor the decoration is considered to be in bad taste.

3 *Il Palio*, The Parade of the Banner, takes place twice a year, on 2nd July and 16th August, in several Italian cities. *Il Palio de Siena* is the most famous.

The main event of this festival is an intensely competitive horse race which dates back to 1275. Before the race itself there is a splendid parade by representatives of the *contrade** of Siena. In the Middle Ages the *contrade* were rival military organisations.

Nowadays all the *contrade* employ professional jockeys who wear fifteenth-century costumes. If a jockey falls off, which happens quite often because no saddles or stirrups are used, the riderless horse can win the race by itself.

Although the race is not a religious event, all the horses are blessed in church, and the winning *contrada* receives the *Palio*, the silk banner of the Virgin Mary.

*contrada/e = area/s of the city

● **Understanding**

Read the three texts again and answer these questions about each of the festivals:

1 Where does the festival take place?
2 When does it take place?
3 What are the main activities?
4 What special food is associated with the festival? (One text does not mention food.)
5 What special objects are associated with the festival?

Now answer the following questions:

Ganjitsu
a) Why do the Japanese think the beginning of the year important?
b) Why do people put decorations at the entrance to their houses?

Day of the Dead
a) What symbols of death are used as decorations and gifts?
b) How would Mexicans themselves describe their view of death?

Il Palio
a) How are the modern *contrade* of Siena different from *contrade* of the past?
b) How do you know that the horses are more important than the jockeys in the race?

---

2 Vocabulary

● Match the words from the text with a suitable meaning.

1 celebrate (*Text 1*)   a something that makes a place look attractive
2 ceremonial (*1*)   b place where dead people are buried
3 feasting (*1*)   c seat on a horse for the rider to sit on
4 decoration(*1*)   d having a special, large meal
5 prosperity (*1*)   e gift
6 cemetery (*2*)   f hold an event to mark a special occasion
7 offering (*2*)   g wealth or success
8 departed (*2*)   h competing
9 rival (*3*)   i formal, ritual
10 saddle (*3*)   j dead

● **Euphemisms**
(*Language review B1, page 63*)

In Text 2, what does the expression *departed relatives* mean?

Why does the writer use the word *departed* instead of the more common word *dead*?

Do you know any more words like this?

Can you think of any examples of euphemisms in your language?

---

3 Proportions
(*Language review A1, page 62*)

Read these sentences from the three texts:

1 *Most people put up special decorations.*
2 *Many people visit cemeteries to leave presents.*
3 *Some families spend whole nights in the cemetery.*
4 *No saddles or stirrups are used.*
5 *All the horses are blessed in church.*

The words in bold refer to proportions of something. Arrange these five words in order, starting with *all*.

What kind of word follows the words in bold type in these sentences?

How is the sentence starting with *all* different from the others?

What do you notice about the verbs in these sentences?

4 None
(*Language review A2, page 62*)

Now look at this sentence from Text 2:

None of these objects compares with the paper skeletons ...

What do you notice about the verb in this sentence?

Which word in the five sentences in Exercise 3 has the same meaning as *none*?

None is often followed by *of the* + a plural noun. Which of the words in bold type in sentences 1-5 in Exercise 3 can also be followed by this construction?

5 Practice

Write answers to these questions by finishing the sentences.

1 How do people in your country celebrate birthdays?
   a Most people ...

   EXAMPLE:
   Most people send cards to people on their birthday.

   b Many people ...
   c Some people ...

2 When do people in your country decorate their homes?
   a Some people ...

   EXAMPLE:
   Some people decorate their homes at Easter.

   b Many people ...
   c Most people ...

6 Class survey

Find out how many of the other students in your class celebrate birthdays and decorate their homes in the ways you have suggested in Exercise 5.

Ask questions like this:

1 *Do you send cards to people on their birthday?*
2 *Do you decorate your home at Easter?*

Make a note of their answers.

Write sentences about other students' customs. Start your sentences with:

All (of) the   Most (of the)
Many (of the)   Some (of the)   None of the

EXAMPLE:

All (of) the students in my class send cards to people on their birthday.

---

7 Listening 🔲

● Look at this photograph of a New Year celebration and discuss these questions with a partner:

1 Which country celebrates New Year in this way?
2 When exactly does this celebration take place?

3 Do you know any other facts about this country's New Year celebrations? Make a list of things you know or think you know.

● Now listen to someone describing this celebration. Listen for the answers to the three questions above.

● **Listening for detail**

Listen to the recording again and finish these sentences:

1 The Chinese New Year is not always on the same date because...
2 The Chinese let off firecrackers at New Year to...
3 To stop evil spirits getting into their houses, people...
4 Dragons are symbols of...
5 The dragons can be made of...
6 Some of the dragons are so big and heavy that it takes...
7 *Sze Tsu* is the name of...
8 It's funnier and more theatrical...

8 Talking points

Work in groups of three.

1 How do people in your country or your family celebrate New Year?

2 Do your New Year celebrations have anything in common with each other or with the Chinese celebrations you have heard about?

9 Both, either, neither
(Language review A3, page 62)

Read these sentences from the texts in Exercise 1 and the recording in Exercise 7:

1 **Both** the cake **and** the soup are made from traditional recipes.
2 **Neither** the food **nor** the decoration is considered to be in bad taste.
3 The dragons are made of **either** paper **or** cloth.

What have the words in bold type in these three sentences got in common?

What do you notice about the verbs in sentences 1 and 2?

Why is there a difference between the verbs used in these sentences?

Choose the correct verb in this sentence and think of a reason for your choice:

Either paper or cloth is/are used to make the dragons.

Now read these sentences:

1 You should try *mochi* cake and *zoni* soup. **Both** are made from traditional recipes.
2 Mexicans buy skulls and skeletons. **Neither** is considered to be in bad taste.
3 They make the dragons from paper and cloth. **Either** is equally good.

What kind of words are *both, neither* and *either* in these sentences?

10 Practice

Make new sentences with *both ... and, either ... or,* or *neither ... nor.*

The first one has been done for you.

1 People can give each other Christmas presents on December 24th, or they can give them on December 25th.
People can give each other Christmas presents either on December 24th or on December 25th.

2 In Scotland some people celebrate Christmas. They also celebrate New Year.
3 In other countries people celebrate Christmas, or they celebrate New Year.
4 Until two years ago my brother believed in Father Christmas, and so did I.
5 Now my brother doesn't believe in him any more. And I don't believe in him.
6 Children think Father Christmas comes down the chimney or he comes through their bedroom window.
7 For Christmas dinner you can eat turkey or you can eat chicken. They're both traditional.
8 My mother doesn't eat meat, and I don't eat meat. We're vegetarians.
9 My mother eats pizza for Christmas dinner and I eat pizza too.
10 Christmas cake is made with dried fruit. Christmas pudding is also made with dried fruit.

11 Personalised practice

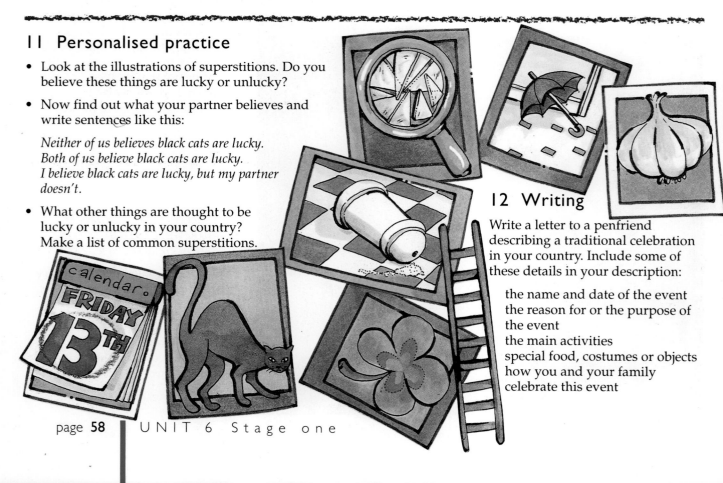

- Look at the illustrations of superstitions. Do you believe these things are lucky or unlucky?

- Now find out what your partner believes and write sentences like this:

Neither of us believes black cats are lucky.
Both of us believe black cats are lucky.
I believe black cats are lucky, but my partner doesn't.

- What other things are thought to be lucky or unlucky in your country? Make a list of common superstitions.

12 Writing

Write a letter to a penfriend describing a traditional celebration in your country. Include some of these details in your description:

the name and date of the event
the reason for or the purpose of the event
the main activities
special food, costumes or objects
how you and your family celebrate this event

National Characteristics

1 Nationalities

Look at these flags. How many of the countries can you identify?

What are the national characteristics commonly associated with people from these countries?

2 Listening

You are going to listen to James, a British person living in Mexico, talking about the national characteristics of Mexicans. Which subjects from this list do you think he will mention?

the family   attitudes to time   religion   friendliness
arguments   stereotypes   children

Now listen to the recording. Does James have a positive or a negative attitude to the subjects he mentions?

● Listening for detail

Listen again. What does James say to illustrate these statements?

1 It is easy to talk to people in Mexico.
2 The immediate friendliness of the Mexican people is not entirely positive.
3 Mexicans do not mind other people knowing their problems.
4 The Mexicans' attitude to time is not as unusual as most people think.
5 Life in Mexico City is more modern than people may imagine.

3 Vocabulary

Match the words or phrases in bold type in the sentences from the recording with their meanings.

1 *I've **got into** conversations on the bus …*
2 *So they **tend** to be a lot more friendly.*
3 *They seem to be willing to **air** their personal feelings …*
4 *… that seems a lot more healthy than the way we **go about** things.*
5 *And that immediately **strikes** you as quite odd.*
6 *I think this 'mañana' business is probably **exaggerated**.*
7 *It doesn't **bother** me at all.*
8 *I'm **in my element** here, you know.*
9 *I was quite **taken aback**.*

   a cause inconvenience   f started
   b shocked   g are inclined
   c over-emphasised   h approach
   d express   i impresses
   e very comfortable

---

4 Pronunciation

Read these words aloud:

of   to   but   for   at

Now listen to these extracts from the recording. How are the same words pronounced in these sentences?

1 *They tend **to** be a lot more friendly …*
2 *Having lived here **for** a while …*
3 *I haven't noticed that Mexicans are that bad **at** keeping appointments.*

4 ***But** I think it depends on the circumstances.*
5 *A Mexican is this sort **of** man with a big sombrero…*

Now work with a partner and take it in turns to repeat the sentences with the same pronunciation.

Read these five new sentences, paying careful attention to the pronunciation of the words in bold type.

6 She doesn't like **to** get up early.
7 I'll see you **at** four o'clock tomorrow afternoon.
8 The food here is great **but** it's a bit pricey.
9 Two cups **of** coffee please.
10 He's lived here **for** three-and-a-half years.

5 Listening

What are the national characteristics commonly associated with British people? Look back at the list you made in Exercise 1.

Now listen to two Mexicans discussing the British, and see how many of your points are mentioned.

Listen to the conversation again and note down what the speakers say about each of these topics:

1 making friends
2 being patient
3 the weather
4 attitudes to rules

Compare notes with a partner.

6 Talking points

Look back at the lists of national characteristics you wrote in Exercise 1 and discuss these questions with a partner:

1 Do you know people from any of these countries? What are they like?
2 Are the characteristics that you listed true or untrue of the individuals you know?

7 Multi-meaning words

(Language review B2, page 63)

The words in bold type in these sentences from the recordings all have several meanings. What is their meaning in these sentences?

What other meanings can they have?

1 *... that's the first thing you **notice** when you come here.*
2 *... waiting to **cross** the street.*
3 *... that's rather superficial in one **way**.*
4 *What else **strikes** you as positive ... ?*
5 *... quite **odd** coming from another culture.*
6 *... how far did you change your **view**?*
7 *... they are extremely **patient** compared to us.*
8 *... I still had to pay a **fine**.*

8 Conjunctions

(Language review A4, page 63)

Look at these extracts from the recordings. What have the underlined words got in common?

1 *They tend to be a lot more friendly, <u>but</u> ... you begin to realise that's rather superficial.*
2 *<u>Although</u> they're more relaxed about time, I think this 'manana' business is probably exaggerated.*
3 *<u>While</u> it was true that outwardly they were cold, when you made contact with them they could be open and friendly.*
4 *If they say 8 o'clock and you arrive at 9, it's really terrible, <u>whereas</u> in Mexico it would even be impolite to arrive exactly at 8 o'clock.*

Each of these four sentences has two clauses. One of these is introduced by the underlined word. What is the relationship between the two clauses in each sentence? Think about the meaning of the two clauses.

Compare ideas with a partner.

9 Practice

Match each sentence in the list on the left with a contrasting sentence in the list on the right. Then rewrite these two sentences as one, using each of the conjunctions from Exercise 8 twice.

EXAMPLE: 1D

Although the Mexicans are friendly when you first meet them, it is difficult to become close friends with them.

1 The Mexicans are friendly when you first meet them.
2 The British appear cold and reserved.
3 The weather is actually quite warm in the summer.
4 British people enjoy going abroad for their holidays.
5 Most countries celebrate New Year's Day on 1st January.
6 The French are famous for their cooking.
7 Americans love travelling to Europe.
8 Scottish people have a reputation for being mean.

A Paris is full of fast food restaurants.
B The Chinese celebrate their New Year between 10th January and 19th February.
C Most of them are actually very kind and generous.
D It is difficult to become close friends with them.
E They often find the way of life slow and old-fashioned.
F They are warm-hearted when you get to know them.
G Many British people go abroad for their holidays.
H They wouldn't like to live permanently in another country.

10 Writing

- Write a list of characteristics that are commonly associated with people of your nationality.

- Compare lists with a partner, and decide which characteristics are true, which are partly true and which are untrue.

- You are going to write the introductory chapter of a guidebook to your country. Using the points you

have listed and any ideas you have discussed, write a description of your national characteristics. Compare and contrast the stereotyped views with your own opinions.

EXAMPLE:

Everyone thinks we're very patriotic and quick-tempered people. Although we are proud of our country, we know that it's not perfect. And it's true that we get angry easily, but that's because we are passionate about everything we do.

Nationalities

1 Reading

Read the passage and try to guess which nationality is being described.

2 Vocabulary

Underline all the adjectives used to describe people's characteristics in paragraphs 1 and 2. Decide whether each one is positive, negative or neutral.

Can you find any pairs of opposites among the words in your list? What are the opposites of the rest of the adjectives? Compare ideas with a partner or use a dictionary to help you.

3 Discussion

Discuss these questions with a partner:

1 In what ways are people in your country similar to or different from the nationality described in the text?
2 Do you think it is possible to describe someone of a different nationality accurately.
3 Do you know of any foreigner who has written about your country and its people? How accurate was this description?

While the _____ often come across as gruff, cold and impersonal in public, in private, with the family and close friends, they are among the warmest, most cheerful, generous, emotional and overwhelmingly hospitable people on earth.

They adopt two very different modes of behaviour for their two lives – whereas in one they are reserved, hypocritical, careful, cagey, passive, in the other they are voluble, honest, direct, open, passionate.

The _____ are a mystical, religious, superstitious people at heart. Many intelligent people I knew swore that leap year is unlucky. The coming of anything as precious as a child invokes all kinds of precautions. It is bad luck to pick a name in advance, bad luck to buy a present ahead of time, even worse to discuss the likely date.

The _____ love a party and use any holiday, and even the unexpected arrival of a stranger, as a pretext for feasting and drinking. Moderation and frugality do not come naturally to the _____; they live for the moment. So when an occasion for partying, and especially drinking, arises, they will throw away an entire bonus or a huge chunk of pay – more than they can sensibly afford – on a single evening of mad jollity and emotional self-indulgence.

Most leisure activities are rather informal and modest. The men, young and old, gather round park benches to play chess or dominoes, usually with a good bit of betting. If they can choose, however, the majority of _____ turn back to nature for relaxation, taking a train out into the country. But their favourite outdoor hobby – one that always puzzles foreigners – is mushroom picking. In autumn, it approaches a national craze. Connoisseurs treat the location of their favourite hunting grounds as top secret.

A Grammar and Use

1 *All, most, many, some, no*

● **Meanings**

These words are all used to refer to proportions of something:

All the horses ...	= 100% of the horses
No saddles ...	= 0% of the saddles

● **Grammatical patterns with *all, most, many, some, no***

1 *All, most,* etc. + plural noun:

> *All children like sweets.*
> *Most people put up special decorations.*

2 When we refer to particular groups, *all, most,* etc. can be followed by *of* + *the, these, my,* etc. + plural noun:

> *All of these people are out of work.*
> *Some of the families in the country spend the whole night in the cemetery.*

3 *All* can be used without *of*:

> *All the contrade employ professional jockeys.*
> *All my friends are coming to my party.*

4 *All* does not always come before the noun or pronoun it refers to:

> *The horses are all blessed in church.*
> *The contrade all employ professional jockeys.*

5 *All, most, many* and *some* can be used as pronouns:

> *Many visit cemeteries to leave presents.*

6 *No* cannot be followed by *the* or *of the*, and cannot be used as a pronoun.

2 *None*

● **Grammatical patterns**

1 *None* is always followed by *of* + *the, these, my,* etc. + plural noun, and is followed by a singular verb:

> *None of these objects compares with the paper skeletons.*

2 *None* can be used as a pronoun:

> *None compares with the paper skeletons.*

Note

In informal speech we often use plural verbs with *none*:

> *None of these objects compare with the paper skeletons.*

3 *Both, either, neither*

● **Meanings**

Both indicates two people or things.

Either means any one of two.

Neither means not one and not the other of two.

● **Grammatical patterns with *both***

1 *Both* + plural noun or *Both* + (*of*) *the, these, my,* etc. + plural noun:

> *Both dishes are made from traditional recipes.*
> *Both (of) my parents speak German.*

2 *Both* can be used as a pronoun:

> *Both are made from traditional recipes.*

3 *Both ... and*

In this pattern *both* emphasises the fact that there are two:

> *Both the cake and the soup are made from traditional recipes.*

● **Grammatical patterns with *either* and *neither***

1 *Either/Neither* + singular noun:

> *Either material can be used.*
> *Neither feature of the festival is considered to be in bad taste.*

2 *Either/Neither* + *of* + *the, these,* etc. + plural noun:

> *Either of the materials can be used.*
> *Neither of these features is considered to be in bad taste.*

3 *Either/Neither* can be used as pronouns:

> *Either can be used.*
> *Neither is considered to be in bad taste.*

4 *either...or/neither...nor*

This pattern is used when the alternatives are specified:

> *The dragons are made from either paper or cloth.*
> *The Mexicans consider neither the food nor the decoration to be in bad taste.*

Note

When the *either...or/neither...nor* phrase is the subject of a sentence, a singular verb is used.

4 Contrasting conjunctions

Although, but, whereas, while and *even though* are conjunctions which are used to connect two contrasting clauses (parts of a sentence):

> *Although the race is not a religious event, all the horses are blessed in church.*

> *They tend to be more friendly, but you begin to realise that's rather superficial.*

> *In Britain people don't like to be late, whereas in Mexico it's impolite to arrive on time.*

> *While it was true that outwardly they were cold, when you made contact with them they could be open and friendly.*

> *Even though I argued with her, I still had to pay a fine.*

Note

Clauses starting with *although, whereas, while* and *even though* can be first or second in the sentence:

> *Even though I argued with her, I still had to pay the fine.*

> *I still had to pay the fine, even though I argued with her.*

Clauses starting with *but* must be second in the sentence.

B Vocabulary

1 Euphemisms

A euphemism is an indirect word or phrase which we use when we prefer not to be too direct. For example, the phrase **departed** *relatives* is more pleasant or more polite than **dead** *relatives*.

Here are some more commonly used euphemisms:

Direct words	Euphemisms
to die	to pass away
mad	disturbed
fat	plump
stupid	less able
bald	thin on top
old	elderly
ugly	plain
rich	well-off
deaf	hard of hearing

2 Multi-meaning words

Here are the most common meanings of the words in Exercise 7 on page 60.

(The first meaning given is the meaning used in the recordings.)

notice	1	(vb.) to see, observe
	2	(n.) a written announcement
cross	1	(vb.) to go from one side to the other
	2	(adj.) angry
	3	(n.) a mark like this: X
way	1	(n.) respect/aspect
	2	(n.) method
	3	(n.) direction
strike	1	(vb.) to impress
	2	(vb.) to hit
	3	(vb. & n.) (to) protest by stopping work
odd	1	(adj.) strange
	2	(adj.) opposite of even (numbers)
view	1	(n.) opinion
	2	(n.) a scene, what you can see from a place
patient	1	(adj.) tolerant, good-tempered, calm
	2	(n.) person receiving medical treatment
fine	1	(n.) money paid as a punishment for breaking the law
	2	(adj.) beautiful, good
	3	(adj.) bright, not raining (weather)

◆ This is how a magazine published in 1990 summarised the early 1960s:

'The Fabulous Sixties,' they say, looking wistful. 'What an amazing time to have been a teenager.' Do you wonder what they're talking about; think they're mad or just old and nostalgic? Or are you intrigued? You've probably seen the photos of those days – the girls in the mini skirts, the guys with long hair. You probably even look a bit sixties yourself. And the music – well you know about Bowie and Jagger, they're still around, and you keep hearing all those oldies on the radio by the Beatles, the Kinks, the Stones and all those others.

◆ How many of the people and events illustrated can you identify? What else do you know about the 1960s?

◆ Work in small groups. If you were the editorial team of a magazine looking back at the late 1980s and early 1990s, how would you summarise this period in words and pictures? Write brief notes, and make a list of photographs you would use.

◆ What is special about being a teenager? In what ways are teenagers different from children or adults? Make a list of differences and then compare lists with a partner.

◆ Look at the photographs. Which of these two situations do you identify most closely with? Compare ideas with a partner.

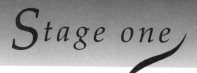

Stage one

Teenagers and Parents

1 Pre-listening

What do parents and their teenage children often have disagreements about?

Discuss your own experience with a partner.

2 Listening 📼

You are going to hear some people talking about their teenage years.

How many of the speakers are still teenagers?

Do the speakers mention any of the kinds of disagreement you discussed?

● Understanding

Listen to Parts 1 and 2 again and answer these questions:

Part 1
1 According to the first speaker, what is being a teenager all about?

Part 2
2 Why didn't the girl want to go out with her parents?

3 According to the boy, why don't teenagers have any freedom?

Now listen to Parts 3 and 4 again and answer these questions:

Part 3
4 What is the one subject of disagreement between the speaker and his parents?

Part 4
5 Why didn't the first speaker enjoy being a teenager?

---

3 Vocabulary
(Language review B1, page 72)

● *Thing*

What do the *'thing'* phrases mean in these extracts from the recording?

That's another thing about being a teenager …
That's the thing … parents actually have quite a lot of power.
… she always told me, 'You look terrible in that,' and that sort of thing.

It is very common in spoken English to use the word *thing* instead of words with a more precise meaning. Replace the *'thing'* phrases in these sentences with more precise words or phrases. Use your imagination.

EXAMPLE: You can't take all those things – we haven't got room in the car.
You can't take *all that luggage/all those bags …*

1 Have you seen that thing we use for cleaning the windows with?
2 What have you done with my swimming things? I left them on the table.
3 That was a really boring programme. I'd heard all those things before.
4 I'll be ready in about ten minutes. I've just got to pack my things.
5 A strange thing happened to me on my way home this evening.

● Synonyms

Look at these extracts from the recording in Exercise 2. Replace the words or phrases in bold type with a word or phrase from the box below:

1 *I can't be seen out with my dad. People will just **laugh at** me.*
2 *… they've got to cook the **tea** …*
3 *… she **didn't have a clue** when it came to understanding what goes on in the teenage mind.*
4 *I was expected to **behave** like an adult.*
5 *… given the **status** of a child in the other …*
6 *I could never **join in with** the fashions.*
7 *It was really **irritating**.*
8 *… he actually **grounded me** for a whole week.*

make fun of	act	annoying
had no idea		
kept me in	evening meal	take part in
importance		

4 Statements, Questions and Commands
(Language review A1, page 70)

Compare these pairs of question sentences. What are the differences between the two sentences in each case?

1 a Where are you going?
  b He asked me where I was going.
2 a What time will you be back?
  b He wanted to know what time I'd be back.

3 a Are you going with anyone?
  b She asked me if I was going with anyone.

Compare ideas with a partner.

Look at these extracts from the recording. Decide whether they are reported statements, questions or commands. Write **S**, **Q** or **C** in the boxes.

1 *My dad asked me where I was going.* ☐
2 *He wanted to know who I was going with.* ☐
3 *My mother always told me what I looked like.* ☐
4 *He told me to be home by midnight at the latest.* ☐

5 Practice

If you could meet the people in these photographs, what questions would you ask them?

Make up indirect questions like this:

I'd ask the man on the bicycle if he was afraid.
I'd ask the stuntmen how much money they got paid.

6 Conversations

● Read this extract from a teenage girl's journal. How old do you think the girl is? Who is John?

Working in groups of three, make up the conversation between the girl and her parents.

● Read this report of a conversation that took place between a boy and his father.

Tuesday: Mentioned that I was thinking about holiday with Sue and Jenny. Mum and Dad just stared at me as if I was mad. Said I was too young. Told them that Sue and Jenny's parents didn't mind. They asked usual questions: where we were thinking of going, who else was going, how long we'd be away for – the usual things.

Ended up getting angry – stormed out of the room. I'm fed up with being treated like a child. Why do parents treat girls differently from boys? John went away with friends when he was 16.

Now write the actual conversation between the boy and his father.

7 Pronunciation 🔊

To make their conversations more lively, speakers often use other people's actual words (direct speech) instead of reported speech. Listen to these examples.

How do the speakers make it clear that they are using another person's words and not their own? Listen to the examples again and compare ideas with a partner.

Now listen to these five examples which contain direct speech. As you listen, add speech marks in the correct places.

1 *He burst through the door and just came out with it. I've passed my exam. It was amazing.*
2 *… of course I had to stop. I got out and waited by my car. Morning, Sir. He had a really booming voice. Did you know you were exceeding the speed limit?*
3 *I'd just got into bed when I heard a voice from the garden. Are you awake? So I called back, No, I've been asleep for nearly an hour. That shut him up.*
4 *With my mother it was always a case of don't do this and don't do that.*
5 *It was always the same old questions, Where have you been? or more often, Who have you been with?*

Tell a partner some of the things your parents or your teachers often say to you. Use their actual words.

---

8 Role play

Work in pairs.

Read this description of a problem a couple are having with their teenage daughter:

Sara is 14 years old and seems to go out of her way to defy her parents. If they ask her to do something, she does the opposite, or becomes stubborn and difficult. Last week, she was seen hitch hiking alone, even though her father had forbidden it, and she didn't get home until midnight after going to a disco with her friends.

Think about what you would do if you were in the same situation as Sara's parents.

Student A: Turn to page 157.

Student B: As a parent you try to take things calmly. You hope your daughter is just going through a difficult phase.

Make a list of some of the things that you might say to Sara. They can be statements, questions or commands.

EXAMPLES: *I'd tell her to start thinking about other people.*
I'd tell her I was very very worried about her.
I'd ask her to stop behaving so selfishly.
I'd ask her if she was unhappy at school.

In pairs discuss how best to deal with Sara. Try to agree on one or two things to say to her.

---

9 Talking about the past
(Language review A2, page 71)

Which of these sentences refer to single past events, and which refer to routines? Write **S** or **R** in the boxes:

a *She used to tell me what to wear.* ☐
b *I took exams a couple of years ago.* ☐
c *We used to hang out quite a lot.* ☐
d *I would spend the day at school and in the evening go and meet up with my friends.* ☐
e *Whenever I was at home, they would moan about me not being there.* ☐
f *My dad always asked me where I was going.* ☐
g *Once, he actually grounded me for a whole week.* ☐

Which words or phrases tell you that the speakers are referring to routines or to single actions?

Compare ideas with a partner.

---

10 Personalised practice

When you were 14 years old, what did your parents use to say to you before you went out for the evening?

Make a list of some of the questions they asked you and some of the things they told you to do, or not to do.

EXAMPLES: *They'd want to know where I was going.*
They used to tell me to phone them if I was going to be home late.

Try and find someone in the class whose parents used to say similar things.

S tage two

Explaining Behaviour and Feelings

1 Listening

Listen to two people talking about the reasons why parents put restrictions on their teenage children. Are the speakers talking from the point of view of a teenager or a parent?

What are the two reasons mentioned by the speakers?

2 Talking point

In your experience, how common are these explanations for parents' attitudes?

Discuss ideas in pairs or groups.

3 Reading

Read this story of a family incident from a mother's point of view.

How would you describe the mother's feelings?

● Understanding

Find evidence in the text that the mother:

1 was worried or anxious
2 felt frightened
3 felt physically sick
4 thought something terrible might have happened to her daughter
5 became emotionally upset
6 was relieved to find that her daughter was at her friend's house
7 felt that she was to blame for her daughter's behaviour

A MOTHER'S FONDNESS

1 I began to worry and fidget by half past five. Two buses had gone by and she had not come home from school. I thought of all the places she could go to and became afraid because there were so many. My husband was in Glasgow and my father, who lived with us, was on holiday. The house was empty. I was frightened, not because I was alone, but because I thought she would have phoned if she was going anywhere. My stomach turned, I felt hungry but could not eat, tired but could not sleep, tormented by my imagination.

2 At six o'clock I phoned her friend but she had no idea where she was and suggested I phone several people who were other schoolfriends. I phoned them all, but no one knew, and they said they would phone back if they found out where she was. I took the car into town. There was a girl she was friendly with who lived in a house on the way to town, so I called in.

3 'Elaine, have you seen Cathie?' It was hard to speak as the cries of pain echoed through my head. I was too embarrassed to stay. I had started to cry and my eyes were red and sore. I went into all the cafés she talked of. It was no use. I went home and found myself waiting for the phone to ring. It did several times. It was always someone asking if I had found her.

4 At nine o'clock I answered the phone for the millionth time. It was Mrs Wilson, Elaine's mother. She said Cathie was at their house. I felt as though the greatest load had been lifted from my heart. Again I took the car and drove back into town.

5 She was very quiet and looked at me coldly. She thanked Elaine and got into the car. We said nothing, but I wanted to be angry, I wanted to show how worried I had been. I knew she would not see my anger as love. It seemed as though she hated me and wanted to hurt me, but I could tell as she sat stiffly and unmoved that she had no idea this was possible. I was as pleasant as I could be and she answered all the countless questions in a calm indifferent manner. I had failed. I could not get through to her. She could not see the agony I had gone through because of her. It was my fault she was as she was. I had brought myself pain.

6 When we got home we watched television and it seemed as though nothing had happened at all. It was forgotten, pushed away out of sight. That night I prayed it would never happen again.

4 Vocabulary
● **Phrasal verbs with** *through*
(Language review B2, page 72)

Choose the correct meaning (from the box below) of the *'through'* verbs in these sentences.

> pass   communicate with
> read carefully   repeat
> recover/survive

1 I've tried explaining, but I just can't get through to her.
2 I'm taking my driving test on Tuesday. I hope I get through.
3 I still don't understand. Can you go through the instructions again?
4 He's been very ill, but the doctors say he's going to pull through.
5 I've looked through the paper twice and I can't see the story anywhere.

---

5 Explanations and reasons
(Language review A3, page 71)

The mother explains why she was frightened:

> *I was frightened, not because I was alone, but because I thought she would have phoned if she was going anywhere.*

Here are some more ways of asking for and giving explanations or reasons. Match these questions with an appropriate explanation:

Question	Explanation
1 Why did the mother begin to worry about her daughter?	a The main reason was that she felt sick.
2 How do you account for the fact that her husband was not at home?	b Because two buses had gone by and Cathie had not come home.
3 How do you explain that although she was hungry, she couldn't eat?	c Maybe it was because the friend didn't have a phone.
4 Can you explain why she didn't telephone her daughter's friend?	d It was because she knew her daughter would not see her anger as love.
5 The mother didn't show her daughter how worried she had been. Why was that?	e It could be because he was away on business.

Why do you think the daughter didn't telephone her mother to tell her where she was? Discuss this question with a partner. Think of several possible answers.

---

6 Practice
Work in small groups.

Work out answers to these questions. Use some of the ways of giving explanations from Exercise 5.

1 Can you explain why so many teenagers seem lazy and selfish?

2 Why do you think that boys are more aggressive than girls?

3 How do you account for the fact that girls learn to speak at an earlier age than boys?

4 Why do teenagers tend to like different clothes and music from everyone else?

5 How do you explain the fact that women live longer than men?

Extension

The Daughter's Story

1 Writing

You have read about a family incident from the mother's point of view. You are now going to write the daughter's view of the same incident. Before you start, plan your composition. Here are some guidelines:

● Content

1 How will the daughter's story differ from her mother's?
2 What will a reader want to find out from reading the girl's story?
3 Will the daughter write mainly about events or about her feelings?

● Structure

Read quickly through the mother's story again and write a sentence summarising what happens in each of the six paragraphs. Now write about six phrases or sentences summarising what you think will be in the daughter's story.

EXAMPLE: *In Paragraph 1 the daughter explains why she didn't go home at the usual time.*

● Language

1 What are the main verb tenses used in the mother's story? Why are these tenses used?
2 In her version of the story, why do you think Cathie might use more direct speech than her mother?
3 Time is very important for the mother, so in her story she uses a lot of time phrases. Would you use as many time phrases in the daughter's story? Why or why not?

Now write a first draft of the daughter's story. Write about 150 words.

Exchange stories with a partner and compare what you have written. Discuss the differences between your versions.

Write your final draft and check it carefully.

2 Reading

Finally, turn to page 157 and read *The Daughter's Story*.

Language review

A Grammar and Use

1 Direct and Reported speech

● Reported statements

Remember the main differences between direct and reported speech:

1 The tense of verbs in reported speech is usually further in the past than the corresponding verbs in direct speech (but see note below).

2 Pronouns become indirect
   I → she, we → they

3 Time references become indirect
   yesterday → the day before

EXAMPLE:

Direct: *'I'm going home tomorrow,' she said.*
Reported: *She said she was going home the following day.*

Note: The present tense can be kept in the reported statement if you are reporting permanent states or facts, just as the Simple Past does not have to change to the Past Perfect if the context is clear. (See Unit 3, Language review A1.)

● Reported questions

1 *Wh-* questions

DIRECT	REPORTED
'Where are you going tomorrow?' she asked	She asked (me) where I was going the following day.
'What time will you be back?' my father asked.	My father asked what time I would / I'd be back.
'Where have you been?' he asked	He asked where I had / I'd been.

2 Other questions

When we report questions which do not have a *wh-*question word, we add *if* or *whether*:

DIRECT	REPORTED
'Are you going with anyone?' he asked	He asked if I was going with anyone.
'Is it a party or a dance?' she wanted to know.	She wanted to know if it was a party or a dance.
If I met Michael Jackson, I'd say, 'Do you prefer making videos or doing live shows?'	I'd ask Michael Jackson whether he prefers making videos or doing live shows.

3 Reporting verbs with reported questions:

He **asked** if I would be late home.
She **wondered** where I was going.
They **wanted to know** who I was going with.

● **Reported commands or requests**

When we report commands (orders) or requests, we often use *tell* or *ask* + infinitive:

DIRECT	REPORTED
'You must be home by midnight,' he said.	He told me to be home by midnight.
'Don't be late!' she said.	She told me not to be late.
'Could you lock the doors when you come in?' she said.	She asked me to lock the doors when I came in.

Notes

1 The verbs *order*, *command* and *request* are not often used as reporting verbs.

2 *say* and *tell*: *say* does not need a personal indirect object, whereas *tell* does:

He said he was emigrating to Australia.
He told **his mother / her** he was emigrating to Australia.

2 Past habits and routines

Remember these ways of referring to past habits and routines:

- *used to:*

  My mother used to tell me what to wear.
  Did your parents use to worry when you were late?
  We didn't use to have arguments.

- A verb in the simple past with a time expression which shows frequency or regularity:

  I always went to school by bike.
  I met up with my friends in the evenings.
  At weekends I went to parties or discos.
  Whenever I wore new clothes my mother said I looked terrible.

- *Would* + infinitive can also be used to refer to past routines or behaviour:

  I would spend the day at school and in the evening go and meet up with my friends.
  Whenever I was at home they would (they'd) moan about me not being there.

Note

Would can only refer to actions, not to states:

I used to live in Paris.
I would/used to walk by the river every day.

3 Explanations and reasons

Here are some common ways of asking for and giving explanations or reasons:

● **Why ...?/Because (of) ...**

Why are you shivering?
  Because I'm cold./Because of the cold.
Why do teenagers prefer to go out without their parents?
  Because they want to be independent.
  Maybe it's because ...
  It could be because ...

● *Reason*

Why didn't the mother eat anything?
  The main reason was that she felt sick.
  One of the reasons was that she was very worried about her daughter.

● *Explain/account for*

Can you explain why she didn't telephone her daughter's friend?
  The only explanation I can think of is that the friend didn't have a phone.
  I can't explain it.

How do you account for/explain Michael Jackson's popularity?
  I can't account for it.
  I'd say it was a combination of his unusual voice and his brilliant dancing.

Note

Explain is followed by a noun or a verb phrase.
Account for can only be followed by a noun or noun phrase.

B Vocabulary

1 Thing

Thing is often used in spoken English instead of other words when a speaker doesn't want to, cannot be bothered to or is unable to be more precise.

Thing is used to refer to an object, an activity, a situation or an idea:

*While I was in town I bought a few **things** I needed for my holiday.*
*Tell me some of the **things** you do at work.*
***Things** are going quite well at the moment.*
*I've just heard an interesting **thing** on the radio.*

Here are some common expressions with *thing*:

*My sister's just won £100, the **lucky thing**.*
*I prefer walking to work. **For one thing** it keeps me fit.*
*I don't like organised holidays. I'd rather **do my own thing**.*
*Jim, I haven't seen you for ages. **How are things**?*
*I can't stand housework, gardening and **things like that**.*
*There's **no such thing** as fairies.*
*We can't go to the meeting tomorrow. **The thing is** we've got some people coming round.*

Other similar words and expressions:

*Where's that **thingummyjig** I was using a minute ago?*
*I was in town yesterday and I saw **thingy**, you know, what's his name – that bloke who lives round the corner.*

2 Phrasal verbs with *through*

Here are some more examples of verbs followed by *through* in addition to those on page 69.

*Unfortunately, our plan to move house has **fallen through**.*
= fail

*However hard I try, I just can't **get through to** him.*
= communicate with

*I hope you **get through** your driving text tomorrow.* = pass

*I had three teeth out yesterday. I never want to **go through** that again.* = experience, suffer

*I can't find your book anywhere. I've **been through** all my drawers and cupboards.*
= look carefully through, search, examine

*For a moment or two I thought he wasn't going to **pull through** after the operation.* = recover, get better

*Could you **run through** the rules once more please?*
= repeat/read quickly

*He said he was a senior police officer, but I **saw through** his disguise immediately.* = not be deceived by

◆ How do you react to these photos? What is the first word that comes into your head,
e.g. *stupid, sad, funny*?

◆ Find someone who has the same reactions to the photos as you.

◆ Read these quotations about animals and human beings.

• *Nothing can be more obvious than that all animals were created solely and exclusively for the use of man.* (Thomas Love Peacock)

• *Wild animals never kill for sport. Man is the only one to whom the torture and death of his fellow creatures is amusing in itself.*
(J.A. Froude)

• *Animals are such agreeable friends – they ask no questions, they pass no criticism.*
(George Eliot)

• *I think I could turn and live with animals,*
They're so placid and self-contained,
I stand and look at them long and long,
They do not sweat and whine about their condition,
They do not lie awake in the dark and weep for their sins …
(Walt Whitman)

• *All animals are equal, but some animals are more equal than others.*
(George Orwell)

◆ Discuss these points in groups:

1 What is the main idea in each of these quotations?
2 Could the photographs above be used to illustrate any of these quotations?
3 Do you strongly agree or disagree with any of these quotations?

◆ What are your opinions on these animal-related subjects?

zoos • animal acts in circuses • hunting • pets

Stage one

Survival

1 Pre-reading

● David Attenborough, who is a famous British naturalist, has spent much of his working life writing about and filming wild animals. His TV series and book, *The Trials of Life*, looks at how animals behave. This is the opening paragraph of Chapter 3, 'Finding Food':

> Animals have to kill to feed. They cannot, like plants, build their bodies from nothing more than minerals from the earth and gases from the air. They must eat plants. Some consume them directly; others do so indirectly by eating the bodies of plant-eating animals. Neither plants nor animals welcome being eaten. So finding food, for an animal, can be a demanding and continuing trial.

● How do animals and plants protect themselves so as to avoid being killed and eaten? Working with a partner, think of as many methods as you can. The photographs opposite may give you some ideas.

2 Reading

Match the four photographs with the texts. How many of the ideas you thought of are mentioned in the texts?

1
Some plants have an ingenious way of deterring animals from destroying their seeds. They pack them with poison. Strychnine, which is one of the deadliest of all poisons, comes from the seeds of a tall Asian evergreen tree. Its fruit is about the size and colour of small oranges, and various animals feed on the fleshy pulp. But these animals have to take great care not to crack the disc-shaped seeds. Macaws, which specialise in eating seeds, also have to deal with this problem. These birds normally live in isolated pairs, but occasionally congregate in large numbers on particular river banks, where they gnaw the soil with their beaks. It has been discovered only recently that they come to these places to gather particular minerals, such as kaolin, in order to neutralise the poison they have absorbed from the seeds they eat.

2
Most animals escape from their predators by getting out of their way. But there are other ways for even the most defenceless animals to improve their chances of survival. In East Africa, for example, grass-eating gazelles manage to find protection among their own number. A gazelle, grazing by itself with its head down, is an easy target for a cheetah. But if the gazelle grazes in a herd of a hundred or so, its chances of survival are dramatically better. In this way, it is more likely to get an early warning of the cheetah's approach; even when its own head is down grazing, other heads are up and scanning the surrounding country ready to sound an alarm. At this signal the herd take flight. The cheetah, which is forced to attack when it is still some distance from the herd, may have to spend crucial moments picking out its chosen target from among the confusing mass of racing bodies. Even when it succeeds, there is still a chance that after pursuing it for some way, another gazelle will impede it, and its first, tiring target will be able to escape.

3
Few mammals have chemical defences, but the skunk is an exception. From glands just beneath its tail it produces considerable quantities of a most evil-smelling liquid. You might imagine that a bad smell would not deter a really hungry hunter, but a full squirt from a skunk is almost unbearable. The stench is so powerful that you feel violently sick, and if it gets into your eyes, you may be unable to see for several hours. The skunk does its best to prevent confrontations with would-be enemies by displaying vivid keep-off signs. It is boldly patterned in black and white. Skunks also give fair warning of their character by deliberately making themselves conspicuous and waving their bushy tails. A skunk can put on an impressive performance. First it stamps vigorously with its front feet and raises its tail. If you get closer, it does a hand-stand, raising its hind legs in the air and pointing its tail over its head towards you. If that does not deter you, it drops back on all fours, turns its back on you and squirts. The jet can travel up to twenty feet.

4
Other animals play tricks to protect themselves. The clear-wing moth, whose appearance resembles that of a wasp or a bee, and which makes a buzzing noise, actually has no sting. By masquerading as a poisonous insect it avoids attacks from birds. This tactic of drawing attention to yourself when you have no deterrent to back up your threat, may seem reckless. And indeed it is not universally successful. Some species of birds have developed the ability to distinguish between the real thing and the mimic, and actually feed on the imposters. Nonetheless, the strategy is generally successful. The caterpillar of a Costa Rican moth, in one of the most extraordinary of all mimicries, has a pattern at its rear that makes it look like a tiny viper.

● Titles

Choose a suitable title for each of the four reading texts:

Animal impersonators
Strychnine kills macaws
Safety in numbers
A natural antidote
Keep away – dangerous liquid!
Animals with chemical defences
Gazelle attacks cheetah
Snake that looks like a caterpillar

● Understanding

1 In what way are macaws different from other animals which eat the fruit of the Asian evergreen tree? (*Text 1*)
2 What makes the gazelle a particularly defenceless animal? (2)
3 In what ways do gazelles protect each other? (2)
4 How are skunks different from most other mammals? (3)
5 How do skunks warn their enemies before they squirt them with their liquid? (3)
6 In what ways is the clear-wing moth similar to bees and wasps? (4)

3 Vocabulary

● Guess the meanings of these phrases from the texts:

a chances of survival (*Text 2*)
b an early warning (2)
c to sound an alarm (2)
d crucial moments (2)
e the skunk is an exception (3)
f would-be enemies (3)
g a hand-stand (3)
h on all fours (3)
i not universally successful (4)

● Attack and defence

Find words in the texts which mean about the same as:

1 to discourage by the use of fear (*Text 1*)
2 to make harmless (1)
3 animals which live by killing and eating other animals (2)
4 unable to protect oneself (2)
5 to follow, chase in order to catch (2)
6 occasion of coming face to face with an enemy(3)
7 easily seen, noticeable (3)
8 to pretend to be something (4)
9 act of imitating another animal's appearance or behaviour (4)

4 Animal idioms
(Language review B1, page 83)

Certain animals are commonly associated with particular characteristics. These animals are used in idioms to refer to certain types of people.

EXAMPLE: *a snake in the grass* = a hidden or treacherous enemy

Match these animal idioms with their meanings:

1 *a wolf in sheep's clothing*
2 *a rogue elephant*
3 *a dark horse*
4 *an eager beaver*
5 *a dog in the manger*
6 *the bee's knees*
7 *a cold fish*

a someone who has no respect for authority
b someone who thinks they are the best
c someone who stops other people from enjoying something they can't enjoy themselves
d a person who keeps their abilities to themselves
e someone who pretends to be friendly but actually has bad intentions
f someone who does not show emotions
g someone who works hard and with enthusiasm

5 Extra information
(Language review A1, page 82)

The underlined words in these sentences from Exercises 1 and 2 are relative pronouns.

Who or what do they refer to?

1 *David Attenborough, <u>who</u> is a famous British naturalist, has spent much of his working life writing about and filming wild animals.*
2 *Strychnine, <u>which</u> is one of the deadliest of all poisons, comes from the seeds of a tall Asian evergreen tree.*
3 *Macaws, <u>which</u> specialise in eating seeds, also have to deal with this problem.*
4 *The cheetah, <u>which</u> is forced to attack when it is still some distance from the herd, may have to spend crucial moments picking out its chosen target.*
5 *The clear-wing moth, <u>whose</u> appearance resembles that of a wasp or a bee, and <u>which</u> makes a buzzing noise, actually has no sting.*

These five sentences consist of two or three clauses. (A clause is part of a sentence which includes a subject and a verb.) One of the clauses in each of the five sentences makes sense on its own. The other(s) only make sense in relation to the main clause. Write down the five main clauses.

What is the function or purpose of the other clause(s)?

Why is *who* used only in the first sentence?

6 Practice

Here are five pairs of sentences. For each pair decide which sentence should be the main clause and which should be the 'extra information' clause. Then rewrite each pair as a single, two-clause sentence.

EXAMPLE:

Beavers live in North America and in parts of Europe. (Extra)
Beavers feed on leaves and the living bark of trees. (Main)
Beavers, which live in North America and in parts of Europe, feed on leaves and the living bark of trees.

1 Beavers use their teeth to cut down young trees.
  Their teeth are chisel-shaped.
2 Dams provide beavers with a safe home and a food store.
  Dams are made out of sticks, stones and mud.
3 Beavers live in lodges.
  These lodges are built on the side of the lake formed by their dam.

4 The only way into a beaver's lodge is from the lake.
  The lodge's entrance is actually underwater.
5 In the winter beavers feed on young trees.
  The young trees have been lying on the lake bed since the previous summer.

7 Negatives

Rewrite these sentences from Exercises 1 and 2 without using the underlined words. Do not change the basic meaning of the sentences.

1 *Neither plants nor animals welcome being eaten.*
2 *They (animals) cannot, like plants, build their bodies from nothing more than minerals from the earth and gases from the air.*
3 *The clear-wing moth actually has no sting.*

Think of suitable endings to these sentences:

a Neither humans nor animals …
b Neither dogs nor cats …

(See Unit 6, Language review A2.)

---

8 Reading and writing

● Read this story of animals threatening human beings. Why do you think agricultural department officials were so worried about these snails?

● Now rewrite the story adding these pieces of extra information.

1 Miami is a famous resort in Florida.
2 The giant snails were as big as a man's hand.
3 The tourist had found the snails in the tropics.
4 The snails have plenty of natural enemies in other parts of the world.
5 The snails began reproducing at a fantastic speed.
6 The officials imagined the snails eating every bit of green vegetation in Miami.
7 The snails' appetite matched their size.
8 A snail mother can produce between 400 and 600 eggs a year.

EXAMPLE:

*The people of Miami, **which is a famous resort in Florida**, thought they had become victims of a science-fiction nightmare when …*

Compare versions of the story with a partner.

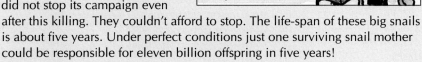

The Invasion of the Giant Snails

THE PEOPLE of Miami thought they had become victims of a science-fiction nightmare when their pleasant residential neighbourhoods were invaded by giant snails. Perhaps 'invaded' is not the right word. The snails were actually brought to Miami by an unsuspecting tourist. In Florida the giant snails found a perfect, safe environment.

But the snails created an enormous problem for officials of the Florida Department of Agriculture. Soon after the discovery of the potential snail plague, the officials launched a massive extermination campaign. Just one week after the poisoning started, 2500 dead snails had been picked up. Two weeks later another 5000 were found. By the end of the year 17,000 snails had been killed.

The Department of Agriculture did not stop its campaign even after this killing. They couldn't afford to stop. The life-span of these big snails is about five years. Under perfect conditions just one surviving snail mother could be responsible for eleven billion offspring in five years!

---

9 Pronunciation

Listen to the first part of the story of the giant snails. As you listen, compare it to your version.

Listen again. Why do you think the speaker pauses before and after the *which* or *who* clauses?

Now read these sentences to each other in pairs, pausing briefly before and after the relative clauses:

1 The giant snails, which began reproducing at a fantastic speed, created an enormous problem for officials in Florida.
2 The officials, who imagined the snails eating every bit of green vegetation in Miami, launched an extermination campaign.
3 The life-span of these snails, whose appetite matched their size, is about five years.
4 One surviving snail mother, which can produce between 400 and 600 eggs a year, could be responsible for eleven billion offspring in five years.

10 Reading and discussion

In what ways are human beings a threat to animals? What can or should be done to protect animals from humans?

Discuss these questions in pairs.

Now read this article in which the biologist Dr Desmond Morris proposes a new set of laws to protect animals. Are any of your ideas mentioned?

Talk about some of the issues raised by Dr Morris. Here are some starting points:

- What animals are thought to have good or evil qualities?

- What kinds of animals do people in your country keep as pets? Do these animals 'adapt easily to the lifestyle of their human owners'?

- What 'heavy duties' are animals in your country forced to do?

- How far do you agree with Dr Morris's ideas? Do you think his proposed laws can or should be put into practice?

Man's contract with the animals
The proposed law of the jungle

No animal should be:

1. endowed with imaginary qualities of good or evil to satisfy our superstitious beliefs or religious prejudices.
2. dominated or degraded to entertain humans.
3. kept in captivity unless provided with an adequate physical and social environment.
4. kept as a companion unless it can adapt easily to the lifestyle of its human owner.
5. driven to extinction by direct persecution or by further increases in population.
6. made to suffer pain or distress to provide humans with sport.
7. subjected to physical or mental suffering for unnecessary experimentation.
8. kept in a deprived environment to provide humans with food or other produce.
9. exploited for its fur, its skin, its ivory or for any other luxury products.
10. forced to carry out heavy duties that cause distress or pain.

S*tage two*

Man's Best Friend

1 Pets

People often accuse pet-owners of spoiling their animals.
Do you know people who spoil animals?
What do they do?

The British have a reputation for being a nation of pet-lovers. Do you find any of the facts in this short text surprising?

How do people in your country compare with the British in this respect?

- Fewer than half of British households have pets.
- 23% of pet-owners have dogs – there are over 6 million dogs in Britain.
- 19% have cats – 6 million cats.
- 8% keep caged birds.
- 8% keep rodents like rabbits, hamsters, mice, etc.
- 8% have fish.
- Reptiles and amphibians, like snakes, frogs, turtles and terrapins, are becoming increasingly popular as pets.
- The British spend £35-£40 million a year on their pets' health. This includes food and vets' bills. On average people spend 66p a day on a dog and 40p on a cat.

'You spoil that dog'

2 Talking point
Work in pairs.

Why do people have pets? Think of as many different reasons as you can.

3 Listening

Listen to Diane and Louisa talking about why they have pets. Do they mention any of the reasons you thought of?

4 Vocabulary

Look at the tapescript for Exercise 3 on page 167 and find words or phrases which mean about the same as:

1 have an understanding with
2 make fun of/laugh at
3 something missing
4 welcome/say hello
5 friendly/loving
6 characteristics

5 Debate

In groups of four discuss this statement:

Most animals have human qualities.

Stage 1: Students **A** and **B** prepare short talks, about two minutes, agreeing with this statement.

Students **C** and **D** prepare short talks disagreeing.

Stage 2: Give your talks to the rest of the group in this order: **A, C, B, D**

Stage 3: Short class discussion.

Final vote: Do you agree or disagree with the original statement after hearing the talks?

6 Listening

As you listen to Louisa, make a note of the main differences between her two dogs. Compare notes with a partner.

Listen again and write down any words or phrases that are more commonly used to describe human beings.

EXAMPLE: The interviewer talks about the dogs' *personalities*.

7 Vocabulary

● **Adjectives and adverbs beginning with** *a-*
(Language review B2, page 83)

Notice how the underlined words are used in these sentences:

I own cats because I live <u>alone</u>.
My two dogs have never been <u>apart</u>.

Which words beginning with *a-* mean:

a sleeping   b the opposite of sleeping   c the opposite of dead
d being frightened   e knowing what is happening around you

Now write sentences including these five words. What do you notice about the word order of these sentences?

● **Instincts**

An instinct is an understanding or a desire that is in a person or an animal from birth. Louisa's dogs show a family instinct.

What other instincts are common in animals and people?

8 Making comparisons
(Language review A2, page 82)

Talking about her two dogs, Louisa says:

One of them is a lot more boisterous and a lot more dominant than the other.

1 Look at the tapescript for Exercise 6 on page 167, and make a list of all the phrases in which the two dogs are compared.
2 Which word occurs in all these phrases?
3 Explain what this phrase means:
   one of them is more of a bodyguard

---

9 Practice
Work in pairs.

Compare the two dogs in the photographs, using phrases similar to those in Exercise 6. As well as comparing their physical appearance, make guesses about their 'personalities'.

---

10 Intensifiers
(Language review A3, page 82)

In this sentence, the word *extremely* is an intensifier. It tells us how big Louisa's dogs are:

They're German Shepherds, or Alsatians some people call them, and they're extremely big.

Read through the tapescripts for Exercises 3 and 6 on page 167, and make a list of all the intensifiers used by the speakers. Add any other intensifiers you know to this list.

11 *Will*
(Language review A4, page 82)

Look at these two extracts from the recording in Exercise 6:

1 *… the other one doesn't really mind who comes in, you know, he'll sniff them and sort of say hello, …*
2 *… the more dominant dog will actually go and defend him …*

How is *will* used in these extracts? Choose the best explanation:

• to talk about the near future
• to talk about something probable or typical
• to talk about a wish

---

12 Practice

Write about the typical behaviour of an animal you know well, (or, if you prefer, a person) in these circumstances:

1 when they are tired
2 at night
3 when they are hungry
4 when they are frightened

EXAMPLE: *My parrot will hide in the corner when she's frightened.*

Extension

Domestic Animals

In groups of four, discuss the problems caused by domestic pets or other animals in your town or country (or the town or country you are studying in) and recommend ways of dealing with these problems.

Task 1: Identify the problems. Write a list in order of importance.
These newspaper extracts may give you some ideas.

Task 2: Discuss what could be done to solve the problems you have identified. Write a list of possible solutions.

Task 3: Discuss each solution in turn. Points to talk about:

    a Is this a practical idea?
    b Do you think most people in your town would agree with the idea?
    c How would you publicise your ideas?

Task 4: Write a formal or semi-formal letter of complaint about one of the problems you have discussed. You can write to local or national authorities or to individuals whose animals are causing problems. Use this letter framework:

- Write your address, the date and the address of the person you are writing to at the top of your letter.

- Start formally:
  Dear Sir/Madam/Mr/Mrs/Ms X

- *Paragraph 1:*
  Say why you are writing. Introduce the subject of your complaint. Express your opinions strongly, but remain formal and polite.

- *Paragraph 2:*
  Give full details of your complaint. Describe the animal or human behaviour or the situation you object to.

- *Paragraph 3:*
  Say what you think the person you are writing to should do to solve the problem.

- End the letter:
  Yours faithfully/sincerely
  Sign the letter, and write your name clearly beneath your signature.

Postmen bite back in vicious dog fight

Every year in Britain more than 6000 postmen and women are bitten by dogs, some so severely that they are forced to leave their jobs. In Gloucester, a 56-year-old post-woman had an ear bitten off.

Noah's Ark Home

Pet-lover had 8 goats, 22 dogs, 12 chickens, 3 sheep, 2 horses, 6 ferrets, 7 rats, a python, a pot-bellied pig, etc. etc. etc.

Rambo Rats

A new type of Super Rat, which can't be killed by normal poison, is swarming through the sewers of London.

MAD CAT

Cats across Britain could be in danger after the first recorded case of 'mad cat disease' killed a Siamese last week.

Ferocious dogs

Five boys were attacked in the corridors and playground of their school by three Rottweiler dogs, which had escaped from the garden of their owner, Mrs Doris Brown. One boy said: 'I couldn't get away, and the two larger dogs cornered me. They were looking at me and growling and had spit round their mouths.' Both dogs jumped up and grabbed his arms in their jaws.

Language review

A Grammar and Use

1 Non-defining relative clauses

1 These provide extra information about a person or a thing, and are an addition to the main clause.

2 They are separated from the main clause by commas and are used mainly in writing.

3 When they are used in speech, the speaker pauses at the beginning and end of the relative clause.

Relative clauses follow the nouns they relate to and can be in the middle or at the end of the main clause. They can begin with these relative pronouns:

1 *who*

   This refers to people:

   *David Attenborough, **who** is a famous British naturalist, has spent much of his life writing about animals.*
   *The snails were brought to Miami by an unsuspecting tourist, **who** had found them in the tropics.*

2 *which*

   This refers to animals or things:

   *Strychnine, **which** is a deadly poison, comes from the seeds of an evergreen tree.*

3 *whose*

   This refers to people, animals and things. It is used like *his, her* or *its*:

   *The clear-wing moth, **whose** appearance resembles that of a wasp, has no sting. (**whose** = of this moth)*

2 Comparisons: uses of the word *more*

More is used when we are comparing two ideas, people, things, etc. It is used:

1 to make the comparative form of longer adjectives and adverbs:

   One of my dogs is more boisterous and more dominant than the other.
   One of the dogs behaves more aggressively than the other.

2 with nouns or as a pronoun:

   He eats a lot more (food) than the other dog.

3 as an adverb:

   The bigger dog looks after the house a lot more (than the smaller dog).

More of a can be used with a noun:

   One of the dogs is more of a bodyguard.

This has two possible meanings:

1 It is more like a bodyguard than the other dog.
2 It is more like a bodyguard than a friend.

3 Intensifiers

Intensifiers are adverbs which strengthen the meaning of adjectives:

   My dogs are extremely big.
   They're so affectionate.
   They're completely/totally different from each other.
   I'm incredibly lucky.
   The bigger dog is very, very friendly.

Quite is normally used to weaken an adjective:

   I'm quite hungry. = not very

But it can also be used as an intensifier:

   They have quite different personalities. = completely

Very is the most commonly-used intensifier, but these words are often used instead:

awfully, dreadfully, extremely, particularly, really, terribly

Here are some more intensifiers which have particular meanings of their own:

absolutely, amazingly, completely, entirely, especially, incredibly, remarkably, surprisingly

Intensifiers are normally used only with gradable adjectives. These are adjectives which can be modified and which have comparative and superlative forms, for example *clean, big, old*, etc.

4 *Will*

Will is sometimes used to talk about behaviour or actions which are predictable, probable or typical:

   Goldfish will swim round and round in their bowls all day.
   Animal lovers will go to extreme lengths to get their message across.

In sentences like these *will* has a similar meaning to the Present Simple and does not refer to the future:

The more dominant dog will defend his weaker brother.
= The more dominant dog defends his weaker brother.

B Vocabulary

I Animal idioms

Here are some more animal idioms in addition to those on page 76.

● **Names of animals used as verbs:**

*to **ape** someone* = to imitate or copy another person

*to **badger** someone* = to persuade someone to do something by worrying or harrassing them

*to **chicken** out of doing something* = to get out of doing something because of fear or cowardice

*to **fox** someone* = to deceive or trick someone

*to **lark** about* = to enjoy yourself doing silly or naughty things   (a lark is a bird)

*to **monkey** with* = to interfere with something (often causing damage)

*to **parrot** something someone says* = to repeat word for word

*to **rat** on someone* = to betray someone to the police or a person in authority

*to **wolf** food (down)* = to eat food very quickly

● **Other common animal expressions:**

I'm in the dog-house.
= I'm in disgrace; people are angry with me.

Let sleeping dogs lie.
= Don't interfere. Avoid mentioning a subject that could cause trouble.

*I'm afraid **I've let the cat out of the bag.***
= given away a secret

*Don't look in the cupboard. Remember, **curiosity killed the cat.***
= Too much interest in something (curiosity) can get you into trouble.

*I should have warned you. He can **talk the hind leg off a donkey**.*
= talk endlessly

*I was paid today. That should **keep the wolf from the door**.*
= provide essential food and/or shelter

A leopard can never change its spots.
= It is impossible to change a person's character.

*When I'm in town, I'll go to the bank, and call to see my mother. That will **kill two birds with one stone**.*
= do two important things at the same time

2 Predicative adjectives

Many adjectives which start with the prefix *a-* normally come **after** the noun. They are called predicative adjectives.

*When we went to the zoo most of the **animals** were **asleep**. Most **children** are **afraid** of big dogs.*

Here are some more:

alike, alight, alive, alone, apart, ashamed, awake, aware

◆ Look at this school report of a ten-year-old girl.
What are her strong and weak points at school?

WINTERSIDE SCHOOL
SUMMER TERM 1991

AGE: 12   CLASS: 3B

Language B+

Claudia has worked hard throughout the school year, and has made noticeable progress. She has become more confident in her own abilities and is always keen to express her opinions in class. This had led to a distinct improvement in her oral skills. She is also a very competent reader – she is quick to absorb and understand what she reads. Although she has handed in some good examples of creative writing, she must realise that handwriting and presentation are also important. There is a need for improvement here.

Mathematics C–

Claudia has found Maths hard going this year. Although her arithmetic continues to be good, she has experienced difficulties in understanding some of the more advanced concepts which are important at this level.

Science C–

Claudia has not made as much effort as she could have this year. Progress has been disappointingly slow. Her homework and written work in general have been carelessly presented and full of inaccuracies.

History C+

Claudia must learn to organise her work more effectively. Some of her ideas were not carefully enough thought out and expressed.

Art B+

Claudia has produced original and creative work – a great improvement on last year. Well done Claudia!

Music A

She has worked well throughout the year and made considerable progress. She has natural ability and a particular talent for playing stringed instruments. Excellent.

P.E. B+

Claudia works well, is keen and has shown good co-ordination. She has a competitive instinct which should help her to succeed.

General remarks

There are some very pleasing comments in this report. Claudia is certainly improving in some areas of work. However there are a few rather negative remarks which spoil an otherwise excellent report. I have no doubt that Claudia is capable of succeeding in all subjects, but clearly she needs to put more effort into areas of weakness.

Barbara Williams
(Class Teacher)

Date: 17th May

◆ Discuss in groups of three or four:

What other subjects do/did you study that aren't included here?

Which subjects do/did you like or dislike most at school?

Should schoolchildren be given regular tests to assess their progress? Can you think of other ways to check progress?

What makes a good school?

1 Pre-reading

Look at this photograph and guess when it was taken.

What do you think school was like in those days? Compare ideas with a partner.

You are going to read a text describing a school around the time these photos were taken. Tick the words you would expect to find and write a cross next to the words you would not expect to find in the text.

arithmetic	laboratory	punish
lesson	coffee	cafeteria
discipline	uniform	computer
cane	bus	money
playground	tests	composition
video	subjects	spelling

2 Reading

Now read the text. In which paragraphs are these topics mentioned?

a the subjects taught ☐

b discipline and punishment ☐

c the teaching staff ☐

d the school buildings ☐

Look quickly through the text again. Were the words you ticked in the text? Were any of the words you put a cross next to used?

1 Fordlow National School was a small grey one-storey building, standing at the crossroads at the entrance to the village. The one large classroom which served all purposes was well lit with several windows. Joined on to the school was a tiny two-roomed cottage for the schoolmistress, and beyond that a playground surrounded by white-painted railings. The school had a lobby with pegs for clothes, boys' and girls' toilets and a backyard with washbasins, although there was no running water. The water supply was contained in a small bucket, filled every morning by the old woman who cleaned the schoolroom. She always looked very grumpy, probably because the children used to finish all the water.

2 The average attendance was 45. Reading, writing and arithmetic were the principal subjects, with a religious lesson every morning, and needlework every afternoon for the girls. Because there was no assistant mistress, Miss Holmes taught all the classes simultaneously, assisted by two monitors – ex-scholars, aged about twelve, who were paid a shilling a week for their services.

3 The writing lesson consisted of neatly copying maxims like 'A fool and his money are soon parted'; 'Waste not, want not'; 'Count ten before you speak', and so on. Once a week the children would do a composition, usually in the form of writing a letter describing some recent event. This was regarded chiefly as a spelling test. As there were no suitable books, geography was not taught. Once a day pupils would be called to read out loud, and this was extremely tedious as many of the children read so slowly and haltingly.

4 When Miss Holmes went from class to class, she carried a cane, which she used to lay on the desk before her. This was not necessarily for use, but served as a reminder since some of the bigger boys were very unruly. Most of them left school at ten or eleven because of the need to work. She punished them by a smart stroke on each hand. 'Put out your hand,' she would say, and some boys would openly spit on each hand before holding it out. She seldom used the cane on the girls and more seldom on the infants. Standing in a corner with their hands on their heads was their punishment.

● Understanding

Choose the correct endings for these sentences:

1 The school mistress lived in a cottage that was ...
   a) ... close to the school.
   b) ... part of the school building.
   c) ... in the school playground.

2 Miss Holmes used to teach ...
   a) ... all the classes herself without any assistance.
   b) ... only one class at a time.
   c) ... with the help of children who had already left the school.

3 In writing lessons the children ...
   a) ... sometimes wrote letters.
   b) ... only did spelling tests.
   c) ... only copied neatly.

4 Geography was not taught at the school because ...
   a) ... it was not a suitable subject.
   b) ... the school hadn't got the right books.
   c) ... there were more important subjects.

5 Miss Holmes' cane ...
   a) ... was never used to punish the girls.
   b) ... was only used to punish the older boys.
   c) ... was hardly ever used to punish the youngest children.

---

3 Talking points
Work in small groups.

Think about the first school you went to. Were there any similarities or differences between your school and the one described in the text?

Compare ideas with the other students in your group.

---

4 Vocabulary
● Compound adjectives
(Language review B1, page 92)

Look at this sentence from paragraph 1 of the text:

*Joined on to the school was a tiny **two-roomed** cottage for the schoolmistress, and beyond that a playground surrounded by **white-painted** railings.*

The words in bold type are compound adjectives. What do they describe?
How are they formed?

Look at the two lists and make compound adjectives by combining a word from list **A** with a word from list **B**. Now make sentences using each compound adjective with one of these nouns:

textbook   classroom   pupil   teacher

A	B
well	heated
old	going
easy	behaved
centrally	fashioned

● *Lay* and *lie*
(Language review B2, page 92)

Look at this example from paragraph 4 of the text:

*When Miss Holmes went from class to class, she carried a cane, which she used to **lay** on the desk before her.*

What do you think *lay* means in this sentence?

Now look at the two meanings of *lie*.

*I'm so tired I think I'll **lie** down for a while.*
*Why did you **lie** to me about where you were last night?*

What are the past simple and past participle forms of the three verbs *lay, lie* (meaning 1) and *lie* (meaning 2)?

● Find words or phrases in the text which mean the same as:
   1 very small (*Para. 1*)
   2 bad-tempered (*1*)   3 main (*2*)
   4 at the same time (*2*)
   5 popular sayings (*3*)
   6 boring (*3*)   7 hesitantly (*3*)
   8 badly-behaved (*4*)

5 *Because, since, as*
(Language review A1, page 91)

Look at these extracts from the text. What do they have in common?

> *Because there was no assistant mistress, Miss Holmes taught all the classes simultaneously.*
> *As there were no suitable books, geography was not taught.*
> *This was not necessarily for use, but served as a reminder since some of the bigger boys were very unruly.*

What do the words *because, since* and *as* have in common?

Which of these three words would you be more likely to use in everyday speech?

Which of these three words do you think is the most formal?

Compare ideas with a partner.

6 Practice

Complete these sentences with an appropriate explanation, starting with one of these words: *because, since, as*.

EXAMPLE:

It was difficult for the children to wash ...
because/since there was a shortage of water.

1 The old woman who cleaned the schoolroom was bad-tempered...
2 Reading aloud wasn't very interesting...

3 Miss Holmes did all the teaching...
4 Miss Holmes had a cane on her desk...
5 She didn't use the cane to punish very young children...

Compare answers with a partner.

7 Personalised practice

Work in pairs.

Write a list of things you (have) always liked or disliked doing at school.

EXAMPLES:

I (have) always liked speaking English.
I (have) always hated maths.

Exchange lists with your partner and discuss the reasons for your likes and dislikes.

EXAMPLE:

I (have) always hated maths, because I (have) never understood what the teacher was talking about.

Now write sentences about your likes and dislikes, using *since* or *as* instead of *because*.

EXAMPLE:

As/Since I (have) never understood what the teacher was talking about, I (have) always hated maths.

---

8 Listening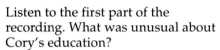

Listen to the first part of the recording. What was unusual about Cory's education?

Now listen again to find out the following details about the school:

> number of students
> nationality of students
> number of buildings
> sports facilities available
> other facilities available

Now listen to the second part of the recording. Why did Cory start to get lower grades? Compare ideas with a partner.

9 Pronunciation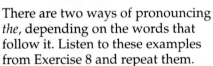

There are two ways of pronouncing *the*, depending on the words that follow it. Listen to these examples from Exercise 8 and repeat them.

> *My father was in the military.*
> *It was called the American school.*
> *It was run by one of the universities.*

How is *the* pronounced if it is followed by:

a a consonant sound?
b a vowel sound?

Now read these phrases aloud, then listen to the recording to check your pronunciation.

a the French teacher
b the students
c the oil industry
d the United States
e the teachers
f the hour   g the infants
h the undergraduates

10 Interview

Work in pairs.

You are going to interview your partner to find out about one of the schools they have been to. (This could include the school they go to now.)

Look at the headings and work out the questions you will have to ask your partner so that you can fill in the information required.

Name of school: _____
Location: _____
Number of students: _____
Buildings: _____
Facilities: _____
Years attended: _____
The standard of education: _____
Best subjects (with reasons): _____
Worst subjects (with reasons): _____

11 Writing

You are going to write about the school you described to your partner in Exercise 10. Follow this plan:

Introduction:
Your attendance at the school. (When did you start? When did you leave?)

Paragraph 1:
Location. Description of the buildings and the atmosphere.

Paragraph 2:
Description of some of the people you knew there.

Paragraph 3:
Description of one or more memorable occasions at the school.

Conclusion:
The best and the worst features of the school from your point of view.

Works of Art

1 Pre-reading

Match the captions to these pictures of works of art. What do you notice about the origin of the objects, and the museums they are found in?

1 Greek black figure vase (British Museum)

2 Mummy of Shepenmut (Exeter Museum, England)

3 *The Terrace at Sainte Adresse*, France (Metropolitan Museum, New York)

2 Reading

Tutankhamun's tomb was the only royal tomb in ancient Egypt to remain untouched for more than 3000 years. Why do you think this was? Make a guess.

Read the text and see if you were right.

The Discovery of Tutankhamun

1 THE discovery of the tomb of Tutankhamun was the work of two very different men: Howard Carter and Lord Carnarvon. Carter was a retired British archaeologist who had opened a small art shop in Luxor, Egypt. Carnarvon came to Egypt from Britain in 1903 to convalesce after a motoring accident. He was wealthy and had amassed a large collection of antiquities. He quickly became fascinated by Egypt's past and was given permission by the Egyptian authorities to excavate – at his own expense – near Luxor.

2 Lord Carnarvon soon realised he needed help in order to locate anything of value, and Howard Carter was the expert he put in charge of the archaeological research. After several years of excavation Carter began to uncover the tombs of six ancient Egyptian royals. Only the tomb of the king Tutankhamun eluded him, and Carter began to give up any hope of finding it. Carnarvon had decided to pay for only one more season's work.

3 Finally, in 1922, Carter's luck changed. His team had been excavating in the Valley of the Kings, where they had found the ruins of several houses used by workmen who had decorated the ancient tomb of Ramesses VI. By chance, these houses had been built on top of the entrance to another tomb that had then been hidden by sand, rubble and time. A staircase led to a sealed doorway. On the other side of the doorway was a passage, filled with rubble. Slowly the debris was cleared. The passage led to another door which had been opened and resealed. On it was the name of Tutankhamun.

4 Carter informed Carnarvon in England, and delayed the ceremonial opening of the tomb for seventeen days, so that Carnarvon could also be present.

5 Carter made a small hole in the door, inserted a candle and peered in. Slowly he began to make out details in the room; he saw strange statues and objects made of gold. It was evident that robbers had ransacked the tomb centuries before, but after being caught in the act had run away and left all the objects behind.

6 The tomb was so magnificent that the Egyptian government changed the law so as to ensure that any objects found in Egypt would remain there, unless specifically given to the excavator. Carter immediately began to catalogue and preserve the hundreds of objects found in the tomb by labelling, treating and photographing each one. In order not to risk damage to the treasures, he erected a steel gate around the site and placed men on guard.

7 It wasn't until 1923 that the mummy of Tutankhamun was found, but by that time Lord Carnarvon had died from a fatal illness which had started soon after the opening of the tomb. Some people believe his death was caused by the Pharaoh's legendary curse, which was put on anyone who disturbed his tomb.

● **Understanding**

These events are all mentioned in the text.

Put them into chronological order, using clues from the language in the text.

The first one has been done for you.

a Howard Carter opened an art shop in Luxor. _____

b Lord Carnarvon came to Egypt. _____

c Lord Carnarvon had a motoring accident. _____

d Lord Carnarvon became fascinated by Egypt's past. _____

e Howard Carter found six royal tombs. _____

f Howard Carter found a hidden entrance to a tomb. _____

g Workmen decorated the tomb of Ramesses VI.   *1*

h Robbers ransacked the tomb. _____

i The mummy of Tutankhamun was found. _____

j Lord Carnarvon died in Cairo. _____

3 Vocabulary

Match these words from the text with the most suitable meaning:

1 convalesce (*Para.1*)	a recover	b study	c explore
2 eluded (*2*)	a abandoned	b avoided	c escaped
3 sealed (*3*)	a broken	b opened	c closed
4 debris (*3*)	a ruins	b waste	c antiques
5 ransacked (*5*)	a cleared	b searched/robbed	c damaged
6 legendary (*7*)	a famous	b historical	c evil

4 Expressing purpose

(Language review A2, page 92)

Which words or phrases in these extracts from the text are used to express a purpose?

> *Lord Carnarvon soon realised he needed help in order to locate anything of value... (Para. 2)*
> *Carter delayed the opening of the tomb for seventeen days, so that Carnarvon could also be present. (4)*
> *The Egyptian government changed the law so as to ensure that any objects found in Egypt would remain there. (6)*
> *In order not to risk damage to the treasures, he erected a steel gate... (6)*

Which of these four expressions is followed by a clause with a subject and a verb?

What are the other three expressions followed by?

Rewrite this sentence, using *so that* and *so as to*:

> *They came here early to find the best bargains.*

5 Practice

Finish these sentences with expressions of purpose, starting with one of these words or phrases:

> *in order (not) to, so as (not) to, so that.*

EXAMPLE:

Lord Carnarvon visited Egypt in 1903 ...
in order to convalesce after a motoring accident.

1 The ruined houses were originally built ...
2 The debris in the passages had to be cleared ...
3 Carter made a small hole in the doorway ...
4 The Egyptian government changed the law ...
5 Every object in the tomb was labelled and photographed ...

6 Talking points

Work in small groups.

Do you think the Egyptian government was right to change the law in order to keep the treasures in Egypt?

Do you think archaeologists deserve some reward for their hard work?

7 Giving an opinion

● **Reading**

1 Read this letter quickly. Which paragraph(s)

  a) summarise the writer's opinion?
  b) introduce the topic?
  c) give the details of the writer's opinion?

2 Which words or phrases does the writer use to order the points he makes?

EXAMPLE:

In the first place ...

Compare answers to these questions with a partner.

● **Writing**

Write a letter expressing your own opinion on the subject of art treasures being removed from their countries of origin. (You may refer to the letter opposite.)

Organise your letter according to the paragraphs outlined above, and remember to order the points in your argument by using the expressions you identified in the letter.

Dear Sir,

1 I am writing about the article in yesterday's *Mail*, suggesting that foreign works of art in the British Museum should be returned to the countries they came from. I totally disagree with this idea.

2 In the first place, most of these pieces were legitimately purchased or removed with official permission. In my opinion this gives the museum the legal right to keep them. In many cases, not only did we restore them and transport them at our own expense, but we also removed them in order to save them from being damaged or destroyed. In addition, the museum has looked after these treasures for more than a century – which is why they are still in excellent condition today.

3 Another point is that many other museums have foreign works of art: the Louvre, the Metropolitan Museum, the Vatican Museum, etc. Anyway, there are still hundreds of fine works left in the countries of origin.

4 Finally, works of art belong to everyone, not just to one nation. If every museum had to give back all its foreign pieces, large sections of major museums would soon be nearly empty.

5 I feel very strongly that there would be only negative implications to taking any of the pieces out of the British Museum and returning them to where they came from. This particular move would have no positive result for anyone, and could start a trend which would destroy the historical collections of the Western world.

Yours faithfully,

J. Thompson (Mr)

Extension

Michelangelo

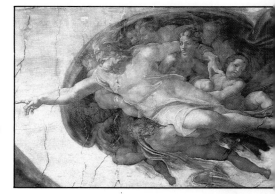

Reading
Work in pairs.

You are going to read about works of art created by the famous sculptor and painter Michelangelo.

Student A: Turn to page 158.
Student B: Look at this picture and read the text.

The picture shows part of the ceiling of the Sistine Chapel in the Vatican, Rome, painted by Michelangelo. When Pope Julius II changed his mind about his tomb, Michelangelo was first disappointed then angry and suspicious. He left Rome in a fury and went to Florence. He wrote the Pope a rude letter saying that if the Pope wanted him, he would have to look for him.

Surprisingly Julius did not lose his temper, but started negotiations with the Head of the city of Florence in order to persuade the young sculptor to return. This succeeded and when Michelangelo returned to Rome, the Pope persuaded him to accept a second commission.

There was a chapel in the Vatican which had been built by Pope Sixtus IV, and was therefore called the Sistine Chapel. The walls of the chapel had been decorated by famous painters such as Botticelli, but the ceiling was still blank. The Pope wanted Michelangelo to paint it.

It took four years of lonely work to complete the masterpiece. Michelangelo had to lie on his back to paint. He covered the whole space with a series of figures painted with imagination and beauty showing, among other stories, the story of the Creation.

He also painted on this ceiling many figures he had originally wanted to sculpt for the Pope's tomb. It was only when he had finished the ceiling in 1512 that he returned to work on the statues for the tomb.

Some of the answers to these questions about Michelangelo and his work are in your text and some are in your partner's text. Read your text and answer as many of the questions as you can. Then ask your partner questions to find the other answers.

1 When was Michelangelo born and when did he die?
2 What was the first work the Pope asked Michelangelo to create?
3 Why did the Pope stop Michelangelo working on this commission?
4 How did Michelangelo react to the Pope's change of mind?
5 What was the second work commissioned by the Pope?
6 How long did it take Michelangelo to finish this work?
7 Where is this work?
8 When did Michelangelo return to his first work?
9 What is the name of the only part of this work that was finished?
10 Where can this be seen now?

*L*anguage review

A Grammar and Use

I *Because, since, as*

● **Meaning**

These three words are used at the beginning of clauses which give reasons for an event or situation:

Miss Holmes taught all the classes herself because there was no assistant mistress.
Geography was not taught as/since there were no suitable books.

● **Use**

Because is the most common of these words in everyday speech.

As and *since* are more formal and more commonly used in writing.
Since is more formal than *as*.

● **Position**

Since and *as* clauses often start a sentence:

As there were no suitable books, geography was not taught.
Since many of the boys were very unruly, Miss Holmes sometimes had to punish them.

Because clauses are only used at the beginning of sentences when we want to emphasise the reason. This is more common in writing than in speaking:

Because there was no assistant mistress, Miss Holmes taught all the classes herself.

Notes

1 The *because, since, as* clause is followed by a comma if it comes before the main clause.
2 *Because* and *because of* were also dealt with in Unit 7 Language review A3 on page 71.

2 Expressions of purpose

● Meaning

In order to, so as to and *so that* are used to express purposes:

Lord Carnarvon needed help in order to locate anything of value.
The Egyptian government changed the law so as to ensure that any objects found in Egypt would remain there.
Carter delayed the opening of the tomb, so that Carnarvon could also be present.

● Grammatical patterns

In order to and *so as to* are followed by infinitive verb forms.
So that is followed by a clause with a subject and verb.

● Negative forms

Notice the position of *not* in these sentences:

In order not to risk damage to the treasures, Carter erected a steel gate.
So as not to risk damage to the treasures, Carter erected a steel gate.
Carter delayed the opening of the tomb, so that Carnarvon would not miss the event.

Note

To + infinitive is also commonly used to express purpose:

Carnarvon came to Egypt in 1903 to convalesce after a car accident.

B Vocabulary

I Compound adjectives

● Form

Compound adjectives are adjectives formed from two words. Here are the most common ways of forming these adjectives:

1 adjective or number + noun + *-ed*:
old-fashioned clothes
a two-roomed cottage

2 adjective or adverb + past participle of verb:
white-painted railings
a centrally-heated room

3 adjective or adverb or noun + *-ing* form of verb:
an easy-going teacher
a well-meaning politician
a record-breaking athlete

Note

Compound adjectives thàt start with an adverb can be used without a hyphen if they come after a noun:
This is a centrally-heated house.
This house is centrally heated.

2 Lay and lie

● Lay

Lay is a transitive verb which means 'to put down carefully or flat':

She used to lay the cane on the desk before her.
We laid the picnic things on the grass.

Here are two other common uses of *lay*:

1 *To lay the table* means 'to put knives, forks, plates, etc. on a table in preparation for a meal'.

2 *Hens lay eggs*

● Lie

Lie has two completely different meanings:

1 *Lie* is an irregular intransitive verb which means 'to be or to move into a flat position':

Don't just lie there in bed. Get up!
The cat lay in the sun all afternoon.

It is often used with *down*:

If you feel ill, why don't you go and lie down?

2 *Lie* is also a regular intransitive verb which means 'not to tell the truth':

When their father asked them if they had eaten the cake, they lied and said they hadn't.

● Summary of forms:

Infinitive	Simple Past	Past Participle
to lay	laid	laid
to lie (meaning 1)	lay	lain
to lie (meaning 2)	lied	lied

UNIT 10

first impressions

◆ Look at these photos of celebrities. Do you know who they are?

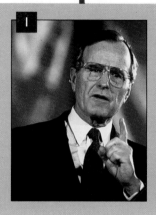

◆ Now look at the same people, photographed when they were babies. Match the adults to the babies.

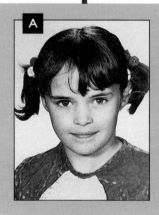

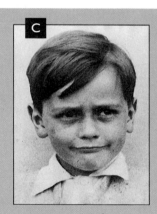

◆ Read these statements about fame:

- *A celebrity is someone who works hard all his life to become known, then wears dark glasses to avoid being recognised.* (Fred Allen)

- *There are many paths to the top of the mountain, but the view is always the same.* (Chinese proverb)

- *What is fame? An empty bubble?* (James Grainger)

- *People that seem so glorious are all show; underneath they're like anybody else.* (Euripides)

- *A plague on eminence! I hardly dare cross the street anymore without a convoy and I am stared at wherever I go like an idiot member of a royal family or an animal in a zoo.* (Stravinsky)

◆ Discuss these points with a partner:

1 What is the main idea in each of these quotations?

2 Do you agree or disagree with any of these ideas?

Stage one

Fame

1 Pre-reading

Work in pairs.

What are typical classical musicians like? Make notes about their appearance and character.

Look at these photos and decide which of the three people is *not* a classical musician.

2 Reading

Read this text. Which of the people in the photographs is Nigel Kennedy?

The Cockney Classicist

1 He said that he was usually stopped at the Customs and it was easy to see why. The plastic bag he was carrying was full of clothes. He was unshaven and haggard-looking after celebrating until 5.30 that morning and the dark glasses he was wearing hid a black eye. His hair was spiked like a worn brush, his black leather jacket was spattered with paint, he had a gold stud in his ear, and there was a football scarf tied round the handle of his violin case.

2 Nigel Kennedy, who is 33, is a baby-faced hero of our times. He is more talented than most, with three records among the top ten classical bestsellers, including his interpretation of Vivaldi's *Four Seasons*, which has sold more than 250,000 copies. Tomorrow he will appear in the final concert of the sellout tour which has established him as a celebrity.

3 Kennedy takes after other members of his family, who were all musical. Both his father and his grandfather were cellists, his great-aunt Daisy was a hotel pianist, and his mother is a music teacher. His father went to Australia before Nigel was born, leaving him to be brought up by his mother.

4 'I knew we didn't have much money at the time I was offered a place at the Menuhin Music School. My mother was going to turn it down, but they offered me a scholarship, which meant I was able to go there when I was seven. There was a lot of pressure on all the kids who were there, but I found I could achieve good results with just two hours' practice a day.'

5 After that, Nigel's wandering took him to the Juillard School of Music in New York, but he returned to London after two years without a diploma, in order to take up the many offers of concert work that were already being made.

6 'My success was weird, man. For two or three years, I tried to do what people wanted me to do. I wore a bow tie and all that stuff. But it didn't work for me. I got no joy. I don't want to be a classical musician if it means having an image which doesn't represent me as a person. I'd rather paint walls or something.'

7 Few musicians reach the same level as Kennedy. 'It's not just talent – lots of people are born with that,' he says. 'What makes the difference is having a performing mentality. I took to being on stage, which isn't the case for every musician, because that's my moment of freedom. The best in me comes out when I'm on stage. That's where I excel.'

8 In spite of the unorthodox image, things have turned out very well for him. 'I can't be *totally* shocking ... All the main conductors in the world want to work with me, and I'm getting better as a violinist.'

● Understanding

Choose the best endings for these sentences:

1 Among the unusual things about Nigel Kennedy's appearance were...
   a ... a leather jacket with holes in.
   b ... an earring and a football scarf.
   c ... a pair of shoes in a plastic bag.

2 At the time this article was written, Nigel Kennedy ...
   a ... was in the middle of a successful tour.
   b ... had just finished a successful tour.
   c ... was about to give the final concert of a successful tour.

3 Nigel nearly didn't go to the Menuhin Music School, because...
   a ... he wasn't good enough.
   b ... his mother was poor.
   c ... he was only seven years old.

4 He studied music in New York ...
   a ... but he didn't finish the course.
   b ... where he was the top student.
   c ... but he didn't practise much.

5 He refused to behave like a typical classical musician because...
   a ... he didn't like wearing smart clothes.
   b ... he was trying to change his image.
   c ... he wanted to be himself.

6 What makes him different as a musician is the fact that ...
   a ... he likes performing.
   b ... he works extremely hard.
   c ... he is very talented.

3 Vocabulary

Guess the meanings of these words from the text:

1 unshaven (*Para. 1*)
2 spattered (*1*) 3 baby-faced (*2*)
4 bestseller (*2*) 5 sellout (*2*)
6 weird (*6*) 7 unorthodox (*8*)
8 shocking (*8*)

● Suffixes
(*Language review B1, page 103*)

Look quickly through the text and make a list of words for people involved in music.

4 Relative clauses (1)
(*Language review A1, page 102*)

Read these extracts from the text and underline the relative clauses:

1 *Nigel Kennedy, who is 33, is a baby-faced hero of our times.*
2 *... his interpretation of Vivaldi's 'Four Seasons', which has sold more than 250,000 copies.*
3 *... he will appear in the final concert of the sellout tour which has established him as a celebrity.*
4 *Kennedy takes after other members of his family, who were all musical.*
5 *There was a lot of pressure on all the kids who were there, but ...*
6 *... he returned to London ..., in order to take up the many offers of concert work that were already being made.*

The words you found end in *-ist*, *-ian* and *-or*. Together with *-er*, these are common endings for words which describe what people do. What are the nouns used for people who are involved in these activities or subjects? Compare ideas with a partner.

EXAMPLE: acting – *actor*

acting art cello drums
football guitar history
languages piano politics
saxophone science sculpture
singing statistics violin writing

7 *I don't want to be a classical musician if it means having an image which doesn't represent me as a person.*

Make a list of the relative pronouns used in these extracts.

Extracts 1, 2 and 4 contain non-defining relative clauses. You learnt about these in Unit 8. How are the relative clauses in the other extracts different from these three?

How is the meaning of these extracts affected if the relative clauses are removed? Think first about extracts 1, 2 and 4, and then about extracts 3, 5, 6 and 7.

Compare ideas with a partner.

5 Practice

These sentences are incomplete. Finish them by replacing the pronouns in the endings A-H with a relative pronoun. The first one has been done for you.

1 Nigel Kennedy is one of the few classical musicians... (F)
   who really enjoys performing.
2 *The Four Seasons* is a famous piece of music...
3 Kennedy comes from a family...
4 Kennedy's mother was married to a man...
5 His grandfather was a man...
6 Kennedy doesn't like wearing clothes...
7 He likes wearing clothes...
8 Classical music is a type of music...

A they reflect his personality
B he went to Australia before Nigel was born
C it is becoming more popular
D it was composed by Vivaldi
E he played the cello
F he really enjoys performing
G it is very musical
H they make him look like a typical classical musician

6 Personalised practice

Finish these definitions with ideas of your own:

1 A friend is someone who...
2 A good teacher is someone who...
3 A classical musician is someone who...

7 Relative clauses (2)

(Language review A1, page 102)

Underline the relative clauses in these extracts from the text:

1 *The plastic bag he was carrying was full of clothes.*
2 *... the dark glasses he was wearing hid a black eye.*

Rewrite these two extracts adding a relative pronoun in the correct place.

In sentences like these it is possible to leave out the relative pronoun. How are these sentences different from the extracts in Exercise 4?

Compare ideas with a partner.

8 Practice

Rewrite these pairs of sentences as one sentence. The first one has been done for you.

1 The music was by Beethoven.   She was playing the music last night.

The music she was playing last night was by Beethoven.

2 The violin was worth £5000.   She was playing the violin this evening.

3 The record is Number 1 in the classical charts.   We've just heard the record.

4 The jacket is his brother's.   He was wearing the jacket yesterday.

5 The concert is the last of the current tour.   We're going to the concert.

6 The earring used to belong to his girlfriend.   Kennedy was wearing the earring on stage.

9 Pre-listening

How much do you know about Mozart? Try answering these questions:

1 What nationality was Mozart?
2 How old was he when he started playing the harpsichord?
3 How old was he when he started giving concerts and composing music?
4 Who was the young Mozart's manager?

Compare answers with a partner.

10 Listening 📼

Listen to the broadcast about Mozart and check your answers to the questions in Exercise 9.

● **Listening for detail**

What does the speaker say Mozart could do at or by the ages listed in the table? Listen to the recording again and make notes. (One of the answers has been done for you.)

Age	Notes
3	
4	*learnt pieces from his sister's harpsichord book*
5	
10	
14	
16	
30	

11 Vocabulary

● *A piece of...*
(Language review B2, page 103)

Music is an uncountable noun. If we want to refer to a single item of music, we say:

a piece of music

Do you know any other uncountable nouns which can be used with the phrase: *a piece of ...?*

● Choose the best meaning for each of these words from the recording:

1 eminent	a elderly	b important	c educated
2 baffled	a shocked	b fascinated	c puzzled
3 prodigy	a performer	b wonder	c musician
4 ailment	a feeling	b illness	c pain
5 flattery	a compliments	b insults	c jokes
6 patron	a employee	b enemy	c sponsor

12 Relative clauses (3)
(Language review A1, page 102)

Read these two extracts from the recording:

His father took him to the most important European cities, where he could show off the boy's talent.
Things were difficult for Leopold: it was a time when musicians in Austria were treated like servants.

Underline the relative clauses in these extracts.

Are they defining or non-defining relative clauses?

Which relative pronouns are used?

Compare ideas with a partner.

13 Practice
Work in pairs.

Student A: Think of a famous town or city and write five sentences about it.

EXAMPLE: *It's the place where you can see the Mona Lisa.*

Student B: Think of a year in the past when a lot of important things happened, and write five sentences about it.

EXAMPLE: *It's the year when the Soviet Union broke up.*

Now exchange sentences with your partner.

Student A tries to guess the year Student B has written about.

Student B tries to guess the place Student A has written about.

14 Discussion
Work in pairs.

Student A: Look back at the text in Exercise 2, and make a list of Nigel Kennedy's personal qualities.

Student B: Look at the tapescript for Exercise 10 on page 168, and make a list of Mozart's personal qualities.

Now discuss these questions with your partner:

1 Do Mozart and Nigel Kennedy have any qualities in common?
2 Were their childhoods similar in any way?
3 Nigel Kennedy says that reaching a high level as a musician does not depend only on talent, and that what makes the difference is having a performing mentality. Do you agree with this statement? Can you think of any other musicians who have this mentality?

Stage two

Original Career Plans

1 Pre-reading
Work in small groups.

What do you know about the artist of this painting?

From the photographs and illustrations, note down as much information as you can about him and his life.

2 Reading
Read the text and check how much of the information you noted down was correct.

GAUGUIN

1 PAUL GAUGUIN was born in Orleans, France in 1848 and lived in Peru for four years. At the age of seventeen he went to sea and for six years sailed around the world in trading-ships or warships. In 1871 he joined a stockbroking firm and two years later he married a young Danish woman. It looked as though Gauguin was going to settle down and become a respectable businessman. But he took up painting and also began to collect Impressionist art. At this time in his life, however, it seemed that painting was going to be just a hobby. Then in 1875 he met Camille Pissarro, and began to work with him. He spent holidays painting with Pissarro and another important Impressionist artist, Paul Cézanne. Gauguin made visible progress in his art. He became more and more absorbed by painting and in 1883, when the Paris Stock Exchange crashed and he lost his job, he decided 'to paint every day'.

2 This decision was to change the course of his life. He had a wife and four children to support, but no income – no one would buy his paintings. He moved to Copenhagen where he was going to make a fresh start, but when his marriage broke up, he returned to Paris. There he lived in poverty and discomfort, and came to despise Europe and its civilisation. Two decisive experiences influenced Gauguin. The first of these was a meeting with Vincent van Gogh. They had similar ideas about painting and were going to paint together. But unfortunately they quarrelled, and as a result van Gogh cut off his own ear.

3 The second experience was Gauguin's journey to Martinique, where he discovered the brilliant colours of the tropics and the attractions of a 'natural' life. In 1891, as a result of this discovery, he moved to Tahiti, where he was to live for nine years. There he developed his 'primitive' style of painting, using bright colours and simple shapes to symbolise ideas.

4 Although he became increasingly ill after 1899, he never returned to civilisation, which he said 'makes you suffer'.

● **Understanding**

1 Read the text again and put these events in Gauguin's life into the right order. Write 1–8 in the boxes.

a The Paris Stock Exchange crashed and he became unemployed. ☐

b He got married to a Danish woman. ☐

c He spent a number of years at sea. ☐

d He started to work with Pissarro. ☐

e He visited the island of Martinique. ☐

f Together with his family he went to Copenhagen. ☐

g He moved to Tahiti. ☐

h He returned to Paris. ☐

2 Answer these questions about Gauguin's life:

a Why did he decide to paint every day?

b Why did he move to Copenhagen?

c Why did he come to hate Europe and 'civilisation'?

d Why did he move to Tahiti?

---

3 Vocabulary

Rewrite these extracts from the text, replacing the words or phrases in bold type with words or phrases which mean the same.

1 *It looked as though Gauguin was going to settle down and become a respectable businessman.* (Para. 1)

2 *Gauguin made visible progress in his art.* (1)

3 *He moved to Copenhagen where he was going to make a fresh start.* (2)

4 *There he lived in poverty and discomfort.* (2)

5 *There he developed his 'primitive' style of painting.* (3)

4 Listening

Listen to the recording and make a list of the main events in the speaker's life after he left university.

● **Understanding**

Read these statements and say if they are true or false. Then listen to the recording again to check your answers.

1 He spent a year abroad after leaving university.

2 During his stay in Italy he became fluent in Italian.

3 He taught English as a hobby in Italy.

4 In the end he decided to do a law course.

5 The course involved a lot of creativity.

6 After the course he started training in an office.

7 The work was difficult but rewarding.

8 His firm was totally opposed to his decision to resign.

---

5 Vocabulary

Look at these extracts from the recording and guess the meaning of the words and phrases in bold type.

1 *I toyed with the idea of doing teaching...*
2 *I picked up some basic Italian...*
3 *I ended up teaching anyway.*
4 *I enrolled for a six-month crash course in London.*
5 *We had to learn everything like parrots...*
6 *I was bored stiff 99% of the time.*
7 *Anyway, to cut a long story short, I started to do a course...*
8 *...I decided, 'That's it.'*

6 Pronunciation

Look at these words from the recording. Which letters are not heard when the words are spoken? Listen to the recording and write down what you hear. The first one has been done for you.

1 interesting ___*intresting*___

2 ironically _____

3 suppose _____

4 library _____

Now work with a partner. Take it in turns to read these words aloud:

5 carefully 6 several 7 secretary 8 police
9 naturally 10 history

Listen to the recording and check your pronunciation.

7 Future-in-the-past
(Language review A2, page 102)

Read these extracts from the text and the recording. Which two verb forms are used to express the idea of the future-in-the-past?

1 *It looked as though Gauguin was going to settle down and become a respectable businessman.*
2 *This decision was to change the course of his life.*
3 *He moved to Copenhagen where he was going to make a fresh start, ...*
4 *The two men had similar ideas about painting and were going to paint together.*
5 *In 1891, as a result of this discovery, he moved to Tahiti, where he was to live for nine years.*
6 *I thought I was going to be dealing with crimes...*

Which of these extracts express:

a intentions b expectations
c unforeseen results

Which of the actions or situations actually came true? Answer Yes or No to these questions:

1 Did Gauguin settle down and become a businessman?
2 Did this decision change the course of Gauguin's life?
3 Did Gauguin make a fresh start in Copenhagen?
4 Did Gauguin and van Gogh paint together?
5 Did Gauguin live in Tahiti for nine years?
6 Did the speaker deal with crimes?

Compare ideas with a partner.

---

8 Practice

● Fill the gaps in this dialogue with suitable *was/were to/going to* phrases. The first one has been done for you.

Jane: Have you always been good at music?

Mike: Yes, I suppose I have. I remember when I was about six my parents thought (1) *I was going to be really brilliant*, you know, like Mozart.

Jane: So what went wrong?

Mike: Nothing went wrong, I just decided (2) _____ different.

Jane: And then I seem to remember that you and Marcia (3) _____ as soon as you were both eighteen.

Mike: That's right. (4) _____ , but we had a terrible argument and split up about a week before. Soon after that I went to Cambridge where I (5) _____ three really exciting years.

Jane: What did you study?

Mike: Languages.

Jane: Did you spend a year abroad?

Mike No, unfortunately not. (6) _____ in a German school, but I was very ill and couldn't go.

Compare answers with a partner.

● Make up suitable beginnings for these sentence endings. (There is no single correct answer.) The first one has been done for you.

1 *I was going to rent a car*, but my brother lent me his.
2 _____ , but I decided to write a letter instead.
3 _____ , but I couldn't stay awake long enough.
4 _____ , but it was too expensive, so I went to Scotland instead.
5 _____ , but it was closed, so we had to cook for ourselves.

9 Personalised practice
Work in pairs.

EXAMPLE:

I was going to leave school when I was 16.

Exchange lists with a partner.

Find out why your partner didn't do the things on their list.

Extension

Famous Dustbins

1 Discussion

Work in pairs.

The objects in this picture were taken from the dustbin of a famous person.

Look at the picture and discuss what kind of person might have thrown these things away. Make brief notes like this:

> *a smoker   a pet-lover*
> *middle-aged*

Now guess which of these famous people threw away the objects.

2 Writing

Look at this picture and write notes about the kind of person who might have thrown these objects away.

Now write a profile of this person by expanding the notes you have just written. Use phrases like this:

> *This person is obviously someone who...*
> *S/he's the sort of person who...*
> *S/he must be a very extravagant/wasteful type of person.*
> *S/he's probably a film star.*
> *S/he might live in a flat in a big city.*

Exchange profiles with a partner. Ask your partner to explain each of the points they have made. Now discuss which of the famous people in the pictures above threw out these things.

Language review

A Grammar and Use

1 Relative clauses

● Non-defining relative clauses

Remember these features of non-defining relative clauses (Unit 8, Language review A1):

1 They give more information about nouns, but are not essential to the meaning of a sentence.

2 They begin with relative pronouns:
who (to refer to people)
which (to refer to animals and things)
whose (to refer to people, animals and things. It is the relative pronoun equivalent of *his, her* or *its*.)

3 They are separated from the main clause by commas and are used mainly in writing.

● Defining relative clauses

1 These give information which *is* essential to the meaning of a sentence. They 'define' or 'identify' the person or thing we are talking about. If a defining relative clause is removed, a sentence changes its meaning or becomes meaningless:

Kennedy will appear in the final concert of the sellout tour which has established him as a celebrity.
There was a lot of pressure on all the kids who were there.
I don't want to be a musician if it means having an image which doesn't represent me as a person.

2 The pronoun *that* can be used instead of *who* or *which*:

There was a lot of pressure on all the kids that were there.
He returned to London to take up the many offers of work that were already being made.

3 They are not separated from the main clause by commas. In speech, the speaker does not pause at the beginning and end of the clause.

4 The relative pronoun can be left out if it is the object, rather than the subject, of the verb in its clause:

The plastic bag (which/that) he was carrying was full of clothes.
The dark glasses (which/that) he was wearing hid a black eye.
He's a musician (who/that) people like to listen to.

Note

Where and *when* can be used in the same way as relative pronouns when the nouns they refer to are places or times:

His father took him to the most important European cities, where he could show off the boy's talent.
It was a time when musicians in Austria were treated like servants.

2 Future-in-the-past

● *was/were going to* + infinitive

The future-in-the-past is used to talk about:

1 predictions or expectations:

It looked as though Gauguin was going to settle down and become a respectable businessman.
I thought I was going to be dealing with crimes...

2 intentions (especially intentions which are prevented from coming true):

He moved to Copenhagen, where he was going to make a fresh start, (but when his marriage broke up, he returned to Paris.)
Gauguin and van Gogh were going to paint together. (But unfortunately they quarrelled...)

● *was/were to* + infinitive

This form of the future-in-the-past is used to talk about events that were not possible to predict before they happened (unforeseen results):

This decision was to change the course of his life.
In 1891 he moved to Tahiti, where he was to live for nine years.

(These were not intentions. Gauguin did not know when he took the decision that his life would change. He did not have any plans to live in Tahiti for nine years.)

B Vocabulary

I Suffixes

● **-or/-er**

These suffixes are often added to verbs to make nouns which refer to people who do things:

actor (act) *sculptor* (sculpt) *sailor* (sail)
singer (sing) *player* (play) *teacher* (teach)

Notes

1 Sometimes verbs have to be modified before the ending *-er* is added:

writer (write) *drummer* (drum)

These nouns are formed in the same ways as the *-ing* form of verbs:

by dropping a final *-e*: *to write/writing/a writer*
by doubling a final consonant: *to drum/drumming/a drummer*

2 There are no reliable rules about when to use an *-er* or an *-or* suffix, but notice that there are some nouns ending in *-or* which are not formed from verbs:

author sponsor donor

● **-ist/-ian**

1 These suffixes are often added to the name of subjects (usually uncountable nouns) to make nouns which refer to people who do things:

artist (art) *scientist* (science)
psychologist (psychology) *linguist* (languages)
statistician (statistics) *musician* (music)
politician (politics) *grammarian* (grammar)

2 *-ist* is often added to the name of a musical instrument:

guitarist (guitar) *cellist* (cello) *pianist* (piano)
saxophonist (saxophone) *violinist* (violin)

Notes

1 There are no reliable rules about how subject words are modified before these suffixes are added, or about which suffix should be used.

2 There are some common exceptions to these general rules:

geographer (geography) *trumpeter* (trumpet)

2 A piece of

This phrase is often used when we refer to single items of uncountable nouns. Here are some common examples:

a piece of advice, information, music, news, poetry, writing, cake.

A bit of is used as a more colloquial alternative to *a piece of*:

I'd like to give you a bit of advice.
That was a brilliant bit of music.

◆ Make a list of everything you know about Saint Valentine's Day. Compare your list with the information given in the text on page 159.

I'd like you to be my Valentine, but I'm not going to beg.

◆ Read these Valentine's Day messages from a British national newspaper.

ROSS: 'Very special hello.' Help needed – please rescue! Friend in need. R. A.

E.S.C. Looking forward to the next five years and the next ... and the next ... and the next ... Love E. J.

SIMON PATRICK HOPKINS: I Love You. Yours, Lucinda Clare Robins (Same address) Guess who...?

PHIL, thank you for sharing this transcending passion. My infinite love!

For Barbara, My Schoolteacher
I love those eyes, they taught my heart that loving needs no scruples. And, when apart, so each must dwell upon my teacher's pupils. **Bob**

PRINCESS: Thanks for kissing a frog. Read my eyes. Forever yours Pxx.

TO OUR great year. Still love you JU! JAP 4TTC.

Gill
Lots of love today, I'll try to listen more.
Richard

REB Must marry you 6-4-92. Any Problems? TEL, the Robber Baron.

NAPOLEON SOLO – Looking forward to our celebration of True Love, 7.7.92.

PAULA BRADLEY, two years eh? Gary was absolutely right! Love you, Dave.

POPPET. – I'm not Tibetan so don't make me blue. Blacksmith.

HARMONIOUS playing keys. Magic moments. Love, Sue. XXX.

SCRUMPLED FACE. Coffee! Coffee! Coffee! Love you. W.W.W.

SWEETPEA. Thank you for your love and seven glorious months. Plums.

SWEETIEPIE. I luvs ya lots 'n' lots. Will you marry me? Hugs 'n' kisses. Growly Bear.

AMANDA. Looking forward to Amsterdam in June. I'll love you forever, JAMES.

◆ Find:
1 three expressions of thanks to someone
2 a promise
3 a request for help
4 a proposal of marriage

◆ Do you have similar customs in your country? Compare ideas with a partner.

Love

1 Listening

Make up a definition of *love* in not more than ten words.

Compare definitions with a partner.

Listen to these people's definitions of love. Which one is closest to your definition?

Now listen again. Which of these definitions do you think were made up by adults and which were made up by children?

Love is ....

2 Listening

Do you believe in love at first sight? Compare ideas with a partner.

Listen to four people discussing this idea. Do any of them believe in love at first sight?

Jeremy   Jenny   Mike   Margaret

● Attitudes and beliefs

Listen again and match these beliefs with the four speakers – Jeremy, Jenny, Mike or Margaret.

1 used to believe in love at first sight but doesn't now
2 believes people can like the look of each other at first sight
3 believes people can fall in love with the idea of love
4 likes the idea, but doesn't believe in it

● Understanding

1 According to Jenny, why is love at first sight impossible?
2 What does she think is possible?
3 What kind of 'horrible habits' do you think Jenny is talking about?
4 What do you think Jeremy learnt from his relationship with the woman he met on a train?
5 According to Mike, why are people likely to fall in love while they are travelling?

3 Vocabulary

● Multi-meaning words

Here are the definitions of some of the words in the recording in Exercise 2.

Look at the tapescript on page 169 to find the words which can have **all** the meanings given below. Then choose the meaning each word has **in the recording**.

1 a an act of seeing, or an occasion on which you see something
  b something worth seeing (a place tourists visit)
  c power of seeing, or ability to see

2 a to behave
  b to perform a part in a play or film
  c to fulfil a particular function

3 a to provide housing
  b to have enough space
  c to accept or put up with

4 a to feel attracted to someone
  b to think or imagine
  c special, unusual, highly decorated

5 a to teach skills needed for a particular activity
  b means of transport which takes passengers from station to station
  c to practise or prepare yourself physically for sports

6 a railway lines or roads that join two places
  b emotional connections between two people
  c rings in a chain

4 Pronunciation 🔲

(Language review B1, page 114)

In the recording in Exercise 1, one of the speakers says:

Love is when someone keeps on smiling at you. And they give you presents.

How is the word *presents* pronounced here?
How else can it be pronounced?

Many two-syllable words in English, like *present*, belong to more than one grammatical category (nouns, adjectives, verbs, etc.). Some of these words also have different meanings. These differences are marked by different stress patterns.

What grammatical category does the word *present* in the example sentence belong to? Does it have the same meaning if it is pronounced differently?

Now work with a partner. Read these sentences to each other. Think carefully about the stress on the words in bold type.

1 *In recent years there has been a steady **increase** in the divorce rate.*
2 *You still owe me £20. I **refuse** to lend you any more money.*
3 *This year there has been a **decrease** in the number of marriages.*
4 *I'm very sorry for what I said. I didn't mean to **insult** you.*
5 *Sociologists say they expect the birth rate to **increase** next year.*
6 *Modern Valentine cards often contain humorous **insults**.*
7 *Marriage is a legal and moral **contract** between two people.*
8 *In the winter Britain **imports** red roses from the Canary Islands.*

Now listen to these sentences in the recording. Did you put the stress on the correct part of the words?

Which grammatical categories do the eight words belong to?

Use a dictionary to check the different meanings of these words.

5 -ing forms

(Language review A1, page 113)

-ing forms can be used in these ways:

a as part of a continuous verb tense
b as nouns or as parts of noun phrases
c after prepositions
d after certain verbs and verb phrases (e.g. *to like*)

In which of these ways are the -ing forms used in these extracts from the recordings in Exercises 1 and 2? Write a, b, c or d in the boxes.

1 *I love **playing** with my friend next door …* ☐
2 *Love is **being** kind, and **holding** hands and **getting** married.* ☐
3 *I'm always **falling** in love.* ☐
4 *There's a big difference between **being** in love with someone and … **liking** someone a lot.* ☐
5 *Love is when someone keeps on **smiling** at you.* ☐
6 *I don't think you can actually love someone without **knowing** them deeply.* ☐
7 ***Travelling** is quite romantic and you form certain links …* ☐

Compare ideas with a partner.

Now for each of these seven sentences write a sentence with a similar meaning, without using -ing forms. The first one has been done for you:

1 *I love it when I'm with my friend next door.*

Compare sentences with a partner.

6 Pre-reading

Look at these photographs and read the headline.

DO WE MARRY OURSELVES?

What do you think the article is about?

7 Reading

Read the text and see if your prediction was correct.

WEDDING PICTURES in newspapers can show a remarkable likeness between partners. Is this just because the lighting angle has thrown similar shadows on their faces, or is there more to it than that? One point of view is that people are so self-centred that when they select their perfect mate they choose as close an image to themselves as they can.

How does this phenomenon arise? Possibly we spend so much time looking at ourselves in the mirror and trying to perfect our looks that we come to think of our own physical appearance as some kind of ideal standard. Assuming that our own appearance is less than perfect, this means that we would have to convert our weaknesses into strengths. So, if we have a large nose ourselves, we must first convince ourselves that big is beautiful and then set out to find an equally 'beautiful' partner. This may be an extreme example, but there's undoubtedly some truth in the suggestion that we are more sympathetic to physical handicaps in others if we ourselves share the same disabilities. Certainly, we are inclined to date and marry partners who are of a physical attractiveness similar to our own.

To investigate this, American psychologists took a selection of wedding photographs and cut them right down the centre to separate the bride and groom. They then analysed the individual photographs into categories of physical attractiveness – and found a high degree of correspondence between actual couples. The beautiful people seemed to have found themselves beautiful partners while plain people had acquired plain mates.

Now try to match the brides and the grooms in the photos on page 106.

Discuss ideas with a partner.

8 Talking points

Discuss these questions in groups:

- Do you agree with the writer of this text, who is a lecturer at the University of London, that most people *'think of their own physical appearance as some kind of ideal standard'*?

- In your experience, is it true that *'beautiful people find themselves beautiful partners'*? Do you know of any exceptions to this 'rule'?

9 Vocabulary

● **Nouns ending in *-ness* and *-ship***
(Language review B2, page 114)

In the text in Exercise 7 the word *likeness* is used to mean 'similarity'.
Look at these nouns ending in *-ness* or *-ship* and match them with their meanings:

1 weakness
2 relationship
3 friendship
4 attractiveness
5 membership
6 happiness
7 partnership

a state of feeling pleasure
b close connection between people or things
c quality of not being strong
d business carried on by two or more people
e feeling between people who like each other
f belonging to an organisation, group or club
g quality of being pleasant to look at

Make a list of any more nouns you know which end in *-ness* and *-ship*, and write a jumbled list of meanings.

Exchange lists with a partner and match each other's words with their correct meanings.

10 Definitions

One of the speakers in Exercise 1 defined *being in love* like this:

I think being in love is really depending on someone.

Using *-ing* forms, make up your own definitions of:

loneliness • friendship • happiness
selfishness • kindness

Now compare and discuss your definitions in groups of three or four.

---

11 Survey of beliefs

(Language review A2, page 113)

In Exercise 2 you heard people talking about 'love at first sight'.

Here are some more commonly-held beliefs:

a sixth sense (intuition)
reincarnation • telepathy
fate • chance • magic

Which of these do you believe in? Do you know of any other similar beliefs?

Ask ten other students about these beliefs and make a note of their answers (yes or no). Ask questions like this:

Do you think there is such a thing as reincarnation?

Do you believe in magic?

12 Writing

Write a brief summary of the results of your survey.

EXAMPLE:

A recent survey carried out in France has shown that a surprisingly high/low percentage/proportion of young people believe in the romantic idea of love at first sight. Although only 10% said they believed in fate, 80% said they thought there was such a thing as chance ...

Compare summaries with a partner.

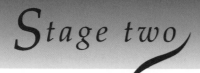

Stage two

A Happy Arrangement?

1 Introduction

Work in pairs.

What do you know about 'arranged marriages'? Here are a few questions to start you thinking:

- How would you define an 'arranged marriage'?
- What other kinds of marriage are there?
- In which countries are or were arranged marriages the custom?

Compare notes with a partner.

Now turn to page 159 and read the text, *Arranged Marriages*.

Does it confirm or contradict any of your ideas?

2 Reading

Work in pairs.

You are going to read some true stories about arranged marriages.

Student A: Read *Mountain Wolf Woman*.

Student B: Read *The Fox Woman*.

MOUNTAIN WOLF WOMAN

MOUNTAIN WOLF WOMAN, a Winnebago Indian, was forced to marry against her will when her brother gave her away to a man who had done him a small favor. Mountain Wolf Woman's mother sympathised with her daughter's situation but admitted there was nothing she could do, as her son had already arranged the marriage. The frightened and upset young woman was advised that if she did not agree to her brother's wishes, he would be embarrassed and disgraced. Because Winnebago girls were taught to have the highest respect for their brothers, Mountain Wolf Woman was finally persuaded. She married the unwelcome lover, but never forgot her mother's words: 'When you are older and know better, you can marry whoever you like.' After the birth of her second child, Mountain Wolf Woman left her husband and married a man she liked better.

Winnebago: the name of a North American Indian tribe

THE FOX WOMAN

IN *Autobiography of a Fox Woman*, the narrator tells how she fell in love with a young man she met secretly while picking fruit. The youth was good and kind, but the young Fox Woman's parents refused to allow her to marry him, saying that he would become a lazy wife-beater just like his father. In fact they threatened to disown their daughter if she even spoke with her sweetheart again. Eventually the girl married a man her parents had chosen for her. After their marriage the husband treated her nicely, but she never loved him, nor did she forget her sweetheart. After their first baby was born, the husband's behavior changed, and eventually the Fox Woman divorced him. Shortly after that, the wife of her former sweetheart died. After a mourning period of several years they married. They lived together happily until the man died suddenly after only a few years.

Fox: the name of a North American Indian tribe

Compare stories with your partner. Without looking at the texts again, tell each other the stories you have read. Make a note of similarities and differences between the two stories.

Understanding

Are these statements about the stories true or false?

1 Mountain Wolf Woman did not mind marrying the man her brother had promised her to.
2 Mountain Wolf Woman married the man for her brother's sake.
3 Mountain Wolf Woman had two children before she left her first husband.
4 The Fox Woman met her first husband while she was picking fruit.
5 The Fox Woman's parents would not let her marry the man she loved.
6 The Fox Woman's first husband was always very good to her.

Now write correct statements to replace the false ones.

● **Inference**
(The answers to these questions are only suggested in the texts.)

1 Why didn't Mountain Wolf Woman's mother help her daughter to get out of her arranged marriage?
2 Why did the Fox Woman wait for several years before marrying her second husband?

---

3 Vocabulary

● **American English**
(Language review B3, page 114)

What evidence is there that the two marriage stories were written by an American writer?

In what ways are American and British English grammar different?

Make a list of any differences you know of and compare with a partner.

What differences in vocabulary do you remember from Unit 2?
(See pages 17 and 23.)

● **Collective nouns**
(Language review B4, page 114)

The word *tribe* ('the Winnebago tribe') is a collective noun. That means it is a singular noun which refers to a group of people. Underline the collective nouns in these sentences and choose a suitable verb to go in the gaps.

1 The Winnebago tribe _____ in the state of Wisconsin.
2 The Johnson family _____ to dinner with us this evening.
3 The government _____ calling an election next year.
4 A young married couple _____ just _____ next door to us.
5 The town council _____ flats for homeless people.

Compare sentences with a partner.

Make a list of any more collective nouns you can think of.

---

4 Reading

Read the text about Benazir Bhutto's arranged marriage. Do you think she is optimistic or pessimistic about her future happiness?

Love by Arrangement

1 ON 29th July 1987 Benazir Bhutto's life changed dramatically when she agreed to an arranged marriage. She knew that her position in Pakistani politics would make it difficult for her to get to know a man in the normal course of events, but her own parents had married for love and she had always believed that she would fall in love and marry a man of her own choice.

2 Benazir made all kinds of objections, but finally agreed to meet Asif Zardari. She remembers the meeting well: 'Asif and I didn't have a conversation by ourselves during the entire evening. I didn't have a single feeling about him, even when he sent me a dozen roses the next day. "What's your answer?" asked my mother. I said I didn't know.'

3 Seven days after she had first met Asif they were engaged. As a politician, Benazir had to spend a lot of her time travelling, but Asif called her every day, and little by little they got to know each other over the phone. 'We had more in common than I thought,' said Benazir. 'We didn't really love each other yet, though my mother assured me that love would come later. Instead there was a mental commitment between us, a realisation that we were accepting each other as husband and wife totally and for always. In a way, I realised that this bond was stronger than love. In love marriages, I imagined, the expectations were so high they were bound to be somewhat dashed. There must also be the fear that love might die and, with it, the marriage. Our love could only grow.'

4 On 17th December Benazir Bhutto and Asif Zardari were married.

● Understanding

Discuss these questions with a partner:

1 Why do you think Benazir Bhutto's lifestyle made it difficult for her to get to know men?
2 What kinds of objections do you think Benazir made?
3 Why do you think Benazir and Asif did not have a conversation by themselves?
4 What did Benazir's mother mean by *'What's your answer?'*

5 Vocabulary

Guess the meaning of these phrases from the text:

1 in the normal course of events (*Para. 1*)
2 a mental commitment (3)
3 for always (3)
4 this bond (3)
5 they (the expectations) were bound to be somewhat dashed (3)

6 Infinitives

(Language review A3, page 113)

Look at these sentences from the texts about arranged marriage.

How are the forms of infinitive different in the two types of sentence?

Type A:
1 *Mountain Wolf Woman was forced to **marry** against her will.*
2 *Winnebago girls were taught to **have** the highest respect for their brothers.*
3 *Benazir agreed to **meet** Asif.*

Type B:
1 *The girl's mother admitted there was nothing she could **do**.*
2 *My mother assured me that love would **come** later.*
3 *Love might **die**.*

Scan the three stories for more infinitives, and then make a list of more **Type A** and **Type B** sentences.

Work with a partner. Finish these sentences:

1 Winnebago girls were taught that it was important …
2 Mountain Wolf Woman's mother thought her daughter was too young …
3 To begin with, the Fox Woman was unwilling …
4 Because of her involvement in politics it was not easy for Benazir Bhutto …

7 Practice

Read this story and fill the spaces with an *-ing* form, an infinitive, or *to* + an infinitive. Choose appropriate verbs from the list below. (You can use any of the verbs more than once.)

A SIGH IS JUST A SIGH

IT is difficult ___(1)___ feelings which are a mixture of 'love' and frustration. For days I have had a strange feeling in my stomach and have not been able ___(2)___ on anything except Nicola Stevens. I haven't known her for long, but my feelings for her have become unbearable.

I couldn't ___(3)___ last night and I didn't stop ___(4)___ about her all morning. I eventually decided ___(5)___ something about it. I got on my bike and cycled all the way to Headley where she lives, though I still don't know what I was intending ___(6)___ there. Anyway, I bought a newspaper and a map in a newsagent's and after about an hour I succeeded in ___(7)___ her house.

I was too frightened ___(8)___ at her door, so I sat on my bike and waited for something ___(9)___. After about half an hour I plucked up enough courage ___(10)___ up the drive to the house.

To my relief there was no one in, so I sat against a tree and started ___(11)___ at my newspaper. I've never really liked ___(12)___ when I'm nervous, and that afternoon it was impossible ___(13)___ at all. My heart leapt into my mouth every time I heard a car. An hour later, I saw Nicola ___(14)___ up the drive in a car. She seemed shocked ___(15)___ me. She carried on up the drive and five minutes later came back with her sister – she obviously didn't want ___(16)___ alone with me. As she reached my tree, my heart nearly stopped ___(17)___.

'What are you doing here?' she said.

The conversation that followed was difficult. We couldn't ___(18)___ for long because a wedding reception was being held at the house, but as we talked I started ___(19)___ more relaxed – my heartbeat slowed and the feeling in my stomach disappeared.

Suddenly I realised that this was the way it was always going to be. I was just her friend and that is how we would ___(20)___ – good friends. As Nicola and her sister walked back to the house, I got on my bike and rode home. I was my old self again.

be	do	happen	remain	think
beat	express	look	see	walk
come	feel	knock	sleep	
concentrate	find	read	talk	

8 Writing

Write your own first-person narrative love story.

If you decide to write a fictional story, choose one of these beginnings and one of these endings:

Possible beginnings	Possible endings
• Your eyes met mine …	• I never saw her/him again.
• My heart sank; I felt so hurt when he/she said …	• Later that evening I planned my revenge.
• When I saw her/him for the first time, I felt like …	• Thank goodness! My first impressions had been right, after all.

Find another student in the class who has written the same beginning and ending as you. Read and discuss each other's stories.

*E*xtension

The Bachelors of Vatersay

Look at the photograph and map and read the Case Study notes.

Case Study: Bachelors of Vatersay

Subjects: (People)	22 single men aged twenty to forty
	All have houses and good jobs as fishermen.
Location:	The island of Vatersay in the Outer Hebrides (See map)
	Population: 80
	Main occupation: fishing
	Nearest island: Barra (*pop. 1800*) – twenty minutes by boat from Vatersay
History:	Two weddings on Vatersay in the last twenty years
	Many younger men have returned to Vatersay after working on the mainland.
Problem:	22 bachelors want to get married and have children.
	No women of marriageable age on Vatersay.
	Nearest nightlife: in Castlebay on Barra.
	Castlebay girls not prepared to move to Vatersay.
Possible solutions:	Proposal to build £3m causeway between Vatersay and Barra.
	Men emigrate from Vatersay.

● **Role play**

Work in groups of four.

Using the above information about Vatersay, discuss the problems of the 22 Vatersay bachelors from the points of view of these people:

Student A: A member of Vatersay council (You want to keep the island alive.)

Student B: A 25-year-old unmarried man (You want a family of your own.)

Student C: A parent of two young children living on Vatersay

Student D: One of the young unmarried women living on Barra

Try to reach agreement about what should be done to solve the situation and improve life on Vatersay. (It is not certain that the causeway between Vatersay and Barra will be built, so think of as many alternative solutions as you can.)

● **Writing**

Write a semi-formal letter to the Editor of Vatersay's local newspaper, suggesting what could be done to solve the problem of the Vatersay men.

*L*anguage review

A Grammar and Use

1 -ing forms

● **Use**

1 As part of a continuous verb tense:
   I'm always falling in love.
   I still don't know what I was intending to do there.

2 As an adjective:
   Love can be a frightening experience.

3 As the subject or complement of a sentence:
   Travelling is quite romantic.
   Love is being kind and getting married.

4 After certain verbs:
   Love is when someone keeps (on) smiling at you.
   Have you ever considered getting married?

   Here are some more common verbs and verb phrases that are followed by the *-ing* form:

   'Liking' verbs: *detest, dislike, enjoy, hate, love, like, mind, can't stand*

   Other verbs: *admit, avoid, consider, deny, face, feel like, finish, give up, can't help, miss, practise, risk, spend time, suggest*

5 After prepositions:
   You can't love someone without knowing them deeply.
   There's a difference between loving someone and liking them.

6 After conjunctions:
   She fell in love with a young man she met while picking fruit.

After leaving her husband, she married her former sweetheart.

7 After perception verbs followed by an object:
   I saw Nicola coming up the drive in her car.
   I heard people talking in loud voices.

2 Expressing beliefs

Here are some common ways of talking about beliefs:

Questions: *Do you believe in reincarnation?*

Do you think there's such a thing as fate?

Statements: *I don't believe in telepathy.*

There's no such thing as luck.

3 Infinitives

Here are some of the uses of the infinitive:

1 Infinitive without *to* after these modal verbs:

   will, shall, would, should, can, could, may, might, must

   She admitted there was nothing she could do.
   His father said he should go and save one for himself.

2 Infinitive with *to* after *ought, used, be able, have:*

   I ought to go now.
   Do you have to leave so early?

3 Infinitive with *to* after certain verbs:

begin, decide, expect, happen, help, hope, intend, learn, manage, offer, prefer, pretend, promise, refuse, seem, start, threaten, try, wish

> I never **expected to see** her again.
> I **refuse to lend** you any more money.

4 Verb + object + *to* + infinitive after certain verbs:

ask, encourage, expect, force, help, invite, order, permit, persuade, remind, teach, tell, want, warn

> Mothers **taught their daughters to have** respect for their brothers.
> Girls **expect their boyfriends to send** them cards on Valentine's Day.

5 After adjectives:

> It is **difficult to express** certain feelings.
> It was **nice to see** you again.

6 With *enough* and *too* phrases:

> I was **too frightened to knock** at her door.
> Some cards were **offensive enough to be classed** as libellous.

7 Expression of purpose:

> **To investigate** this, American psychologists did some research.
> He goes to parties (so as) **to meet** new people.

(See Unit 9, Language review A2.)

B Vocabulary

1 Words with different stress patterns

In the examples in the pronunciation exercise on page 106, the stress is on the first syllable of nouns, and on the second syllable of verbs:

Nouns: *present, increase, decrease, refuse, insult, contract, import*

Verbs: *present, increase, decrease, refuse, insult, contract, import*

Other patterns are also possible:

Adjectives: *frequent, perfect*

Verbs: *frequent, perfect*

2 Nouns ending in *-ness* and *-ship*

- The suffix *-ness* can be added to some adjectives to make nouns which refer to a state or a quality.

  EXAMPLES:
  dampness, darkness, friendliness, kindness, suddenness

- The suffix *-ship* can be added to some nouns to make other nouns. Nouns ending in *-ship* can have three possible meanings:

  1 They can refer to a person's status or official position:
  apprenticeship, chairmanship, membership

  2 They can refer to relations between people or things:
  friendship, partnership, relationship

  3 They can refer to abilities or skills:
  craftsmanship, musicianship, statesmanship

3 American English

These are a few examples of some of the grammatical differences between British and American English:

British	American
I've just eaten.	*I just ate.*
to teach in a school	*to teach school*
I've got a new car.	*I've gotten a new car.*
to visit	*to visit with*
to speak to	*to speak with*
He dived into the lake.	*He dove into the lake.*

4 Collective nouns

- Collective nouns are singular nouns which refer to a group:

  audience, committee, couple, family, government, tribe

Most of these nouns can be followed by a singular or a plural verb.

If this group is thought of impersonally as a single unit, we use a singular verb:

> The council is considering new parking regulations.

If groups are thought of as a number of individuals, we use plural verbs:

> The audience are enjoying the film.

- Some collective nouns, e.g. *cattle, people, the police* always take plural verbs.

  EXAMPLE: *The police have arrested two men for murder.*

◆ Match these captions with the three cartoons:

1 *Know what really makes me mad? Thinking of them living it up on the insurance money!*

2 *You chaps going to be here long?*

3 *What difference does it make whether I'm an old lady or just dressed up as one?*

◆ What crimes do the three cartoons illustrate? Choose from this list:

arson   blackmail   burglary   kidnapping   mugging
murder   robbery   shoplifting   theft   vandalism

What do we call the criminals who commit these ten crimes?

EXAMPLE: arson – *arsonist*

◆ Now put these five crimes in order of seriousness, starting with the most serious:
a *arson* – a man sets fire to his own house to collect £100,000 insurance money.
b *mugging* – a youth hits an old lady over the head in the street and steals £20 from her handbag.
c *murder* – a woman kills her husband after a family argument.
d *theft* – an employee steals £50,000 from the company he works for over a period of five years.
e *kidnapping* – political terrorists kidnap the ten-year-old daughter of a millionaire and demand a ransom of £1 million.

Find another student who has put the crimes in the same order as you.

*S*tage one

Creative Sentencing

1 Pre-reading

Where do you think this notice appeared? What do you think its purpose was?

Public apologies like this are sometimes used as an alternative to prison as a way of punishing criminals in the USA.

What other alternatives to prison do you know about? Make a list of alternatives, and compare ideas with a partner.

'I, Tom Kirby, wish to apologise to the people of Newport for all the problems I have caused. I know now that taking those cars was selfish and wrong. I also realise I have caused a lot of hardship to people that were my friends and also to my own family. I want to thank the courts for a second chance to prove I can be an honest person. My apologies again for causing any inconvenience to anyone.'

2 Reading

Read this article about experimental sentencing in the United States. Are any of your alternative types of punishment mentioned?

● Understanding

Read the text again and answer these questions:

1 According to the text, what three alternatives to imprisonment originated in the USA? (*Para. 1*)
2 What three examples of probation violations are mentioned in connection with the Indiana judge? (2)
3 Why might the Texas woman have been sent to prison? (3)
4 In what way was the 15-day sentence passed on the New York landlord successful? (4)
5 In what three ways was the wealthy industrialist punished? (5)
6 What alternatives to imprisonment are used by Oregon courts? Who decides on the final form of punishment? (6)

The personal touch in punishment

1 In many countries of the world criminals are simply sent to prison, but the USA has a long tradition of introducing new approaches for the treatment of offenders. Probation, parole and fitting the punishment to the crime were all first tried in America.

2 Judges in the United States are expected to act independently. Appeal against sentences is almost impossible and the law gives judges great freedom. The result is a mixture of constructive and cranky sentences. An Indiana judge, for example, has declared war on young offenders. There is nothing strange about the fact that he gives prison sentences to juvenile criminals who break the conditions of their probation. What is unusual, however, is that, in addition to curfew violations and positive drug tests, low school grades also anger the judge. Offenders on probation who score D grades or lower may be sent to gaol for up to six months.

3 A Texas woman with five children faced the possibility of a prison sentence because she had not reported to her probation officer. The court discovered that, although the woman had no job and was getting welfare payments, she was a smoker. The judge said, 'This woman's addiction shouldn't be subsidised by taxpayers.' He ordered her to stop smoking within thirty days.

4 Some judges also think of appropriate punishments for the rich. A New York landlord who had refused to do maintenance work on his apartments was sentenced to live in one of his own buildings for fifteen days. The man was fitted with an electronic monitor until his sentence was completed. The penalty was a success: within a month, all the building's defects had been corrected. In a more traditional court the man might just have been fined.

5 Another famous sentence was imposed on a wealthy industrialist who had evaded more than $600,000 in income tax. He was ordered to pay fines and interest of $1.9 million. In addition he agreed to set up a fund of $1.5 million for homeless men, women and children, and to spend 20 hours a week for five years working with them. But not all Americans agreed with this sentence. Many people thought the industrialist should have been given a long prison sentence.

6 Some judges have made shame a central feature of their sentences. Courts in Oregon, for example, give offenders a choice between prison and a combination of fine, probation, compensation to their victims, and community service, all with an apology. This takes the form of an advertisement in a local newspaper and includes details of the crime and a personally-worded apology. Each advertisement is accompanied by a photo of the offender and mentions the street or area where they live.

● **Inference**
(The answers to these questions are only suggested in the text.)

1 Why do you think the Indiana judge considers good school grades to be so important?

2 Do you think the Texas woman was sent to prison or not?

3 What was the purpose of the electronic monitor fitted to the New York landlord?

4 Why do you think some judges order criminals to make a public apology?

---

3 Vocabulary

● **Law and order**

List these people connected with crime under the appropriate headings:

criminal   judge   offender
policeman   prisoner
prison officer   probationer
probation officer   victim

Wrong side of the law	Right side of the law
criminal	judge

Which two words in the left-hand list mean approximately the same?

Find pairs of people (one from each list), and write sentences which show how they are related.

EXAMPLE: judge/criminal
Judges sentence criminals.

● **Crime and punishment**
(Language review B1, page 124)

Match these methods of treatment with their meanings:

1 community service

2 compensation to victims

3 curfew

4 electronic monitoring

5 fine

6 fitting the punishment to the crime

7 parole

8 probation

a a time after which people must stay at home

b sentence which is specially suited to the offence committed

c organised work to help other people

d the payment of money

e period of time during which the offender must stay out of trouble

f method of checking exactly where a person is at any time

g payment of money to people who have suffered as the result of a crime

h early release of a prisoner who behaves well

---

4 Adjectives as nouns
(Language review B2, page 124)

Some judges also think of appropriate punishments for the rich.

The word *rich* in this sentence is an adjective used with the definite article to refer to a group of people.
The rich = rich people

Think of adjectives used after *the* to mean:

1 people with no jobs
2 people who have very little money
3 people who are no longer young
4 people who cannot see
5 people who cannot hear

5 Talking points
Work in pairs.

• The text in Exercise 2 describes the new punishments either as *constructive* (positive) or *cranky* (crazy or eccentric). Which of the punishments mentioned in the article do you think are constructive and which are cranky?

• Do you think the law treats rich people and poor people as equals?

• What do you think should be the main purpose of a judge's sentence?

1 to punish the criminal

2 to rehabilitate the criminal

3 to protect society

6 Passive verbs

(Language review A1, page 123)

Read these two sentences to remind yourself of the differences between active and passive sentences:

Active: *In the past, judges sentenced murderers to death.*

Passive: *In the past, murderers were sentenced to death.*

Make a list of the passive verbs in the text in Exercise 2.
(Some of them are 'modal passives', for example, *may be sent to gaol*.)

Read the sentences containing passives again carefully and decide in each case why you think a passive verb is used. Which of these three reasons is most probable? Sometimes more than one reason is possible.

Reasons:

a The action or the person affected by the action is more important than the person who does the action (the agent).

b The writer does not know or cannot reveal the identity of the agent.

c The agent is obvious and does not need to be mentioned.

Finally rewrite these sentences using active verbs. If no agent is mentioned in the passive sentence, you will have to think of a subject for your active sentence.

EXAMPLE: Judges in the United States are expected to act independently.
The people of the United States expect judges to act independently.

7 Listening

Listen to these four crime stories which were reported on the weekly TV programme *Crimespot*. As you listen, make a note of the crime and information about the possible suspect in each case.

Story	Crime	Information about possible suspects
1		
2		
3		
4		*medium height*

8 Talking points

Decide on suitable punishments for the criminals involved in these four stories. Write down your own ideas.

EXAMPLE: *I think the hoax caller should be sent to prison for six months.*

Now compare ideas with a partner. Try to reach agreement about appropriate punishments.

9 Reading and writing

Look at these six newspaper headlines. Which four stories were mentioned in the crime report in Exercise 7?

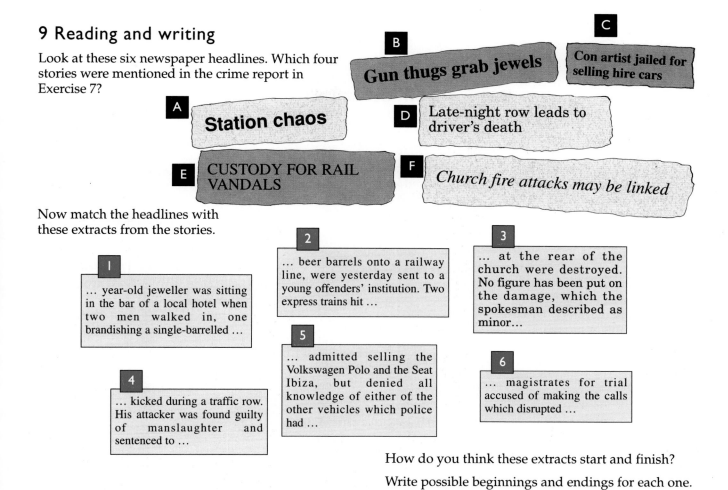

A Station chaos

B Gun thugs grab jewels

C Con artist jailed for selling hire cars

D Late-night row leads to driver's death

E CUSTODY FOR RAIL VANDALS

F Church fire attacks may be linked

Now match the headlines with these extracts from the stories.

1 ... year-old jeweller was sitting in the bar of a local hotel when two men walked in, one brandishing a single-barrelled ...

2 ... beer barrels onto a railway line, were yesterday sent to a young offenders' institution. Two express trains hit ...

3 ... at the rear of the church were destroyed. No figure has been put on the damage, which the spokesman described as minor...

4 ... kicked during a traffic row. His attacker was found guilty of manslaughter and sentenced to ...

5 ... admitted selling the Volkswagen Polo and the Seat Ibiza, but denied all knowledge of either of the other vehicles which police had ...

6 ... magistrates for trial accused of making the calls which disrupted ...

How do you think these extracts start and finish?

Write possible beginnings and endings for each one.

Compare ideas with a partner.

---

10 Role play

Work in groups of four.

● The offenders in the six cases reported above were given these prison sentences:

1	five years	4	four years
2	six months	5	six months
3	three years	6	one year

Read your role descriptions and think of some alternative punishments.

Students B, C, D: Turn to page 159 and follow the instructions.

Student A: Read these instructions.

You agree with the prison sentences imposed by the courts in these cases. Think about why you are not keen on alternative punishments.

● **Discussion**

Make your suggestions or express strong opinions about alternative punishments for the offenders.

11 Writing

Choose one of the four cases from the recording in Exercise 7, and write a defence speech explaining or justifying the 'crime'. Write the speech from the point of view of a defence lawyer. Here are some suggestions for the structure of your speech:

- **Opening remarks:** Introduce your client and try to establish that they have a good character.

- **Background to the crime:** Describe the circumstances that led up to the offence.

- **The incident:** Describe the crime itself in detail. Mention your client's motives and state of mind.

- **Explanation:** Give an explanation for your client's behaviour, but do not try to claim that they are innocent.

- **Concluding remarks:** Summarise the main points of the case for the defence. Emphasise that your client is unlikely to commit another offence.

Stage two

Self-defence

1 Pre-listening

Staying safe on the streets can be difficult these days. In America, for example, one woman in four will be attacked at some time in her life, and in certain European cities attacks of this kind are on the increase.

What advice would you give to someone who was worried about being attacked in the street? Discuss your ideas in pairs or groups.

2 Listening

Now listen to a youth worker talking about ways of avoiding danger. Are any of the ideas you discussed mentioned?

Why is it always useful to carry coins with you? Make a guess. Listen to find out the answer.

● **Understanding**

Listen again and make a list of *Dos and Don'ts* mentioned by the speaker.

Compare lists with a partner and together make a *Dos and Don'ts* poster to put on the classroom wall.

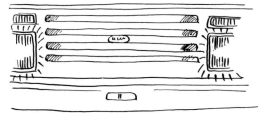

3 Vocabulary

● **'Loud voice' verbs**

One of the pieces of advice in the recording was to: *scream, shout and generally make as much noise as possible.*

Here are the dictionary definitions of the verbs *scream* and *shout*. Which is which?

• to give a loud high-pitched cry to show fear or pain
• to call or say something very loudly

Make up definitions for some more 'loud voice' verbs:

1 to cry 2 to howl 3 to shriek
4 to squeal 5 to yell

Finally, use your dictionary to check your definitions, and to make sure you understand the differences in meaning between these verbs.

● **Verbs and parts of the body**

Match these verbs with the parts of the body used in doing the actions.

1 scratch   a shoulder
2 kick   b teeth
3 slap   c fist (closed hand)
4 bite   d fingernails
5 punch   e palm (open hand)
6 barge   f foot

● **Phrasal verbs with *run***
(Language review B3, page 124)

The speaker in the recording in Exercise 2 says:

***Run away** as soon as you get the chance.*
to run away = to escape/leave

Rewrite these sentences replacing the words in italics with one of the verbs from the box.

1 Yesterday I *ran into* someone I met two years ago.

2 Don't *run* yourself *down*. You're a very good tennis player.

3 My father spends hours on the telephone. He must be *running up* a huge bill.

4 Have we got much further to go? We've almost *run out of* petrol.

5 Can you *run through* the arrangements again, please? I'm still not exactly sure what we're doing first.

6 So far so good. We haven't *run up against* any serious problems yet.

7 When I was in town yesterday I saw a taxi *run over* a cat.

to use all of something
to meet by chance
to drive over
to criticise
to encounter/discover
to review/summarise
to incur (a debt)

4 Pronunciation

Remember that the parts of sentences which are stressed are the words which the speaker thinks contain new or important information.

Read these sentences from the recording in Exercise 2.

In pairs, try to work out or remember which words were stressed.

1 *I'd advise you against trying to use physical violence yourself.*
2 *This really should be a last resort.*
3 *Whenever you travel on a bus at night, make sure you sit near the driver.*
4 *Run away as soon as you get the chance.*
5 *The way I see it, no amount of money is worth getting hurt for.*

Now listen to these sentences in the recording and check which words are stressed.

Work in pairs. Read out the list of *Dos and Don'ts* you wrote in Exercise 2. Decide which are the important words and stress them as you read.

---

5 Giving advice

(Language review A2 and 3, page 123)

Here are two sentences giving advice from the recording in Exercise 2:

1 *Whatever you do, don't accept lifts in strangers' cars.*
2 *Whenever you travel on a bus at night, make sure you sit near the driver.*

What do you think the *Wh-ever* words in these sentences mean? How could these sentences be rewritten without using *whatever* and *whenever*?

Start your sentences like this:

1 *It doesn't matter …*
2 *Every …*

Compare ideas with a partner.

Now look at the tapescript for Exercise 2 on page 000. Make a list of all the expressions used by the speaker to give advice. Group the expressions under these headings:

Advising someone what to do
Advising someone what not to do

Work in pairs, and add any more advice expressions you know to your list.

---

6 Practice

Work in pairs.

Give advice to people in these situations. Use some of the expressions you listed in Exercise 5.

7 Writing

These illustrations show ways of preventing two different types of theft. Write clear instructions for each illustration, explaining exactly what to do or what not to do in each.

EXAMPLE: *Make sure you keep your bag zipped up …*

1 *Beware pickpockets.*

2 *Lock it or lose it!*

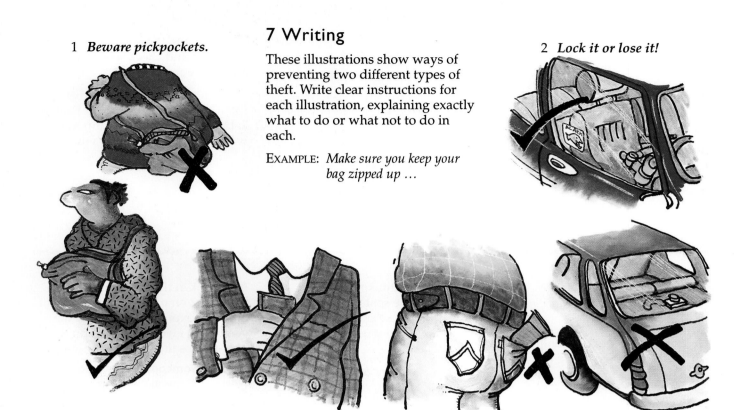

Debate

- You are going to debate this motion in groups of four:

  We believe that murder is always wrong and should always be punished.

- **Students A** and **B** (Proposers): You are going to speak **for** this motion. Write short speeches lasting not more than two minutes, giving your reasons for agreeing with the motion.
  Students C and **D** (Opposers): You are going to speak **against** the motion. Write short speeches lasting not more than two minutes, giving your reasons for disagreeing with the motion.

- When you have prepared your speeches, you should speak in this order:
  A, C, B, D

- When all four members of the group have spoken, have a general discussion of the issues, followed by a vote.

- Now turn to page 160 and read the Case Study notes on a real-life murder which took place in New York a few years ago.

  When you have read the notes, discuss these questions:

  1 Should the bystander give himself up to the police?
  2 If he is found guilty of murder, how should he be punished?

*L*anguage review

A Grammar and Use

1 Passive verbs

● **Passive verb forms**

Remember that the passive is formed like this:

the verb *to be* + past participle:

> Judges **are expected** to act independently.
> (Present Simple)
> A New York landlord **was sentenced** to live in one of his
> own buildings. (Past Simple)
> Within a month, all the building's defects **had been
> corrected.** (Past Perfect.)

● **Modal passives**

Use passive infinitives after modal verbs:

> This woman's addiction **shouldn't be subsidised** by the
> taxpayers.
> A reward **may be given** for information which leads to an
> arrest.

To form a perfect modal passive, use the perfect
infinitive (*have been*) + past participle:

> In a more traditional court the man **might have been
> fined.**
> The industrialist **should have been given** a long prison
> sentence.

● **Uses of the passive**

Remember that passive verbs are often used:

1   when the action or the person affected by the action
is more important than the person who does the
action (the agent):

> In the past murderers were sentenced to death.

2   when we do not know or cannot reveal the identity
of the agent:

> The man has been seen wearing a leather jacket.

3   when the agent is obvious and does not need to be
mentioned:

> A famous sentence was imposed on a wealthy
> industrialist.

2 Giving advice

Here are some common ways of advising people to do
or not to do something:

● **Imperatives**

> Try to go around in groups of two or more.
> Don't accept lifts in strangers' cars.

● *If clauses*

> If I were you, I'd (would) telephone the police.
> If I were in your position, I wouldn't go out alone.

● *Should or ought to*

> You should always carry some coins with you.
> You ought not to/shouldn't walk home late at night.
> I don't think you should carry a lot of money with you.

● **Using the noun** *advice* **or the verb** *advise*

> My advice would be to make sure your parents know
> where you are going.
> I'd advise you to knock on the nearest door.
> I'd advise you against trying to use physical violence
> yourself.

Notice the difference in spelling between the noun
advice and the verb *advise*.

● *Suggest*

> I suggest (that) you always carry some coins with you.

3 Wh-ever words

*   Words like *whatever* and *whenever* can be pronouns or
conjunctions:

> Whatever you do, don't accept lifts in strangers' cars.
> Whenever you travel on a bus, always sit near the
> driver.

*   The suffix *-ever* adds the meaning 'it doesn't matter':

> Whatever you do ... = It doesn't matter what
> (other things) you do ...
> Whenever you travel ... = It doesn't matter when
> you travel/Every time you travel ...

*   Here are some more examples:

> Wherever you are, I'll be thinking of you. (It doesn't
> matter where you are ...)
> Whoever is at the door, tell them I'm not in. (It doesn't
> matter who is at the door ...)

B Vocabulary

1 Crime and punishment

- commit:
  to commit a crime/a murder/suicide

- compensation:
  to pay compensation to someone

- fine:
  to pay a fine of £200/to pay a £200 fine
  to fine someone £200 for committing a crime

- parole/probation:
  to be on parole/probation
  to put someone on parole/probation

- (im)prison/jail/gaol:
  to send someone to prison/jail/gaol for two years
  to gaol/imprison/jail someone
  to go to prison/gaol/jail

- sentence:
  to give someone a 10-year sentence
  to impose a sentence on someone
  to sentence someone to life imprisonment
  to sentence someone to go to prison

2 Adjectives as nouns

We use some adjectives with the definite article to refer to groups of people:

the blind = people who are blind
the dead = people who have died
the deaf = people who cannot hear

Although these words look singular (and never take a plural -*s*), they have a plural meaning and are used with plural verbs:

The rich sometimes receive special punishments in the USA.
The old are often ignored or neglected by society.

Here is a list of the most commonly used adjectival nouns:

the blind, the dead, the deaf, the handicapped, the living, the mentally ill, the sick, the old, the poor, the rich, the unemployed

3 Phrasal verbs with three parts

Run up against and *run out of* are examples of three-part phrasal verbs.

These verbs consist of:
verb + adverb + preposition

The three parts always stay together and cannot be separated. Here are some more examples to learn:

*I've had to walk very fast to **catch up with** you.*
= reach someone who is in front of you

*That's brilliant! Did you **come up with** the idea yourself?*
= invent, discover, produce (something new)

*I wish they would **do away with** school uniform. It's so boring.*
= discontinue, abolish, get rid of

*I never see my brother. We **fell out with** each other years ago.*
= quarrel and stop being friendly with someone

*You don't look well. Are you sure you **feel up to** the journey?*
= feel healthy or energetic enough/feel capable of

*I wish I could **get out of** going to that meeting.*
= avoid (doing something)

*The Australians **go in for** long holidays in Europe.*
= do something regularly, usually for pleasure

*I always **keep up with** the sports news.*
= stay informed about

*We're really **looking forward to** coming to see you.*
= await something with interest or excitement

*I don't know how you **put up with** the noise. It's deafening.*
= tolerate, stand, be patient about

first impressions

◆ Look at the illustrations of inventions in their earliest forms.
Can you recognise the objects?

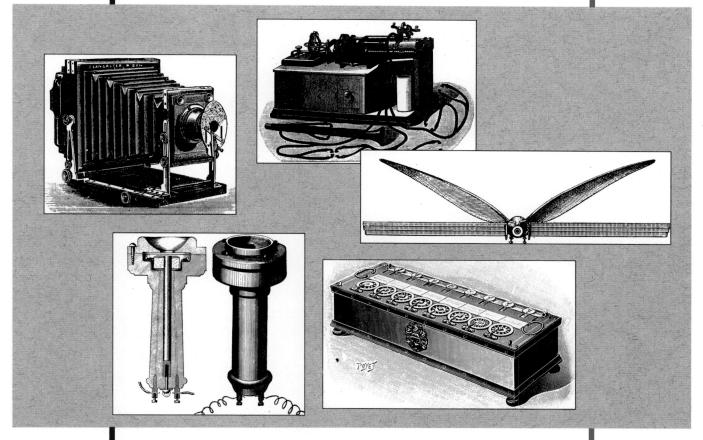

◆ In which ways do you think these objects will be different in the future?

◆ Read this article about an invention. What kind of problem will it solve?

Matsushita Electric Industrial Co. of Osaka, Japan, has just developed a sleep sensor that may help insomniacs get a good night's sleep. The sensor is a thin band containing electronic circuitry, that can be positioned either on top of, or within, the bed mattress. The device monitors the body's movements to determine exactly when the user falls asleep. (Sleep sensors currently in use are attached to the body, restricting body motion and making sleep difficult.) Using the sensor, any noise level or uncomfortable room temperature can be adjusted to create an ideal sleeping environment. For example, once the sensor has determined that the user is asleep, it will be able to turn off a TV or stereo, dim the lights or adjust the air-conditioner. Matsushita plans to market its sensor in the near future.

◆ What sort of object would you like to invent to make life more comfortable, or to solve a problem?

Future Communications

1 Pre-reading

Work in pairs.

Look at the cartoon. How do you think TV has affected people's lives? Think of different areas where it is used.

2 Reading

Read the text and guess which word has been replaced by ****. What experiment is being described, and why do you think Waddington was chosen for it?

Guinea-pig villagers goggle-eyed at the prospect of 30 TV ****

1 THE 14th century village of Waddington in Lancashire is to be sent into the 21st century by an experiment which will give its inhabitants 30 television **** from next month. The villagers will be able to tune in to most of the British and European satellite ****, as well as their own Waddington one, which will show events such as council meetings, weddings and soccer games.

2 The 47 homes involved will have **** from Britain, France, Germany, Luxembourg and Italy, including Sky, Discovery (nature programmes), Landscape (scenery with music), Home Video (movies) and a large variety of entertainment programmes. Granada Television, the main backer of the project, says it will have to shield the people of Waddington from 'blue' European films.

3 This time next week the company will be installing the latest equipment for receiving high-definition pictures of cinema screen quality, and wide-screen television sets in some houses. Most homes will be cabled, although some will have satellite dishes. Villagers will be receiving special devices to monitor what they watch, and they will also be answering questions about whether they like or dislike a programme. The pub car park will house the main dish, which receives all the satellite ****. From there they will be fed by cable to local homes.

4 Waddington was chosen because it had the socio-economic mix that the broadcasters required. The European Institute for the Media will be monitoring the two-month experiment and will produce a report of the results.

5 Most locals are happy with the experiment, but a few are worried about spoiling the village with electronic spaghetti, as well as TV crews, researchers and tourists upsetting the tranquillity.

One 17-year-old TV addict, David Walker, is keenly looking forward to life as a 'couch potato'.

6 'I think it will be great. I can't wait for it to start. I reckon it could change the way people think about TV. I'm going to be watching it as much as possible.'

7 Tricia Hargreaves, a teacher in the local primary school, says, 'I'm sure it won't make a lot of difference to me as I don't watch that much TV anyway. I might watch some films.'

8 Garage owner Eric Edmondson is quite positive about the idea. 'I feel it will be a good thing for the community, and it would be nice to go down in history as pioneers of the future in television.'

● **Understanding**

1 Read the text again and note down the following:

   a Site for experiment:

   b **** from:

   c Local events to be televised:

   d Number of homes involved:

   e Duration of experiment:

   f Monitoring body:

   g Special equipment being used:

   h Site for main dish:

2 Find evidence in the text to support these statements:

   a Waddington is an old-fashioned village.

   b A lot of alterations will have to take place in the village.

   c Waddington was chosen for the experiment because of its residents.

   d Some residents are worried about the physical side effects of the experiment.

   e The people of Waddington have a variety of responses to the project.

3 Talking points

Discuss these questions with a partner:

1 How would you feel about having so many TV channels to choose from?

2 How many TV channels do you have to choose from where you live? How many of these channels do you watch regularly?

3 How do you think the experiment affected the people of Waddington?

4 Vocabulary

1 These 'television' words from the text all have other meanings. In pairs, explain their meaning in the context of TV, and think of at least one other meaning.

    a screen b dish c addict
    d set e crew f programme
    g channel

2 Guess the meaning of these words and phrases from the text:

    a goggle-eyed (*Title*)
    b the main backer (*Para. 2*)
    c electronic spaghetti (*5*)
    d 'couch potato' (*5*)
    e to go down in history (*8*)

● **Colours**
(Language review B1, page 135)

Characteristics, feelings, or qualities are often associated with certain colours. For example, the word *blue* can mean:

    pornographic (sexy): *blue films*
    unhappy: *I'm feeling blue.*

What qualities are associated with these colours?

    a red b green c black
    d yellow e white

Compare ideas with a partner.

5 Talking about the future
(Language review A1, page 134)

Look at these extracts from the text:

1 *The Waddington channel will show events such as council meetings. (Para. 1)*
2 *The 47 homes involved will have channels from Britain, France ... (2)*
3 *The company will be installing the latest equipment in some houses. (3)*
4 *They will be answering questions about whether they like or dislike a programme. (3)*
5 *The European Institute for the Media will be monitoring the experiment. (4)*
6 *The Institute will produce a report of the results. (4)*

Now discuss these questions in pairs:

1 What is the main difference between extracts 1, 2, 6, and extracts 3, 4, 5? Think about the form and the meaning of the extracts.

2 Look back at the text. Try to find sentences which include the future forms of *can* and *must*.

3 What do the expressions in bold type in these extracts have in common?

    I think *it will be great. (6)*
    I'm sure *it won't make a lot of difference to me ... (7)*
    I feel *it will be a good thing for the community ... (8)*

Can you think of any other expressions like this that are commonly used before *will*?

6 Practice

Here are a number of possible results of the Waddington experiment. Decide which of these things you think the people of Waddington will do and the things you think they won't do, and put a tick or a cross in the box.

1 watch foreign films □
2 spend less time with friends □
3 find out about local events □
4 learn other languages from foreign programmes □
5 go out in the evening □
6 talk to their neighbours more □

Now write sentences like this:

1 *The people of Waddington will be watching foreign films.*
The people of Waddington won't be watching foreign films.

7 Discussion
Work in pairs.

How do you think the children of Waddington will be affected by the experiment? Write five sentences of your own starting with *I think ...* or *I'm sure ...*

EXAMPLES:

I think they'll be spending more time indoors.
I'm sure they'll do less homework.

Discuss ideas with a partner.

8 Personalised practice

● How do you think these aspects of life will develop and change in the next fifty years?

> education   entertainment   environment   food
> medicine   politics   science   transport

● Think about how these changes will affect you and your family. Make brief notes under these headings:

aspect	change	effects on me and my family
education		
entertainment		

● Now interview a partner: ask questions about the changes they think will take place and how they think these changes will affect them personally.

EXAMPLE:

A *What do you think will happen to the environment?*

B *I think cities will become much more polluted, so I'm sure most people who can afford it will be living in the country. I expect I'll move to the country myself in a few years.*

9 Listening

● You are going to hear a poem about the negative effects that watching too much television can have on children. Before you listen, make a list of some of the points you think will be mentioned. Compare ideas with a partner.

● Now listen to the poem and check how many of the points on your list are mentioned.

● Listen to the poem again and then rewrite your list adding as many of the points from the poem as you can remember.

10 Talking points

Work in pairs.

1 How many of the negative effects mentioned in the poem do you agree with?

2 Can you think of any positive points of TV?

11 Vocabulary

(Language review B2, page 135)

In the first six lines of the poem, four different 'seeing' expressions are used. Look at the tapescript on page 170 to find these expressions, and then match them with these meanings:

1 to look mindlessly at something
2 to look at something for a long time
3 to look attentively at something
4 to notice or perceive something, maybe unintentionally

Now fill the gaps in these sentences with the correct form of a suitable 'seeing' verb. Use the four verbs from the poem and these three verbs:

> *to notice   to observe   to gaze*

Use a different verb in each gap.

1 What are you going to _____ on TV tonight?
2 When she met the TV star, she _____ at him admiringly.
3 Why is that man _____ at me? Is there something wrong with me?
4 Did you _____ what time the film starts?
5 Oh dear, I can't _____ the screen. I'd better put my glasses on.
6 He _____ her behaviour very closely for a week before making his report.
7 Why don't you go and play with your friends instead of _____ at the TV?

Compare answers with a partner.

12 Pronunciation 📼

1 The poem about television has a traditional pattern: the last words of each pair of lines rhyme with each other.

Here are ten words (from the poem) that end the first line of a pair. Which of the three words given ends the second line of the pair.

If you can't remember the poem, make sure you choose a word that rhymes. Follow the example:

1	**been**	a seen	b win	(c) screen
2	**about**	a shout	b out	c route
3	**saw**	a fur	b for	c floor
4	**drunk**	a junk	b tank	c punk
5	**still**	a steal	b sill	c seal
6	**punch**	a munch	b lunch	c ranch
7	**what**	a cat	b hut	c tot
8	**head**	a dead	b lead	c said
9	**mind**	a tinned	b signed	c blind
10	**cheese**	a peace	b freeze	c knees

When you have chosen the rhyming words, listen to the poem again to check your answers.

2 In each of these sets of three words only two rhyme. Circle the word in each set that does not rhyme. (Follow the example.)

1	food	(good)	rude
2	cough	rough	tough
3	caught	thought	doubt
4	shot	what	chat
5	bread	bleed	tread
6	dare	here	fear
7	peace	please	police
8	blue	two	toe

---

13 Writing a poem
Work in pairs.

You are now going to write a three-verse poem about the advantages of TV.

● Verse 1: Fill in the rhyming words:

TV's bad it's often said,
It makes you crazy in the _____.
For some folk that may well be true,
But not for others like me and _____.
What's so good about TV?
Read this poem and you will _____.

● Verse 2: Fill in all the gaps:

TV keeps people off the _____.
People _____ you'd hate to meet.
Provides relief from _____ and strain.
And stimulation for the _____.
The old and sick would be so bored
With entertainment they couldn't _____.

● Verse 3: Compose an original final verse of your own.

It should consist of 6 lines (three rhyming pairs). Try and make your verse sound like the first two verses.

Stage two

Life-cycles

1 Pre-reading

Work in pairs.

● The figures in this table show how human beings in the developed world have changed over the last 3000 years. The figures for 1990 are missing. Estimate what you think they are.

● What do you think are the main reasons for the increases in life expectancy and height?

	1150 B.C.	650 B.C.	120 A.D.	1400 A.D.	1820 A.D.	1990
Average male life expectancy	38.6 years	45.0 years	40.2 years	37.7 years	40.2 years	?
Average height for men	1m 67 cm	1m 70 cm	1m 69 cm	1m 69 cm	1m 70 cm	?
Average female life expectancy	31.3 years	36.2 years	34.6 years	31.1 years	37.3 years	?
Average height for women	1m 55 cm	1m 56 cm	1m 57 cm	1m 57 cm	1m 58 cm	?
World population	–	–	250 million	300 million	900 million	?

2 Reading

Read this text. Are any of the reasons you thought of in Exercise 1 mentioned?

Life goes on ... and on ...

How long we live, how tall we grow, how fast we run, and how intelligent we are all depend partly on the genes we inherit, and partly on the way we live.

A child will not grow to its full potential adult size unless there is optimum nutrition, freedom from disease, and family stability. In the early years of this century, children commonly grew to be taller than their parents, as each generation had a healthier upbringing than the previous one. In the professional classes this process has now virtually stopped, but in almost every country in the world the children of manual workers, the poor and the unemployed still grow less tall than children from wealthy families.

The big change in the West in the past hundred years has been the successful struggle against the spread of infection. This has meant that most people live beyond 70. Formerly, death in infancy was commonplace, and many young adults died from infectious diseases such as tuberculosis, typhoid and pneumonia.

● **Understanding**

Read the text again. Are these statements true or false? Put a ✔ or ✗ in the boxes.

1 People's lifestyle is the only factor which determines how long they live. ☐
2 Children's home environment can affect their development. ☐
3 In earlier times, children were always taller than their parents. ☐
4 Children from wealthier families are normally the same height as children from poorer families. ☐
5 People are living longer these days mainly because they eat better food. ☐
6 Diseases like typhoid have been controlled only in certain parts of the world. ☐

3 Vocabulary

Work in pairs.

The text you have just read is written in rather formal English. Think of more informal ways of expressing these words and phrases. The first one has been done for you.

1 intelligent – *clever*
2 optimum nutrition
3 disease
4 family stability
5 commonly
6 professional classes
7 formerly
8 infancy
9 commonplace

4 Pre-listening

In your experience, what common problems do old people face?

How do you think these problems could be solved?

Compare ideas with a partner.

5 Listening

Listen to the recording. According to the expert, what is the main problem for many people when they retire? Are any of the problems you thought of mentioned?

● Understanding

Answer these questions:

1 How long have most men and women worked for by the time they retire?
2 In what way can this be a problem for them when they retire?
3 What sort of changes do elderly people make when they retire?
4 What opportunities are open to retired people in some countries?
5 According to the speaker, what are the three 'golden rules' for retired people?

Compare answers with a partner.

Now listen to the recording again to check your answers.

6 Talking points

Discuss these questions in pairs:

1 Do retired people in your country face any of these problems?
2 What role does the family or the community play in looking after the elderly?

7 Vocabulary

● Noun suffixes
(Language review B3, page 135)

Nouns formed from verbs often end in *-ment* or *-ion*.

What are the verbs related to these nouns from the texts in this unit?

1 retirement 2 decision 3 education
4 movement 5 infection

What common nouns (ending in one the suffixes above) are formed from these verbs:

1 agree 2 entertain 3 define 4 inform
5 describe 6 involve 7 excite 8 attract
9 converse 10 disappoint

8 Talking about the future

(Language review A2, page 134)

Look at these extracts from the recording:

By the time you retire you will probably have worked for, oh, 45 or 50 years of your life.

You'll have been following a routine based mainly on your work.

But you probably won't have sorted out exactly what you're going to do after you stop working.

Discuss these questions with a partner:

1 What future tense is used in these three extracts?
2 What are the two forms of this tense? How do they differ in meaning?
3 Now look at these three sentences. How do they differ in meaning from the three sentences opposite?

You will probably work for 45 to 50 years of your life.
You will be following a routine based mainly on your work.
You probably won't sort out exactly what you're going to do after you stop working.

9 Information gap

Work in pairs.

George has worked all his life and is retiring next week.
You are going to find out about his life.

Student A: Turn to page 160.

Student B: Follow these instructions:

This table contains information about George's life. Ask your partner questions to find out the missing information.

EXAMPLES:

What did George do in 1957?
When did George move to Ford for a manager's job?
What's the situation now?

Now make Future Perfect sentences saying how long George will have done or have been doing something for when he retires next week.

EXAMPLE:

When George retires, he will have been working in the car industry for X years.

Compare sentences with your partner.

Date	Event	Situation now
1957	▶	works in car industry
1965	married Edna	▶
▶	moved to Ford for manager's job	manager at Ford
1990	started smoking a pipe	▶
This January	▶	lives in a small house
This April	started evening class	

10 Discussion

Work in pairs.

Look at these photos of two people. The first photo shows them in their teens and the second in their forties.

Describe how they have changed between their teens and their forties, and then say how you think they will have changed by the time they retire.

11 Writing

● Choose one of these ages: 25, 45 or 65.

Make predictions about yourself at the age you have chosen. Write note-form answers to questions like these:

What will you have done by this age?
What won't you have done by this age?
How long will you have been doing certain things for by this age?
How will you have changed personally by this age?

● Now write a profile of yourself at the age you have chosen. Follow this paragraph plan:

1 Which age have you chosen to write about and why?
2 Changes in personal appearance
3 Changes in personal situation (family etc.)
4 Career changes
5 Do you think you will be happy at the age you have chosen?

Starting Out

1 Group work

Work in groups of three.

Look at the list below and match each activity with one of the illustrations.

Now put the activities in order, starting with what you think a baby learns to do first.

Compare ideas with another group.

A baby's activities

a feeds only three times a day
b sits alone
c reaches for objects
d visually recognises mother
e says *dada* and/or *mama* as specific names
f tries to walk

2 Reading

Read the following text and check your answers from Exercise 1.

In the next twelve months you will see your baby changing faster and working harder than at any other time in his life. They have a lot to learn. In about half that time the little creature you see now will probably sit alone, reach for and grasp a toy, recognise a familiar face, smile, laugh and hold up their end of a conversation with you by babbling and cooing. By the end of the year they will stand, probably walk, handle a toy or spoon, say a few words, and, being a sociable person, distinguish between strangers and people they know, and form strong attachments to some of them. They will even have settled down to a routine of three meals a day, an afternoon nap, and sleeping through the night. They will have learnt that something heard is something that may be seen, that things seen may be grasped, and that things grasped have a permanence even when out of hand and sight. They will have begun to understand what part of the world is 'them' and what part is not, and how to influence both parts.

Language review

A Grammar and use

1 *Will* future

● Remember these uses of the *will* future:

1 to talk about things that (you think) are certain to happen:

   The pub car park will house the main dish.

2 to express predictions or expectations based on your opinions:

   I think it will be great.
   I'm sure it won't make a lot of difference to me.

3 to talk about something decided on at the moment of speaking:

   I'll telephone you as soon as I get back.

4 to express strong intentions:

   I'll definitely have more than one child.

● The continuous form of the *will* future can be used in these ways:

1 to describe actions which will be in progress at some time in the future:

   This time next week the company will be installing the latest equipment.

2 to describe continuous actions which have been planned:

   Villagers will be receiving special devices to monitor what they watch and will also be answering questions.
   The European Institute for the Media will be monitoring the experiment.

Note

Going to followed by the continuous form can also be used to express intentions:

I'm going to be watching it as much as possible.

● **The future of modal verbs**

The future of *can* is *will be able to*:

The villagers will be able to tune in to most satellite channels.

The future of *must* is *will have to*:

Granada Television will have to shield the people of Waddington from blue films.

Notes

1 *will be able to* is also the future form of *to be able to.*
2 *will have to* is also the future form of *to have to.*

2 Future Perfect

● **Form**

There are simple and continuous forms of the Future Perfect tense:

Simple: *will + have + past participle:*

             You will have worked for 50 years.

Continuous: *will + have been + -ing form:*

             You will have been working for 50 years.

● **Use**

The Future Perfect is used to refer to the past as we see it from the future.

• The simple form is used to talk about an action that will already be completed by a particular time in the future:

   You will probably have made some plans for when you retire.
   You probably won't have sorted out exactly what you're going to do …

• The continuous form is used to emphasise the continuous nature of an activity:

   You will have been following a routine based mainly on your work.
   This time next week I'll have been working here for 40 years.

Note

The Future Perfect is often used with these time expressions:

By the time + clause / (By) this time next week …

B Vocabulary

1 Colours

Common qualities associated with colours:

● *red*

embarrassed: *to go red in the face*
angry: *to see red (= to become angry)*
socialist, left-wing: *the red flag*
danger, warning, prohibition: *Flashing red lights mean a train is coming.*

● *green*

envious: *to be green with envy*
friendly to the environment: *the Green Party*
safe, healthy: *Cross the road when you see the green light.*

● *black*

disapproving, resentful: *He gave me a black look.*
sad, unhappy (to do with death): *in a black mood, to wear black*
bad, evil: *black magic, black humour*

● *yellow*

cowardly, not brave: *I always knew he was yellow.*

● *white*

afraid, shocked: *to go as white as a sheet, white with fear*
purity: *a white wedding*

2 'Seeing' verbs

The most common 'seeing' verbs in English are *look at*, *watch* and *see*.

1 **look** means: to direct your eyes deliberately at something or someone:

   *I **looked at** the clock. I was already five minutes late.*

2 **watch** means: to look at for a period of time:

   *I **watched** TV for five hours last night.*

3 **see** means: to become aware of something with your eyes:

   *When I was in town, I **saw** three people I knew.*

Here are some more 'seeing' verbs:

gape	– look at in surprise:	*Everyone **gaped at** the plane, which was falling in flames towards the town.*
gaze	– look admiringly at:	*He's **gazing at** that car as if he's in love with it.*
glance	– look quickly at:	*I've only had time to **glance at** the newspaper.*
glare	– look angrily at:	*Why are you **glaring at** me like that?*
notice	– see by chance:	*Did you **notice** what time the film starts?*
observe	– watch carefully:	*Ssh! I'm **observing** the behaviour of that bird.*
peep	– look at secretly:	*Close your eyes and don't **peep**. I'm wrapping your birthday present.*
stare	– look at for a long time:	*It's impolite to **stare at** people even if they look very strange.*

3 Noun suffixes

● The suffix -*ment* is often added to verbs to form nouns which refer to:

1 the making (or doing) of something, or things which are made (or done):

   agreement (agree)   *retirement* (retire)
   movement (move)   *replacement* (replace)
   entertainment (entertain)

2 feelings or states of mind:

   disappointment (disappoint)   *excitement* (excite)
   amazement (amaze)

● The suffix -*ion* is often added to verbs to form nouns which refer to a state or a process. Some verbs have to be modified before these suffixes are added:

   education (educate)   *conversation* (converse)
   attraction (attract)   *description* (describe)
   definition (define)   *decision* (decide)

first impressions

◆ Look at these photographs of twentieth century fashions. When did people look like this? Match the fashions with the dates.

1920s   1940s   1960s   1970s

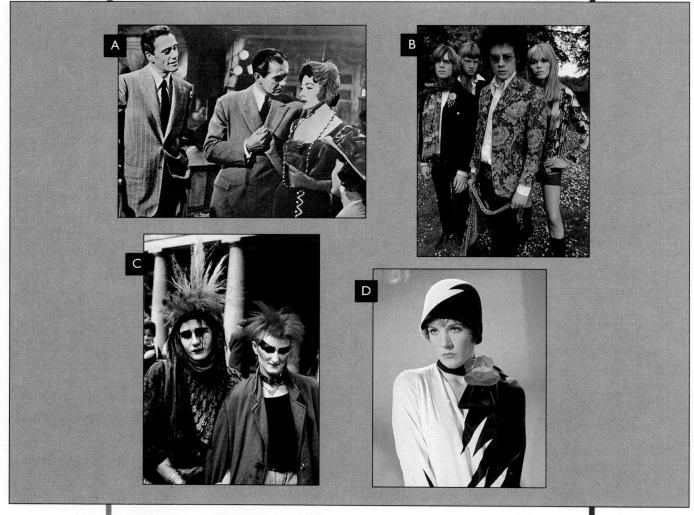

◆ How have styles changed during this century? Can you think of reasons for these changes?

◆ How do you think fashions will change in the future?

◆ Make a list of the different factors that affect people's appearance.

EXAMPLES: *length of hair, weight*

◆ Discuss these statements with your partners.

You can't judge a person by their appearance.
In matters of grave importance, style, not sincerity, is the vital thing.
(Oscar Wilde)
Feeling comfortable is more important than being fashionable.

Stage one

Appearances

1 Pre-reading

Can you think of any examples of fashions which are particularly uncomfortable or impractical?

EXAMPLE:
high-heeled shoes

Compare ideas with a partner.

2 Reading

You are going to read five short texts about strange fashions. Look at these five titles and try to guess what each text will be about.

Read the texts quickly and match them with the correct titles and illustrations.

Denture Difficulties

Stuffed Clothes

Bound to be Trouble

Of course it's tight!

Trendy Toupees

1

During the reign of Queen Mary, the fashions worn by the Spanish became popular throughout Europe. Fashionable English gentlemen had their doublets and hose swelled out with stuffing called 'bombast', which was made from rags, horsehair, cotton or bran. The only trouble was that if they tore their clothes, the stuffing fell out.

2

Small feet used to be very fashionable in China. Until quite recently baby girls had their feet bound. The crippling bandages forced the soft, growing toes to curve under the soles. By adulthood the feet of women treated in this way had completely doubled over and they were barely able to walk any distance.

A

B

C

3

Wigs have often been popular with both men and women. Louis XIV of France popularised wigs for men and set fashion trends which were copied all over Europe. The rich got their wigs specially made for them by wigmakers, who used goat's hair, horsehair or vegetable fibres. Not only were these wigs very hot to wear, but since people hardly ever washed their hair in those days, they were probably crawling with lice and other parasites.

4

In the 18th century, some women put little pieces of cork into their mouths to replace lost teeth. Poor people sometimes sold their teeth to rich people for implantation. These teeth were not always boiled, so when they were implanted into other people's mouths, diseases could be passed on. False teeth did not appear until the late 18th century. Rich people had them made from bone, ivory or even wood, and they were tied to adjoining teeth with gold wire. These teeth often did not fit well. George Washington's false teeth were hinged, and had an unnerving tendency to leap out of his mouth when he least expected it. Wax impressions of the mouth and properly fitting false teeth did not appear until the late 19th century.

5 The great days of the corset were in the 18th and 19th centuries when women struggled and suffered to make their waists smaller. The corsets, which were stiffened with whalebone or even steel, were very hard to fasten. Mothers were advised to make their daughters lie face down on the floor, and then place a foot on the daughter's back to pull in the laces. In later years some people fastened their corsets by using a winch. Tight corsets restricted the blood supply, damaged internal organs and even caused cracked ribs. It is no wonder women at this time seemed to faint so frequently! In many cases, they could hardly breathe.

D

E

● **Understanding**

1 Which text describes …

a … things which made women look slim?

b … something painful which was done to very young children?

c … a fashion that originated in France and was very unhygienic?

d … a fashion that originated in Spain?

e … things that poor people sold to rich people who had lost their own?

2 What were the main disadvantages of each of these fashions or customs?

3 Talking points
Work in pairs.

1 Which of the fashions described in the texts do you find most peculiar?

2 Can you think of any present-day equivalents of these fashions?

4 Vocabulary

Explain the meaning of these phrases from the texts.

1 swelled out with stuffing (*Text 1*)
2 crippling bandages (2)
3 by adulthood (2)
4 (their feet) had doubled over (2)
5 crawling with lice (3)
6 face down on the floor (5)
7 internal organs (5)
8 restricted the blood supply (5)

5 *Hardly* and *barely*
(*Language review A1, page 144*)

Look at these extracts from the texts:

*They were **barely** able to walk any distance.*
*People **hardly** ever washed their hair in those days.*
*In many cases, they could **hardly** breathe.*

What do you think *hardly* and *barely* mean? Try rephrasing the three sentences without using these words.

What kinds of words are *hardly* and *barely*? What other words do you know that can be used in the same position in a sentence?

What is the difference in meaning between these two sentences:

He hardly worked all morning.
He worked hard all morning.

Compare ideas with a partner.

6 Pre-listening

How is appearance or 'image' important to people with these jobs?

air cabin crew   fashion model
TV newsreader
business executive

What are the advantages and disadvantages of being a fashion model?

Compare ideas with a partner.

7 Listening

You are going to hear a model talking about her work. Does she mention any of the advantages or disadvantages you discussed in Exercise 6?

● Understanding

Listen to the recording again and answer these questions:

1 Which of these kinds of clothes does the speaker **not** model?

formal clothes   swimwear
skirts   hats   beachwear
jeans   dresses

2 Which of these people sometimes criticise models?

other models   agents
instructors   audiences
friends

3 Which of these kinds of food does the model try **not** to eat?

snacks   green vegetables
fruit   sweets

4 Which of these clothes does the speaker wear in her free time?

shorts   dresses   jeans

5 Which of these advantages of her work are mentioned by the model?

getting to know people
finding out about clothes
learning how to dress
travelling all over the world
becoming more self-confident
learning about hairstyles and make-up

8 Vocabulary

● 'Clothes' idioms
(Language review B1, page 145)

What do you think this expression from the recording means?

*People think … if you're a model, you're **too big for your boots**.*

Try and work out the meaning of these 'clothes' idioms:

1 I'm tired of *living on a shoestring*. I can't wait to start work.
2 He's already got three prizes *under his belt*, and he's preparing for another competition now.
3 I'd heard everything he said before. It was all *old hat*.
4 Getting promoted was a real *feather in your cap*. You must be pleased.
5 He earns more money than his wife, but she *wears the trousers*.

● Get
(Language review B2, page 145)

Listen to the recording again and fill in the gaps in these sentences:

1 *You get _____ _____ who just go to fashion shows to criticise.*
2 *You get _____, you know, by your own colleagues.*
3 *I need **to get** _____ _____ _____ _____.*
4 *You have **to get** _____ applied too.*
5 *You get to know a _____ _____ _____.*

Which of these words and phrases can replace the phrases in bold type in the five sentences:

to have   you are   to have you meet and find out about there are

9 Pronunciation

Listen to Part 1 and repeat these words which all contain the letter **o**:

show   some   model

Now work with a partner. Take it in turns to pronounce these words. Decide whether they sound like *show, some* or *model*.

clothes   come   company
confident   cope   done   gold
growing   know   love   only
other   popular   socialising
soft   soles   toes   wonder

Now listen to Part 2 to check your answers.

10 Causatives

(Language review A2, page 144)

Read these extracts from the texts (Exercise 2) and the recording (Exercise 7):

1 *Until quite recently baby girls had their feet bound.*
2 *Louis XIV popularised wigs for men.*
3 *The rich got their wigs specially made for them by wig-makers.*
4 *Rich people had them (teeth) made from bone, ivory or even wood.*
5 *Women struggled and suffered to make their waists smaller.*
6 *Everyone needs to have their hair done in the same style.*
7 *You have to get make-up applied too.*

Answer these questions about the extracts. Tick the boxes to show who does the action.

1 Who bound the baby girls' feet?   The baby girls ☐   Other people ☐
2 Who popularised wigs for men?   Louis XIV ☐   Someone else ☐
3 Who made the wigs?   The rich ☐   Other people ☐
4 Who made the teeth?   Rich people ☐   Other people ☐
5 Who struggled and suffered?   Women ☐   Other people ☐
6 Who does everyone's hair?   Everyone ☐   Someone else ☐
7 Who applies the make-up?   You ☐   Someone else ☐

Compare answers with a partner, and then discuss these questions:

a What do extracts 1, 3, 4, 6, 7 have in common?
b What verb forms are used in these extracts?
c What other verb form is this similar to?

11 Practice

You want to look your best because you are entering a competition to model some clothes for a magazine. Look at this list of things that need doing. Decide whether you will do them yourself or get someone else to do them for you. Write M (myself) or S (someone else) next to each item.

jeans need washing
pullover needs repairing
hair needs washing
hair needs cutting
teeth need cleaning
shoes need polishing
shoes need mending

Now write sentences like this:

> *I'm going to wash my jeans.*

or: *I'm going to have/get my jeans washed.*

---

12 Personalised practice

Write a list of things you do for yourself, but which many other people have done for them.

EXAMPLE: *I repair my own car.*

Now ask other students whether they do these things themselves or have them done by someone else. Make conversations like this:

A *Do you repair your own car, or do you get/have it repaired by someone else?*
B *I do it myself.* **or:** *I get/have it repaired at my local garage.*

13 Discussion

Work in groups of three.

An increasing number of people – especially rich film actors and pop stars – are having their appearance changed in some way to make themselves look more attractive.

Can you think of any famous personalities who have changed their appearance? What have they had done?

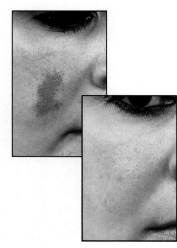

What do you think of this trend?

If you were rich, would you change your appearance? How?

14 Writing

Write a short compostion (about 200 words) giving your opinion about plastic surgery for cosmetic purposes.

Before you start writing, make notes under these headings:

Introduction: Common changes made to people's appearance by plastic surgery
Paragraph 1: Your explanation for why people have changes made
Paragraph 2: The advantages of plastic surgery
Paragraph 3: The disadvantages of plastic surgery
Conclusion: Your personal opinions on this subject

Stage two

Fortune-telling

1 Pre-listening

What do you know about these methods of telling people's fortunes?

**cards   crystal ball   I Ching
palm reading   horoscopes**

Do you know of any other methods?

---

2 Listening

Listen to a woman talking about having her fortune told.

What method did the fortune-teller use? *coffee stains*

What two pieces of information convinced the woman that the fortune-teller had 'special powers'? *2 children*
husband (away), test on 25th

● **Listening for detail**

Listen to the recording again and note the following:

Fortune-teller		Speaker	
Age: *middle aged*		Lucky number: *5*	
Appearance: *normal*		Number of children: *2*	
Profession: *teacher*		Important date: *25th Oct*	
Duration of session: *20 mins*		Reason for importance: *Exam*	
Number of people seen in one session: *2* *1*		Big change described by fortune-teller: *House move*	

---

3 Vocabulary

Choose the best meaning for these words from the recording. (If necessary, check the tapescript on page 171.)

1	exotic-looking	a	ordinary	(b)	unusual	c	ugly
2	stains	(a)	marks	b	flavours	c	aromas
3	earth-shattering	a	destructive	b	loud	(c)	astonishing
4	threat	a	misfortune	(b)	danger	c	help
5	convinced	(a)	certain	b	doubtful	c	confused

---

4 Reading

Read the text and say which method the fortune-teller uses to predict the future. What was Kitty most interested in finding out about?

Because the room was so dark, Kitty was aware of the brightness and stillness of the afternoon. Madame Eva put her hand into a leather bag and produced a small crystal ball. She leaned
5 over Kitty's cupped hands.

'I see a man,' she said. Kitty's heart began to beat rather hard. With alarm and surprise she found herself surrendering to the occasion.

'A man,' repeated Madame Eva. 'Very tall.
10 Nice looking. Clever. You met him through your work.'

Kitty nodded. The woman breathed heavily. 'Now I'm getting a relative. Elderly lady. Bit of trouble there. But not yet. In the future.' She
15 bent over Kitty's hands again. 'I see a tall building. Like a church. I see you going in. Might be a wedding. Don't think so. Might be. Can't see. Hold on, darling. I'll have a drop more tea.'
20 'You're very clever,' said the fortune-teller.

'There's a lot of success ahead. You've no need to worry about money.'

Kitty did not want her to continue with this. She wasn't interested in this information but
25 supposed it was this that people came to hear.

'Was there anything you wanted to ask me, dear?'

'Tell me about the man,' said Kitty, lost to all sense of propriety.
30 Madame Eva sighed and bent once more over the crystal ball. 'I think he loves you,' she said. 'But it's not clear. Someone's holding him back. Is he married?'

Kitty shook her head, unable to speak.
35 'He's connected to someone,' said the medium. She seemed suddenly abstracted. 'Very clever,' she said vaguely. 'Ends badly. Try your luck, dear.'

Kitty handed over ten pounds in a daze of
40 gratitude.

● **Understanding**

1 Read the text again and say whether these statements are true or false.

a It was a dark, calm afternoon.
b Madame Eva put her hands on the crystal ball to tell Kitty's fortune.
c Kitty didn't expect to be convinced by Madame Eva.
d Madame Eva talked about a member of Kitty's family.
e Madame Eva said Kitty was going to do well professionally.
f Kitty was surprised by the information about her success.
g Kitty was interested in finding out more about the man.
h At the end of the session Kitty felt disappointed.

2 What are the main differences between the session described in the reading text and the one you heard about in Exercise 2? Make a list and then compare lists with a partner.

5 Vocabulary

● **Phrasal verbs with *hold***

(Language review B3, page 145)

Look at these sentences from the text and guess what they mean:

> *Hold on, darling. (l.18)*
> *Someone's holding him back. (l.32)*

Replace the *hold* phrases in each of these sentences with another suitable verb, keeping the same meaning:

1 He can't *hold down* a job; this is his fourth in two years.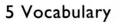
2 She tried to *hold in* her anger, but it was impossible.
3 An armed gang *held up* a bank in the city yesterday.
4 I hope the rain *holds off* until the football match is over.

● Read these sentences from the text and try to demonstrate their meanings with actions. Work in pairs.

(Student A is Madame Eva, Student B is Kitty.)

a *She leaned over Kitty's cupped hands. (l.4)*
b *Kitty nodded. (l.12)*
c *The woman breathed heavily. (l.12)*
d *Madame Eva sighed and bent over the crystal ball. (l.30)*
e *Kitty shook her head. (l.34)*
f *Kitty handed over ten pounds. (l.39)*

6 The definite article

(Language review A3, page 144)

Look at these sentences from the texts and recordings in this unit:

1 ***The rich** got their wigs specially made for them.*
2 *You have to be able to cope with **criticism.***
3 ***The woman** was, well, normal, not exotic-looking, or anything like that.*
4 *I let the remains of the coffee drip down onto **the saucer.***
5 *With **alarm** and **surprise** she found herself surrendering.*
6 *... she said **the most surprising** things.*
7 *Because **the room** was so dark ...*
8 *Tell me about **the man.***

Now match the sentences with one of the following rules about the use of the definite article:

a Use with superlatives.
b Use with adjectives to make them nouns.
c Use when there is only one in the context.
d Use when the noun has been mentioned before.
e Do not use with abstract nouns used in a general sense.

7 Practice

Read and correct this text. There are several kinds of errors involving the use of the definite article.

- *the* is used instead of *a*.
- *a* is used instead of *the*.
- *the* is used when there should be no article.
- *the* has been left out and should be added.

Some articles are used correctly.

8 Talking points

Work in pairs.

1 Have you, or has anyone you know, ever been to a fortune-teller? What happened?

2 What questions would you ask if you went to see a fortune-teller?

I've only once visited a fortune-teller; in fact she was a palm-reader. I was only sixteen and I was very frightened. A palm-reader lived in the caravan and wore long, flowing clothes. She was most exotic-looking person I had ever met. I should have realised she was a fake because there was a sign outside caravan saying: 'Only strong should enter here.' No real fortune-teller would do that. She showed me into a kitchen in the caravan and sat me down at the table. I was trembling with the fear. She asked me to hold out my left hand and she turned it over and looked at a palm. After telling me a few obvious details about myself, she said I would have the accident in the near future which would cause a lot of problems. I burst into tears and ran out. For weeks, I was in the deep despair, until one day I read that she'd been arrested for fraud.

Extension

The Crystal Ball

1 Role play
Work in pairs.

Student A: You want to have your fortune told. Turn to page 160.

Student B: You are a fortune-teller. Read these instructions:

You are going to look into your crystal ball for a subject who wants to know about their future.

Read this information which your special powers have told you about the subject.

Age: Born around 1964

Character: Careful, methodical, organised

Family: Elderly parents, one brother who is three years younger. This brother is a problem, and money is involved, but eventually his problems will be solved.
Father is ill at the moment and will have to go into hospital. His operation will be a success, and he'll make a complete recovery.

Job: Well-paid and secure, but there is a possible change: an opportunity which promises success and fulfilment.

Romance: There is a romantic attachment, but it won't last. There will be a marriage in about eighteen months.

Travel: A journey in the near future, possibly abroad.

Try to make your partner feel relaxed, and be prepared to answer questions about their future.

2 Writing

Write a letter to a friend describing the fortune-telling session you have just taken part in.

Describe what happened including the questions that were asked and the answers and advice that were given.

Student A: Write your letter from the point of view of the subject.

Student B: Write your letter from the point of view of the fortune-teller.

When you have finished writing, exchange letters with your partner, and compare descriptions of the session.

Language review

A Grammar and Use

1 Hardly and barely

● Meanings

These are adverbs which mean *almost not* or *only just*:

They could hardly/barely breathe.

This means: They almost couldn't breathe; they could only just breathe.

Hardly is more commonly used than *barely*.

● Position

The position of these words in sentences is similar to the position of frequency adverbs:

They were barely able to walk any distance.
In many cases, they could hardly breathe.

Notes

1 The expression *hardly ever* is commonly used to mean *almost never*:

> *People hardly ever washed their hair in those days.*

Notice these similar expressions:

> *hardly anybody* = almost nobody
> *hardly anything* = almost nothing

2 There is no connection in meaning between *hardly* and *hard*, which is used both as an adverb and as an adjective:

> *She worked hard.*
> *It was hard work.*

2 Causatives

● *have/get* + direct object + past participle

This structure is used to describe actions which we do not do ourselves, but which we ask or tell someone else to do for us:

> *Rich people had teeth made from bone, ivory or even wood.*
> *Everyone needs to have their hair done in the same style.*
> *The rich got their wigs specially made for them.*
> *You have to get make-up applied too.*

Get is more informal than *have*.

Notes

1 Causative constructions are similar to passives, but are used to emphasise that although a person does not do something for themselves, they cause it to be done. Compare these three sentences:

A wig-maker *is making* him a new wig. (Active)
A new wig *is being made* by a wig-maker. (Passive)
He *is having a new wig made* by a wig-maker. (Causative)

2 *Have something done* and *get something done* are not always used as causatives. They can be used to describe events which happened to us but were beyond our control.

> *In China, baby girls used to have their feet bound.*
> *If you stand too near the fire, you may get your face burnt.*

3 The definite article

In this unit the definite article is used:

* with superlatives:

> *... she said **the most surprising** thing ...*
> *It was **the oldest** one I could find.*

* with adjectives, to make a noun representing a whole group:

> ***The rich** got their wigs specially made for them.*
> ***The very young** appreciate this kind of humour.*

(See Unit 12, Language review B2.)

* when the noun is unique in the context:

> *Because **the room** was so dark ...* (This can only refer to one room – the one the person is in.)
> *She's probably in **the garden**.* (There is only one attached to the house.)

* when the noun has already been mentioned:

> *Tell me about **the man**.*
> *She's bought a second-hand car for only £5000. **The car's** in quite good condition.*

The article is not used with abstract nouns used in a general sense:

> *You have to be able to cope with **criticism**.*
> *We can't live without **hope**.*

B Vocabulary

1 'Clothes' idioms

Here are some more 'clothes' idioms in addition to those on page 139:

> He was always **licking** the director's **boots** – it's no wonder he got that promotion. = trying to gain favour

> I wish you'd come to the point, and stop **skirting around** *the issue.* = avoiding

> I'm not very good at speaking **off the cuff** – I'd like to prepare my speech beforehand. = unprepared

> **I take my hat off to** them for handling the crisis so well. = admire

2 Meanings of get

The verb *get* has many different meanings and uses. Here are some of the most common ones:

receive: *I got a letter this morning.*

become: *He gets really angry if you argue with him.*

there is/are: *You get people who go to fashion shows to criticise.*

understand: *I don't get what you mean.*

buy: *What did you get your mother for her birthday.*

catch (an illness): *I got flu and had to stay in bed.*

catch (a train etc.): *It was too far to walk so I got the bus.*

move: *There's a car coming. Get out of the way!*

Note

Get can also be used as a causative (see Section A2 above):

> When are you going to get your car repaired?

This is not the same as the use of *get* to form 'passive' sentences:

> You get criticised by your own colleagues.

3 Phrasal verbs with *hold*

Here are some more *hold* verbs in addition to those on page 142:

> If we can just **hold on** for a few more days, I'm sure someone will rescue us. (survive)

> **Hold on** a minute. Can you give me a lift. (wait)

> I know she made a mistake, but you can't **hold it against her** forever. (blame/have ill feelings towards)

> To save money, the company is trying to **hold down** wage increases. (keep low)

> I was **held up** for over an hour in the traffic. That's why I'm late. (delay)

UNIT 15

first impressions

◆ The careers officer in this cartoon is replying to something the young man has just said. What do you think this was?

◆ In what ways are – or were – these people famous or successful? Match the people with the symbols of their success.

"Yes, but famous at what?"

A

B

C

D

1

2

3

4

Compare answers with a partner.

◆ Which of these people do you most admire? Why?

◆ Would you like to be famous? Why? Why not?

◆ Read these short texts about world-famous geniuses. Who are they?

◆ What makes a person successful? Put these qualities in order of importance (add any other qualities you think are important):

intelligence • hard work
good luck • inspiration
family background • education
natural talent • determination
ruthlessness • self-confidence

Try to think of famous people who have been successful because of some of these qualities.

1564-1642 Italian astronomer, mathematician and physicist. In 1609 he constructed the first astronomical telescope.
A

1749-1832 German poet, dramatist, novelist and scientist. He studied law in Leipzig and Strasbourg, where he also collected folk songs and began a life-long study of plants and animals. For ten years he was chief minister of state at Weimar. His most famous work was the play *Faust*.
B

1770-1827 German classical composer and virtuoso pianist. As a young man his musical gifts were recognised by Mozart and Haydn. Despite becoming totally deaf in 1817, he continued to compose until his death.
C

1879-1955 Theoretical physicist. He was born in Germany, but in 1934 had his property confiscated and his citizenship revoked because he was Jewish. In 1940 he became an American citizen. He is most famous for his theory of relativity.
D

Talent or Hard Work?

1 Reading

As you read about Gata Kamsky, make a list of ways in which you think his life is different from that of most children of his age.

Daddy Dearest

1 TRY asking Gata Kamsky, who is seventeen, if he has ever had a friend, and he translates the question into Russian and puts it to his father. Gata listens to his father's reply and then translates again, giving the reply half in his own voice and half in his father's. 'Chess has not allowed me to see friends. My father doesn't think I've missed them; and I think the same.'

2 In three years' time Gata will be nearly 21 and, if he completes the timetable his father has set out, he will become the youngest ever world chess champion. Gata is currently the top-ranked chess player in the United States and number thirteen in the world. He has five years in which to improve on Gary Kasparov's record of winning the world championship at the age of 22.

3 Rustam Kamsky explains his son's success: 'Talent is one per cent. What matters is work, work, work. I have given up my life for my son. I have no life for myself. I do not matter.' Speaking through his child, Rustam plays down Gata's achievements in becoming one of the top chess players in the world. 'Any child could do such things if the parents worked with him; work, work and have patience. The most terrible thing is when people don't allow young talent to grow, or block it.'

4 Rustam was divorced from Gata's mother when Gata was eight months old. The boy has always lived with his father; and his father, apparently, has always lived through him, enforcing disciplines which would make the child what the man had always wanted to be. When Gata was eighteen months old, Rustam showed him how to ride a bicycle. He had taught him to read a book before he was two. 'I was trying to develop his brains,' he says. Gata could play the piano by the time he was five. 'He played best between the ages of six and seven. Music was doing a lot for his soul, but nothing for his brains.' So Rustam introduced Gata to chess when he was eight. From the age of five to eight, Gata did not go to school at all, but studied at home under Rustam's direction. He went to school only between the ages of nine and ten, but the experiment was a failure, as Gata explains: 'My teachers were jealous of our success and when I had to travel to a chess tournament and come back and make up the lost lessons, it was a problem.'

5 At the age of nine, Gata started beating adults at a chess club in Leningrad. Later he beat some Russian grand masters. When he was twelve he won the under-20s competition for the whole of the Soviet Union. Only one person had ever done that before: Kasparov. Yet Gata says: 'My father didn't believe I had any talent. It was just hard work. The man who works hardest succeeds most, that's all.'

6 The family moved to New York where Rustam thought Gata would have a greater chance of success. But now Rustam is obsessed with Kasparov: 'Our talent has been blocked by Kasparov. He knows we can't go to Moscow to play.' He doesn't mention the fact that Kasparov has already beaten Gata – in a two-game match in New York in 1988. After the match Kasparov was contemptuous of Gata, saying that he had no potential to be world champion. As if in reply Gata produced perhaps the best result ever achieved by a fifteen-year-old when he finished ahead of 152 grand masters and came second in a tournament in Mallorca. After this triumph Rustam told journalists that his son would not only beat Kasparov, he would 'crush him like a fly.'

7 An American businessman has subsidised Gata and his father with enough money to cover their travel and hotel expenses. Apart from that, Gata's winnings in tournaments and exhibitions are their only source of income. Rustam dictates Gata's day. Up at 7 a.m. for an hour's gymnastic exercises; breakfast at 8; studying chess problems and moves 8.30 a.m.; running 1-2 p.m.; main meal of the day 2.30 p.m.; more chess problems 3-8 or 9 p.m.; resting and walking 9-10 p.m.; bed 10.30 p.m. All day, every day, for seven days a week.

● Understanding

Match seven of these summaries (a-h) with the seven paragraphs of the text. Write the paragraph numbers in the boxes.

a Rustam's plan for his son's future ☐

b Rustam's feelings about his son's main rival ☐

c An example of the relationship between Gata and his father, which mentions one of the effects of chess on the boy's life ☐

d Gata's daily routine ☐

e Gata's personal feelings about his success at chess ☐

f Rustam's early attempts to turn his son into something special ☐

g The first evidence that Gata is a chess genius and his father's explanation of this ☐

h Rustam's philosophy of the relationship between parents and children ☐

● **Inference**

(The answers to these questions are only suggested in the text.)

1 Do you think Gata has any friends?
2 Is Gata unhappy with the life his father has planned for him?
3 Does Rustam believe that his son is especially clever?
4 What does the text suggest as Rustam's main reason for pushing his son to succeed?
5 Why did Rustam stop Gata playing the piano?
6 What image does the text present of the world of competitive chess?

2 Vocabulary

● **Competitive games**

Fill the gaps in these sentences with one of the words from the list below.

1 Kasparov _____ Gata Kamsky in New York in 1988.
2 Rustam expects Gata to be the chess _____ of the world when he is only 21 years old.
3 Currently Kasparov holds the _____ as the youngest ever world champion.
4 He won the world _____ when he was only 22 years old.
5 While still in Russia, Gata _____ a young persons' chess _____.

won   beat   championship   competition   record   champion

3 Prepositions following adjectives

Fill the gaps after these adjectives with the correct prepositions. (Only 1-3 are used in the text.)

1 Gata's father is obsessed _____ Gary Kasparov.
2 They were jealous _____ his success.
3 After the match Kasparov was contemptuous _____ Gata.
4 Rustam is responsible _____ his son's success.
5 Gata seems quite satisfied _____ his life.
6 He doesn't seem particularly interested _____ other people.

---

4 Talking points

Work in pairs.

- Why do you think some parents push their children so hard to succeed?
  Are they right or wrong to do this?

*"It's a father's **right** to help his son.'*

- Do you agree that parents have the right to help their children? What rights do or should children have?

5 -ing clauses

(Language review A1, page 154)

Read these sentences from the text.

1 *Gata translates Rustam's answer, giving the reply half in his own voice and half in his father's. (Para. 1)*
2 *Speaking through his child, Rustam plays down Gata's achievements. (3)*
3 *His father has lived through him, enforcing disciplines which would make the child what the man had always wanted to be. (4)*
4 *After the match Kasparov was contemptuous of Gata, saying that he had no potential to be world champion. (6)*

What can you say about the -ing clauses in these four sentences? Think about these points:

- The subject of the -ing verbs. For example, in the first sentence, who gives the reply?
- The relationship between the main clause and the -ing clause.

Compare ideas with a partner.

Now rewrite the four sentences above. Replace the -ing forms with full verbs. There is often more than one possible way of doing this. The following sentence can be rewritten in at least four ways:

Gata has devoted his life to chess, practising for ten hours a day.

1 *Gata has devoted his life to chess and practises for ten hours a day.*
2 *Gata has devoted his life to chess. He practises for ten hours a day.*
3 *Gata has devoted his life to chess, so he practises for ten hours a day.*
4 *Gata practises for ten hours a day because he has devoted his life to chess.*

6 Practice

Read this short text about Bala Ambati.

In what ways is he similar to Gata Kamsky?

If you ask Bala Ambati whether he ever goes out in the evening – for entertainment, for fun, or just to get away from his family – he doesn't know what you're talking about. There is a puzzled pause while he examines you through his thick glasses, and then he asks, 'In what respect?' It is very likely that Bala will become the world's youngest qualified doctor at the age of seventeen.

The thirteen-year-old is currently an undergraduate at New York University. This year, along with his fellow students, most of whom are twenty years old, he is expected to graduate with a degree in biology. He will then begin four years' study at medical school to qualify as a doctor.

Here is some more information about Bala Ambati and his family. Rewrite these pairs of sentences as single sentences, using *-ing* clauses.

1 Dr Ambati Rao decided to leave India. He thought his sons would do better in America.

2 Dr Rao has moved his family around the country several times. He has advanced his own career on each occasion.

3 Dr Rao allows his sons to decide their own future. He supports whatever interests them.

4 Bala used to sit in his father's study. He listened to him giving private maths lessons.

5 Dr Rao has had arguments with Bala's teachers. He has accused them of slowing up his son's progress.

6 Bala's mother is a quiet woman. She speaks only when someone talks to her.

---

7 Listening

Listen to an interview with Dr Ambati Rao, who is accused of pushing his son too hard. How do you think he defends himself against this accusation? Make a prediction.

8 Future hopes
(Language review A2, page 154)

How did Dr Rao use the word *hope* in his answers to these questions?

And are your sons going to succeed? Don't you think that your interference might turn the school against your son?

(If you can't remember, listen to the recording again or look at the tapescript on page 171.)

Which answer means he **doesn't want** this to happen?
Which one means he **wants** this to happen?

Answer these questions about yourself using the word *hope*.

1 Are you going to fail your exams?
2 Are you going to get a good job?
3 Are you going to get married?
4 Are you going to have children?
5 Are you going to have to work at the weekend?

---

9 Role play
Work in groups of four.

Students A and B: You are the parents of a child you think is a genius. (Model yourselves on what you have read about Rustam Kamsky and Dr Ambati Rao.) You have asked for a meeting to discuss your child's progress at the school. You want to be sure that your child is getting the best education possible. (You are thinking of taking them away from the school unless you are satisfied.)

Students C and D: You are teachers who believe that, however bright the child is, they would benefit from the same treatment as all the other children in your school.

10 Writing: Opinions

Do you agree with Rustam Kamsky's definition of success?

> *Talent is one per cent. What matters is work, work, work.*

- Work out your opinions. What is the relationship between these factors?

  talent   success   hard work

Discuss your opinions briefly with a partner.

- Write an outline composition plan. Decide on paragraph headings.

EXAMPLE:

Paragraph 1 Introduction: What is success? (Give examples of successful people you know.)

Paragraph 2 How have these people become successful? Because of a natural talent, or because they have worked hard?

Paragraph 3 Talent: how important is it?

Paragraph 4 Hard work: how necessary is it?

Paragraph 5 Conclusion: Summarise the main points of your argument. Finish by saying whether or not you agree with Rustam Kamsky's definition.

- Write a first draft composition of about 150 words on this subject.

Language notes:

1 Use different 'opinion-giving' expressions.

2 If you are not sure that what you are saying is true, use one of these expressions:

> *Apparently,...   According to X,...*
> *It seems that ...   People say that ...*

- Exchange, compare and discuss first drafts with a partner.

- Write the final draft of your composition.

Stage two

Wishes and Regrets

1 Pre-listening

What is the person in the cartoon saying?

Working in pairs, think of as many endings to this sentence as possible.

2 Listening

Now listen to ten people talking about their wishes. One of the speakers is like the person in the cartoon. What does he say his problem is?

● **Listening for detail**

Listen to the ten speakers again, and then fill in a table like this:

Speaker	Wish	Reason for wish
1		
2		
3		

3 *Get* + past participle
(Language review B1, page 155)

One of the speakers says she wishes her parents hadn't **got divorced**.
Fill the gaps in these sentences with expressions consisting of **get/got** + past participle:

1 My sister has just ____ ____ to a boy she has only known for three weeks. They're planning a June wedding.
2 Marriage is still popular. Last year more couples than ever ____ ____.
3 I ____ ____ in a hurry this morning. It wasn't until I got to work that I realised I was wearing my brother's jeans.
4 An increasing number of people ____ ____ in road accidents. This year there have already been fifty fatal accidents in our town.
5 When I went shopping with my mother I was always ____ ____. She often spent hours looking for me.
6 I'll never forget ____ ____ in a lift between the thirteenth and fourteenth floors of the building I work in. It took them two hours to free me.

4 *Speak* and *talk*
(Language review B2, page 155)

The last speaker says:

I often wish I could speak Portuguese so that I could talk to her family and friends.

When do we use *speak* and when do we use *talk*?

Compare ideas with a partner. Now choose the best verb in these sentences:

1 My brother can speak/talk four languages fluently.
2 The doctor's waiting room was silent. No one spoke/talked.
3 My nine-month-old daughter has just started to speak/talk.
4 I'm sorry, I can't agree. You're speaking/talking nonsense.
5 It was a brilliant party. Everyone spoke/talked to everyone else.

5 Wishes and regrets
(Language review A3, page 154)

Read these extracts from the recording in Exercise 2 and say whether they refer to regrets about the past or wishes about the present or the future.

1 *I wish I wasn't an only child.*
2 *I wish I could afford to travel more.*
3 *I wish I hadn't changed jobs last year.*
4 *I wish my parents would stop treating me like a child.*
5 *I wish I'd gone to university.*
6 *I wish I could stop smoking.*
7 *I wish my parents hadn't got divorced.*
8 *I wish I could spend more time with my school friends.*
9 *I wish I were a bit taller.*
10 *I often wish I could speak Portuguese.*

Now make a note of the verb forms that are used to talk about the past, present and future.

What do you notice about these verb forms? Compare ideas with a partner.

6 Personalised practice

The last speaker says:

I often wish I could speak Portuguese so that I could talk to her family and friends.

Make up a sentence like this for yourself:

I sometimes/often wish I could ... so that I could ...

Compare sentences in groups of four. Make suggestions about how your partners could make their wishes come true.

EXAMPLE:
A: *I wish I could speak Portuguese.*
B: *If you really want to speak Portuguese, why don't you ask your girlfriend to teach you?*

7 Pre-reading

If it was possible, how would you change yourself? Make up five sentences like this about yourself.

EXAMPLE: *I wish I was/were taller.*

Say what would happen or what you would be able to do if your wish came true.

EXAMPLE: *If I was/were taller, people would notice me at parties and at meetings.*

8 Reading and writing

How would the writer of this text like to change herself? Read and find out.

Misery of an honorary lad*

ANOTHER grumpy tear-soaked diary page. Why am I so ugly? Why do I have to be the one that cracks the jokes and keeps laughing? I want to be a sylph like Sarah, or like Maria who has managed to make herself look more like Madonna than anyone. I'm the sort that gets two Valentine cards and everyone tries not to snigger, but I'm sure they guess that one says 'Love from Mum' and the other 'Love from Dad'.

I thought I would save up and buy myself something for Christmas and wear it at school and say a boy gave it to me – but they'd only guess. The boys talk to me more than to Sarah or Maria, but that's only because they're not frightened of me because they don't fancy me. They treat me like an honorary lad. I suppose I like it, but it's not the same as having them adoring the ground on which I tread. I long for them to look at me the way they look at Sarah or Maria.

I never tell anyone these things. And then I eat sweets. It makes me feel better while they're in my mouth, but not much longer. I was going to write a diary-style thing for this newspaper about something serious and important, like seeing a homeless person in a cardboard box, or world hunger. I sat on my bed, the only private place in the house, and chewed the pen for thought. I got nowhere.

Then I glanced in the mirror and saw all this blue sticky biro ink around my mouth.

I decided to try and not care inside as well as outside, so on Saturday I went to the party with Trudi and I wore a mini skirt. On the way to the party as we walked along, two boys whistled. Trudi turned her head the other way, pretending she didn't approve or care, while I secretly smiled, hoping it was partly for me. A few seconds later, they could see the whole of us, not just our faces – we'd been behind the wall before – and one of them said, 'Hey, Fatty – shame about the legs.' It still makes me cry to think about it.

*lad = boy

Now write a summary of this text. Write in the third person and mention all the things the writer wishes. Start like this:

The writer is not a happy person. She wishes …

---

9 Listening

Listen to these three interviews. Listen for the answer to these questions.

1 How does the first speaker describe the people he met in Spain?
2 Was the second speaker an only child?
3 What sort of job did the third speaker want to do when she was young?

● **Understanding**

Listen again and answer these questions about the three interviews:

Interview 1

1 Why did the speaker leave Spain?
2 Why did he go to South America?

Interview 2

3 When she was a young child, what was the speaker's ambition?
4 Why didn't she play football at school?
5 Why was her father disappointed?

Interview 3

6 Why is the speaker dissatisfied with her life?
7 How old do you think she is?
8 She wants to travel, but why doesn't she want to live abroad?

● Look at the tapescript of the three interviews on page 172. There are several places where the speakers do not finish what they are saying. (These are marked in the tapescript.) Guess what the speakers were going to say.

Discuss ideas in pairs.

10 Vocabulary

Look at the tapescript and find expressions which mean:

1 a strong wish (to do something) (*Interview 1*)
2 (people who are) lively and natural (1)
3 the same in some way (1)
4 strong hopes for success in the future (2)
5 children (2)
6 real/final (2)
7 trapped (3)
8 to think of (3)
9 special (3)
10 schools where pupils live as well as study (3)

11 Pronunciation

Listen to these questions which were asked by the interviewer in Exercise 9.

How does the interviewer sound? Choose suitable words from this list to describe her attitude to the people she is interviewing:

> bored   enthusiastic   encouraging   fed up
> happy   interested   lively   sarcastic
> surprised   sympathetic   tired

Listen to the recording again and repeat the five questions.

Now practise asking your partner questions using the same tone of voice as the interviewer.

Here are some sample questions to start off with:

1 Did you have any career ideas when you were a child then?
2 So, what were you interested in at school then?
3 Do you regret not going to university?

Now think of some of your own questions.

12 Regrets
(Language review A3, page 154)

Look at this extract from Interview 1:

> *Is there anything you regret in your life?*
> *Well, I regret leaving Spain.*

Make up similar answers, using the verb *regret*, that the other speakers might have given to the same question. Remember:

1 The second speaker isn't a boy.
2 She didn't play football for Liverpool.
3 The third speaker got married quite young.

Now rewrite your three 'regret' sentences using the verb *wish*.

EXAMPLE: *I wish I hadn't left Spain.*

13 Personalised practice

Now make up some sentences about yourself starting like this:

> *I regret + -ing/I regret not + -ing*

or

> *I wish I hadn't …/I wish I had …*

Compare regrets with a partner.

Extension

Advice

You are going to write a semi-formal letter giving some advice to one of the speakers in Exercise 9. Work with a partner.

- Look at the tapescripts of Interviews 1 and 3 on page 172, and decide with your partner whether to write to Mick or Jenny.
- Before you write anything, plan your letter together. Here are some ideas to help you:

Discuss what advice you might give Mick or Jenny.

Think of a polite way of starting this letter. Remember it is to someone you have never met.

- Now work individually. Here is a possible paragraph plan:

Paragraph 1 Introduce yourself and explain that you heard the speaker in a radio interview. Explain that you have been in a similar situation yourself and would like to be of help.

Paragraph 2 Describe the similar situation you refer to in *Paragraph 1*.

Paragraph 3 Give advice; be polite, but not too direct.

Paragraph 4 Wish Mick or Jenny good luck in the future.

- Now exchange letters with the partner you worked with earlier. Compare what you have written.

*L*anguage review

A Grammar and Use

1 *–ing* clauses (Present participle clauses)

-ing clauses are used, like adverbs, to give more information about the action of the main verb in a sentence.

- The *-ing* clause can come before or after the main clause:

  Speaking through his child, *Rustam plays down Gata's achievements.*
  His father has lived through him, **enforcing disciplines which would make the child what the man had always wanted to be.**

- An *-ing* clause does not have a main verb, and can only be used as part of a longer sentence.

- The *-ing* clause and the main clause of the sentence have the same subject:

  Kasparov *was contemptuous of Gata,* **saying** *that he had no potential to be world champion.*

- *-ing* clauses of this kind can be used instead of:

1 separate sentences:

  Rustam speaks through his child. He plays down Gata's achievements.
  Speaking through his child, *Rustam plays down Gata's achievements.*

2 *and* clauses:

  His father has lived through him and enforced …
  His father has lived through him, **enforcing** *…*

- *-ing* clauses can be used:

1 to describe actions which take place at the same time as each other:

  Walking to work *the other morning,* **I saw** *an accident.*

2 to describe one action that happened after another:

  Picking up my pen, I started *to write a letter.*

3 to give a reason:

  Wanting to develop his son's brain, *Rustam taught Gata to read at the age of two.*

-ing clauses are rather formal and are more often used in written English than in speech.

2 Expressing hopes

Notice how we express positive and negative hopes in short answers to questions about the future:

Positive hopes: Are you going to pass your exam?
I (certainly) hope so. I need to pass to get into university.
Negative hopes: Do you think Sally knows you're going to the party?
I hope not. I want it to be a surprise for her.

3 Expressing wishes and regrets

● *Wish* + Past Perfect
Use *wish* + Past Perfect to talk about things that happened or did not happen in the past:

  I wish I hadn't changed jobs.
  = I changed jobs and now I regret it.
  Jane wishes she'd worked harder at school.
  = She didn't work hard and now she regrets it.

● *Wish* + Past Simple
Use *wish* + Past Simple to talk about things which are true or not true now:

  I wish I knew my father.
  = I don't know my father and I'd like to.
  I wish he didn't live so far away.
  = He lives a long way off.

  I wish I had a sister.
  = I haven't got a sister and I'd like one.
  I wish I were* a bit taller/weren't* so short.
  = I'd like to be taller than I am.

* *Were* and *weren't* can be used here instead of *was* and *wasn't* because the Past Simple is being used to talk about unreal or hypothetical situations. This is the same as the use of *were* in second conditional clauses:

  If I were you, …

● *Wish* + *would/could*
Use *wish* + *would* or *could* + infinitive to talk about things you would like to happen:

  I wish my parents would stop treating me like a child.
  I wish Mike wouldn't leave his things all over the place.
  I wish I could stop smoking.

Wish + *would/wouldn't* usually refers to other people's annoying habits.
Could has the same meaning as *was/were able to.*

● **The verb** *regret*

There are several different ways of using the verb *regret* to talk about things you wish you had or hadn't done in the past.

1 *Regret + -ing* form

> *I regret leaving Spain.*
> *I regret having left Spain.*

2 *Regret + that* clause

> *I regret that I didn't stay in Spain.*

3 *Regret +* noun object

> *I regret my decision to leave Spain.*

B Vocabulary

1 *Get* + past participle

Get + past participle is often used instead of *be* or *become* + past participle, especially in informal spoken English. It is similar in meaning to a passive construction, but includes the idea of action:

> *I **got lost** in London.* = I became lost

Here are some more common examples of this construction:

> *to get arrested, to get caught, to get cut off (during a telephone conversation), to get delayed, to get divorced, to get dressed, to get drowned, to get elected, to get engaged (become someone's fiancé/e), to get fined, to get killed, to get married, to get promoted, to get stuck (e.g. in a traffic jam)*

Some of these verbs can also be used with reflexive pronouns:

> *After three months hard work, the politician **got himself elected**.*
> *I've been in this job long enough. I'd like to **get myself promoted**.*

2 *Speak* and *talk*

There is not always a very clear distinction between *speak* and *talk*.

● *Speak*

1 *Speak* is more formal than *talk*:

> *The president often spoke to his ministers about the country's economic problems.*

2 If you use *speak* without mentioning *to somebody* or *about something*, it usually suggests that there is a particular topic:

> *The professor spoke without a break for two hours.*

3 Other uses of *speak*:

> *My brother can speak four languages fluently.*
> = have a knowledge of a language
> *I was so shocked I couldn't speak.*
> = have the physical ability to produce words

● *Talk*

1 *Talk* suggests a two-way conversation, speaking with meaning, giving information:

> *It was a brilliant party. Everyone talked to everyone else.*
> *We talked all the way home.*
> *My nine-month-old daughter has just started talking.**

2 Other uses of talk:

> *Can we meet soon? We need to talk.*
> = discuss something important
> *We mustn't be seen together. People will talk.*
> = gossip

*Although *speak* is usually used to mean 'have the physical ability to produce words', we use *talk* when referring to babies' and young children's ability to do this.

Dinosaurs (Unit 3, page 24)

Dinosaurs were a large group of reptiles that dominated the earth for nearly 150 million years before becoming extinct. Dinosaurs ranged in length from the 60cm *Compsognathus* to the 27m *Diplodocus*, and in weight up to the 75 ton *Brachiosaurus*. They are traditionally classified as cold-blooded reptiles, but recent evidence on posture, skeleton and eating habits suggests that some may have been warm-blooded. All dinosaurs were probably egg-layers. Some, like *Allosaurus* and *Tyrannosaurus* were meat-eating bipeds, while others, for example *Brontosaurus* and *Diplodocus*, were plant-eating quadrupeds. Quite suddenly, about 60 million years ago, dinosaurs became extinct.

Deductions Practice (Unit 4, page 36)

Use these illustrations in conjunction with the ones on page 36 to make more accurate deductions about what the people are doing.

Departures	
FLIGHT NO	**DESTINATION**
BA.4071	PARIS
DA.6611	MADRID
AI.1994	ROME

Questionnaire
(Unit 5, page 47)

Students A and B: Read questions 5 – 8 opposite and make sure you understand them. Answer the questions for yourselves.

When you have finished, work in different pairs: **A** with **C**, and **B** with **D**. Ask each other the questions you have read and note your partner's answers. Then check your scores on page 158.

Finally, write two more questions of a similar nature to ask your groups.

5 If you saw someone shoplifting, would you:
a not worry about it, as the store has insurance anyway?
b pretend that you hadn't seen anything – you wouldn't want to get involved?
c report it to the manager immediately?

6 If a good friend of yours left their diary in your flat by mistake, would you:
a look through it quickly to see if there was anything about you in it?
b read the diary from cover to cover?
c put it in a drawer till you saw your friend again?

7 If, by mistake, you were given the bill from another table at a restaurant, and it was much cheaper than your bill, would you:
a pay the wrong bill and leave a large tip because you felt guilty?
b tell the waiter about his mistake?
c pay the bill quickly and go?

8 If you forgot your promise to water a friend's plants while she was away, and they all died, would you:
a tell her the truth and offer some compensation?
b rush out and buy identical plants and flowers so that she wouldn't know?
c tell her that you watered them but that they all caught a disease and died?

Role Play (Unit 7, page 67)

Student A: As a parent you are rather strict. You become very upset when your daughter does not do as she is told.

Make a list of some of the things that you might say to Sara. They can be statements, questions, or commands.

EXAMPLES:

I'd tell her to behave herself.
I'd tell her she couldn't go out for a week.
I'd ask her to do as she was told.
I'd ask her if she enjoyed upsetting me.

In pairs, discuss how best to deal with Sara. Try to agree on one or two things to say to her.

The Daughter's Story (Unit 7, page 70)

After school I met Caroline and as she had borrowed some records of mine I decided to go round to her house and collect them. I didn't really know her all that well, but she was very easy to get on with. She didn't go to the same places as I did but occasionally invited me to her house and things like that. I didn't usually go, simply because I couldn't be bothered. I hardly even saw her because we were at different schools, but when we met we had a good long chat and told each other all our news.

I didn't feel like going home anyway – perhaps it was because I was getting annoyed with my mother – well, not annoyed but it had become too tense being with her. We couldn't have a conversation without it becoming a row. I think she resented me a bit. I don't know why. It made things easier when I went out: I didn't have to face up to her. She really annoyed me sometimes because any row was forgotten too quickly, as though it was a routine, as though she wasn't bothered. Any arguments were never about anything important but she made them seem trivial immediately afterwards. She made me feel foolish and small. It was horrible, I hated it happening. I had begun to keep out of her way as much as possible.

Caroline and I had a good long talk about school and other things that worried us. We listened to records for ages in complete silence, not saying a word. I suddenly realised I had missed both buses and would have to try and get the eight o'clock one.

Caroline decided we should go to the loch until it was time for my bus. By the time we had walked across the causeway and back I had missed it.

'Mum'll go daft,' I said suddenly, beginning to worry.

'Look, she's going to be mad anyway, so it doesn't matter how late you are.'

That was fair reasoning, but I was hungry and cold and I thought I'd like to get home.

'No, I'd better go now,' I said and started walking through town. I was passing Elaine's house so I went in to see her.

'Your mother's going daft, she's been phoning everyone. She was here, she was in town twice, she's even been to the police station.' Elaine stopped and took my arm.

'Oh God,' I said. 'Oh no, you're joking.'

'Come in.'

I sat down and buried my face in my hands. She would be furious. What was I going to say to her? This meant another row.

'Elaine, I don't want to go home. Can't I stay here?'

'You'll have to face up to her as soon as possible. That's typical of you, Cathie, you run away from everything. You'll have to face up to it.'

Mrs Wilson came in. I was scared she would be angry too.

'Cathie, I'm going to the phone box to phone your mother now.'

My mother knocked on the door and Elaine answered. She stood quietly at the living-room door.

I was angry. There had been so much fuss and now she was acting as if nothing had happened. I thanked Elaine and got into the car. I didn't see any point in talking about it so I kept very quiet and pretended I wasn't bothered. She didn't even ask where I'd been until we were halfway home.

There was no way I could show her how hurt I really was. She simply didn't care about me and I couldn't let her see how much that hurt. It was no good: she had already forgotten it – just like everything else.

Story by Marion Rachel Stewart (14)

Michelangelo (Unit 9, page 90)

Student A: Look at this picture and read the text.

The picture shows a marble sculpture by Michelangelo Buonarotti (1475 – 1564). Michelangelo spent many years studying the human body so that he could master the secrets of the ancient sculptors of Greece and Rome. By the time he was 30 he was generally recognised as one of the outstanding masters of the age. At this time Pope Julius II asked Michelangelo to go to Rome to erect a magnificent tomb for him.

The project was an exciting one, and with the Pope's permission the young artist travelled to Carrara to select the blocks of marble from which he would carve the figures for the tomb. He spent more than six months buying, selecting and rejecting pieces of marble and planning a series of sculptures.

But when he returned to Rome and started to work, he soon discovered that the Pope's enthusiasm had cooled. We now know that the Pope's plan for a tomb had come into conflict with a plan even dearer to his heart: the ceiling of the Sistine Chapel.

It wasn't until he had completed his second commission that Michelangelo was able to return to his marble blocks and begin work on one of the figures – the 'Dying Slave'. Unfortunately he was then so famous that he was never allowed to finish the tomb he had dreamed about, although he did complete the sculpture of the 'Dying Slave' in 1516.

The 'Dying Slave' is now in Paris in the Louvre.

Some of the answers to these questions about Michelangelo and his work are in your text and some are in your partner's text. Read your text and answer as many of the questions as you can. Then ask your partner questions to find the other answers.

1 When was Michelangelo born and when did he die?
2 What was the first work the Pope asked Michelangelo to create?
3 Why did the Pope stop Michelangelo working on this commission?
4 How did Michelangelo react to the Pope's change of mind?
5 What was the second work commissioned by the Pope?
6 How long did it take Michelangelo to finish this work?
7 Where is this work?
8 When did Michelangelo return to his first work?
9 What is the name of the only part of this work that was finished?
10 Where can this be seen now?

Questionnaire Scores (Unit 5, page 47)

Add up your scores and then find out how honest you are!

1	a 3	b 2	c 1	5 a 1	b 2	c 3
2	a 2	b 1	c 3	6 a 1	b 2	c 3
3	a 1	b 2	c 3	7 a 2	b 3	c 1
4	a 1	b 2	c 3	8 a 3	b 2	c 1

If you scored 18 – 24, you are as honest as the day is long. Everyone can trust you and you have a clear conscience.

If you scored 13 – 27, you try to be honest, but don't find it easy. On the whole you try to do the right thing and you feel bad if you don't.

If you scored 8 – 12 points, honesty is certainly not your strong point. But you're probably just taking advantage of circumstances.

Valentine's Day Facts (Unit 11, page 104)

Valentine's Day is thought to derive from the unfortunate saint who fell in love with his executioner's blind daughter. He restored her sight by a miracle, but was still clubbed to death.

In the Middle Ages, people exchanged love tokens on 14th February, because it was believed to be the day when birds chose their mates.

The first recorded Valentine card was sent by Samuel Pepys, who wrote about it in his diary. In those days, people didn't choose their Valentine, they cast lots for them, and were expected to send them a present, usually a pair of gloves.

In the 19th century in Britain, people made an art form out of Valentine cards, but not all took the hearts and flowers approach. In 1827, when postage was paid on delivery, the Post Office received hundreds of complaints about insulting cards. Some of these were offensive enough to be classed as libellous, and in these cases, postage costs were refunded.

The Victoria and Albert Museum in London has a huge collection of Valentine cards, mostly from Victorian times. Some are very elaborate hand-cut paper constructions, often a bunch of flowers, which open to show a cage with a bird inside.

In Britain in 1990, £15 million was spent on 16 million Valentine cards, £1.04 million on postage, and £50 million on chocolates. Men spent more on cards than women, but women bought 56% of all cards. The Americans spent £446 million on cards and chocolates.

A survey carried out in Britain showed a 30% rise in teenagers trying to kill themselves on Valentine's Day.

A New York company has devised a clever way to make money out of flowers that are not sold on February 14. It offers a 'Drop dead' message service, sending wilted roses tied with a black ribbon.

A small village called Lover is the most romantic place in Britain on Valentine's Day. The post office handles thousands of cards and gives them the special village postmark: the name 'Lover' surrounded by doves and a heart. A few years ago a man from Saudi Arabia arrived in Lover and posted 64 cards.

There is now a new alternative: the Personal Columns of national newspapers. On 14th February, *The Guardian* usually has three or four pages of Valentine messages. (There are some examples on page 104.)

Arranged Marriages (Unit 11, page 109)

Arranged marriages are the rule in most of the Islamic world, Africa, South East Asia, India and Japan. Young people in these societies may not like the idea of such non-romantic practices, but they continue, not only because of cultural resistance to change, but also because they seem to serve the population's needs best. In Japan and India love marriages are accepted, but they account for fewer than half of all marriages.

In most North American Indian societies marriage was less a matter of romantic love than a practical economic arrangement. The conventional union of a young Indian woman to a man of her tribe was usually arranged by her family with great attention to what was best for the prosperity of the families, the tribe, and only incidentally, the woman herself. Often the young woman did not agree with her parents about who would be the best husband for her. Most Indian tribes had traditional stories which warned of terrible things that would happen to a young woman who did not accept her parents' choice of a husband.

Role Play (Unit 12, page 119)

Students B, C and D

Remembering the American cases mentioned in the article in Exercise 2, think of more imaginative punishments for these six crimes.

Work out your own ideas about how these offenders could or should have been punished.

Student B: You believe in making the punishment fit the crime.

Student C: You think the criminal should repay his debt to society, but you do not believe in prison.

Student D: You believe that criminals should pay some kind of compensation to the victims of their crimes (or to their relatives).

Now turn back to page 119 and discuss possible sentences in your groups.

Case Study (Unit 12, page 122)

Case Study Notes

Location: New York subway station

Time: 5 o'clock in the evening

Sequence of events:
1. Two young thugs were beating up an elderly man.
2. A bystander shouted to the young men to stop.
3. The thugs continued hitting the old man.
4. The bystander took out a knife and attacked one of the thugs.
5. In the fight one of the thugs was stabbed. His accomplice escaped.
6. The bystander dropped the knife and ran away.
7. The wounded man was taken to hospital where he died.

Current situation: Hundreds of people witnessed the incident, but no one has given the police a clear description of the bystander.
The police are appealing to the bystander to give himself up.

Information Gap (Unit 13, page 132)

Student A:
This table contains information about George's life. Ask your partner questions to find out the missing information.

EXAMPLES:

What did George do in 1990?
When did George marry Edna?
What's the situation now?

Date	Event	Situation now
1957	started job in car factory	▶
▶	married Edna	still married to Edna
1978	moved to Ford for manager's job	▶
1990	▶	smokes a pipe
This January	moved house	▶
▶	started evening class	attending evening class

Now make Future Perfect sentences saying how long George will have done or have been doing something for when he retires next week.

EXAMPLE:

When George retires, he will have been working in the car industry for X years.

Compare sentences with you partner.

The Crystal Ball (Unit 14, page 143)

Student A: You want to consult a fortune-teller.

You are 28 years old; your astrological sign is Virgo; you are thinking of getting married but have some doubts. You have a good job in an advertising agency but one of your colleagues has offered you the chance of going into a partnership with them. It could be a great opportunity, but it is risky and you are a very careful person by nature.

Apart from this, you have a younger brother who is a real problem. He didn't finish school; you've lent him a lot of money and he doesn't really want to work. Your parents are very worried about him too, and your father has to have a serious operation soon. You are thinking about taking a holiday abroad to get away from everything, as you feel exhausted.

You want to know:

- about the job.
- what to do about your brother.
- whether your father is going to be all right.
- whether you should get married or not.

Have some questions ready to ask the fortune-teller.

Now consult the fortune-teller.

Unit 1, Stage one, 9

I call myself a househusband. I'm at home all the time, and I do everything a housewife would do. When we first got married it was obvious my wife didn't enjoy housework, so it was common sense that I should start to do it while she went out to work. My wife's a lawyer. I trained as a horticulturalist. Being at home is sometimes pretty monotonous to say the least, but I like to see things clean and tidy so I keep busy. I did have to learn how to cook – my wife is a very good cook in fact and she often likes to take over the cooking at weekends – fortunately for me!

It isn't possible that we should all be the same, but I know a lot of men who'd love to do what I do. You'd be surprised. I'd imagine a lot of women don't want to be housewives or mothers. Some women would accept that they are not very good at looking after children. My wife admits she couldn't cope with it. I'm always losing my temper with the kids and it's a strain at times. I always thought I was very calm, but really, children push you to the limit. Men frequently don't realise this, I mean how hard it is being at home all the time.

Unit 1, Stage two, 2

Emma

Everyone says I'm quiet and shy. When I was young my sisters used to boss me around. Now they know I won't take any notice. It's good being the youngest because I can watch what they do wrong at school and at work. I'm not going to make the same mistakes. I suppose I take after my mother more than my sisters in most things. She's sensible and I am too. Well, most of the time. Only Alison is living at home at the moment but she's out a lot and she's starting a course at university this autumn. But I'm sure I won't mind being on my own. My sisters are much older than me so I've always done things on my own. The age gap means I've always been given a lot more attention. I wouldn't like to be an only child, though, because it would be boring.

Sara

When we were younger it normally used to be Alison and I who played together. I was always a hard worker at school so my parents didn't pressurise me too much. I think this helped Alison as she was always given a lot of freedom. I'm sure she'll do well at university as she's got a lot of confidence. Much more than me. She's got a mind of her own. I'm more like my younger sister – only she's much quieter. She spends a lot more time on her own and is a lot more tied to my mother's apron strings. Well, not independent is what I really want to say. She's going to France for a month with the school. Her flight leaves on Friday actually. Let's see how she gets on away from home for the first time. I always hung around with friends of my own age whereas she's often with Mum and Dad. She's hyper-intelligent; I know she'll get really good results at school. Being the oldest sister has helped me to be more responsible and I do feel protective towards my sisters. I'm certainly not going to get married for some time, but when I do I'll definitely have more than one child. I think it's good to grow up with brothers or sisters. You're never alone.

Alison

I'm more outgoing than my younger sister and Sara's more sensible than me. Actually Sara and I are like chalk and cheese in many ways. We've always had our ups and downs but basically we get on really well. My parents kept more of a check on what Sara was doing than they did with me. They used to have a lot of rows. But with me they gave me more freedom to make up my own mind about what I wanted to do. Sara had to grow up a lot faster. I don't think I'll settle down as quickly as she has. I'm starting a course in economics at university in the autumn. Term starts in October and I know I'll enjoy being independent. I think Emma has grown up more slowly because she's got older sisters but fewer responsibilities. Because Sara and I aren't at home a lot, Emma's like an only child in many ways and I think she might find it more difficult to leave. I like having two sisters because it's easier to relate to them than boys. But the worst thing about being in the middle is that you end up being compared to your sisters on both sides and being squashed between them. I have to live up to Sara and be compared to Emma. I'm going to miss them when I'm away I'm sure.

Unit 1, Stage two, 4

1 Everyone says I'm quiet and shy.
2 I'm sure she'll do well at university.
3 Her flight leaves on Friday actually.
4 They used to have a lot of rows.
5 Term starts in October and I know I'll enjoy being independent.

Unit 2, Stage one, 5

a She talks very fast indeed.
b We don't have much leisure time these days.
c The coffee is over there on the table.
d It's really hot today.
e It won't be necessary to take the car today.

Unit 2, Stage one, 8

I'll never forget arriving in Brazil. It was half past five in the morning and it was just getting light when my plane touched down at Rio airport. Even at that time of the morning the airport was busy. Everyone got off the plane and crowded into the airport bus. Five minutes later we were all waiting in a queue to have our passports stamped. Next, baggage retrieval and the long wait for our cases. On this occasion my case did not appear for at least ten minutes. I was sure it had been sent to Australia or Japan. Five minutes later I was in the busy Arrivals Hall. Everything was very strange – people were rushing here and there, everyone was speaking a language I didn't recognise. I went straight to the tourist information desk and asked about taxis to the city centre. The receptionist was telling me where to find a taxi, when a short man with a cap grabbed my suitcase and said, 'Taxi? This way, please.'

Unit 2, Stage two, 2

Man

Well, I suppose when I think about learning a language I remember my experience at school. Like most people in England I learnt French at school, well didn't learn it actually. So when I started French they never really bothered about us being able to speak the language … or understand it. No, we had to basically learn the grammar and do a lot of translation from French to English and vice versa. I also remember learning all the verbs by heart … *Je suis, tu es, il est, nous sommes, vous êtes,* you know, and we had to do this with all the tenses. Then the teacher used to always give us a test in class. Smith *avoir* or Ferguson *acheter.* And the exams, the exams were mainly grammar, essays and oh yes translation, translation of course. Then of course the first time I went to France, well, disaster – I couldn't understand a thing and I could say even less. I felt really bad and very frustrated. I just hadn't had enough practice and everyone spoke so … fast, for me at least.

Girl

I've never been much good at languages; at school I found it really hard work. But when I got a job in Italy I had a real incentive to learn the language. I bought a lot of books and I did a course at a language school. All the teachers were Italian of course and it was very useful. There was a lot of conversation and practising in class. We also did dialogues in situations which we were going to meet outside. Obviously it's a tremendous help living in the country, hearing the language all the time and having to speak it as well. I had a lot of Italian friends so I had plenty of opportunity to speak. You make mistakes, it's unavoidable, but it's part of learning. I remember going into a chemist, a *farmacia,* to try and get some shampoo. I didn't know the word for this in Italian. So I said, '*Vorrei sappone per i cappeli,*' which means 'soap for the hair'. The woman who was serving me looked puzzled and said, '*Scusi?*' or something like that so I repeated the same thing again nervously. Well, she thought for a bit and said, 'Ah, shampoo!' and I said yes, feeling like a right idiot. Still, that's all part of picking up a language, isn't it? I also found it a bit difficult to use the polite forms for *you* in Italian, um, *lei* and *loro* I think, but I've forgotten a lot. It's hard to know when to use the polite form and when to stop using it and say *tu.* We don't have that problem in English, it's just *you* all the time. Another thing: I think the language introduces you to the culture of a country. With Italian I could discover more about the food, the history, the art and the people, their customs and character.

Unit 3, Stage one, 7

There were five of us on the *Rose-Noelle* when we set sail on the 21st of June. For the first hundred miles or so everything was fine. Then suddenly on the third day, completely without warning, a huge wave crashed into us and we capsized. I came up quite near the overturned boat. It only took me a minute or two to swim to it. We all climbed on to the upturned hull and held on tightly. To start with we ate rice and drank sea water, then someone managed to catch a fish, which we had to eat raw. It tasted terrible, but at least it kept us alive. We floated about for eighteen days before we hit North Island. It's incredible that we all survived.

Unit 3, Stage two, 1

1 I couldn't believe it. I thought he was having me on, you know. I mean, as far as I was concerned we were still getting to know each other. After all, we'd been going out together for only three months. We'd never spent more than an evening together. He said he felt as if he'd always known me. When he asked me, I just felt like laughing, until I realised he was serious. In the end I surprised myself by saying …

2 She'd been staying with a friend, or so she said, but I never really believed her. As soon as I saw her again, she seemed different – I couldn't quite put my finger on it – just different – happier, more relaxed, I don't know what it was. At the time I was just glad she'd come back. I didn't say anything; I made out that everything was normal. Things got worse pretty quickly after that. About a week later she just came out with it. She told me she'd been …

3 I'll never forget that day. It had started quite normally, the usual rush; I stumbled out of bed, grabbed a quick cup of coffee. I didn't have time to open the post or look at the newspaper. I didn't even say goodbye properly. I can't remember anything about the drive to the station – I suppose it was like every other day. I know I managed to get a seat right at the back. We'd only been travelling for about twenty minutes when it happened. The next thing I remember was coming round in hospital. One of the nurses said I'd been very lucky. Apparently, the man I'd been sitting next to …

4 Of course I never really thought it'd happen to me, but no one ever does, do they? The funny thing is, the evening before the phone call I'd been thinking about what I'd do if my number came up. I suppose everyone does that, don't they? The usual fantasies, you know, buying a bigger house, giving up work, having a long holiday, I'd even planned what I was going to say …

Unit 3, Stage two, 4

1 I thought he was having me on.
2 I didn't have time to open the post.
3 Last year I went to Canada and the USA.

a me and you
b No I don't
c in the end
d It's an idea of his
e So is she
f He's in Australia or New Zealand
g easy to understand
h He isn't late
i a law of nature

Unit 4, Stage one, 1

John

I've had this fear for as long as I can remember. My father was scared of dogs, so that must be where I got my phobia from. He used to tell me that all dogs were dangerous even if they looked friendly and were wagging their tails. Consequently I was convinced that any dog I saw would attack me, and I organised my whole life around this fear. Parks were a complete no-go area, and I could never walk along roads with long drives in case any dogs ran out.

Sue

My mother says I loved dolls until I was about five, so it can't be something I was born with. It just crept up on me. I know when I was seven my aunt tried to 'help' me get over my fear. It was awful: she got a doll and pulled it to pieces to show me that it wasn't a real person. Of course I went absolutely crazy, and I had all these nightmares about dolls' bodies, you know, with their arms and legs all scattered about. Yes, that must be when my fear turned into a real phobia. Now, whenever I see a doll, I feel sick and dizzy, and I feel I'm going to die. I just have to get away from it.

Nigel

When I was sixteen I was in London and I had to travel on the underground. The train I was in – it's horrible even talking about it – it just stopped in a tunnel. I just couldn't stand it, and ran up and down the carriage screaming my head off. Eventually, of course, it started moving again, and I got off at the next station. I felt so weak I thought I was going to pass out. Since then I've avoided travelling by tube. I hate feeling trapped so I suppose that must be why I'm phobic about lifts, too. In my last job I worked on the 14th floor of an office block, but I used the stairs, not the lift. I occasionally took the lift just to prove to myself that I could do it, but I always made sure there were other people in it. Once the lift stopped between floors and hovered there for several seconds. I couldn't handle it, and I started clawing at the doors to get out.

Maureen

I come over all panicky. I get this awful feeling that I'm not really there. I can cope quite happily with the local corner shop, but a trip to the supermarket can become a nightmare. I hear my own voice saying: 'I must get out!' That's why I think I might be suffering from a kind of agoraphobia.

Unit 4, Stage one, 7

1 One of my main fears is mid-air collisions, because I live quite near to Gatwick Airport and from my bedroom window I can see all the planes landing and taking off and I wonder how on earth they miss each other. And when I'm flying along I'm forever looking out of the window to see if anything's near that we might collide with, you know.

2 I regularly fly all over the world in my job, but I must say I'm not entirely happy. I still get butterflies in my tummy, and I think anybody who says, 'I'm not frightened' must be kidding themselves – I mean, I think we've all got human emotions and you have to have a little bit of fear because it's not a natural thing to get into a heavier-than-air machine and go up into the sky.

3 All other modes of transport you can stop and get out, but once you get into an aeroplane you can't say, 'Excuse me, I want to get off' or 'Excuse me, I'm leaving.'

4 I think a lot of it's to do with the fear of stormy weather and turbulence and what the aircraft can stand as regards turbulence.

5 Basically you're putting yourself into the hands of other people. You've got no control. You can't even see them. You get on the plane. They strap you in and that's that. They say things like, 'Don't worry, we'll be doing this and that.' And then off you go. You never even see them. As far as we know there may be no one there at all on the flight deck. That's what I don't like.

6 My husband's all right, it's me that's holding him back. We are offered lots of holidays, but I won't go. I flew for a while and it just got worse and worse every time. I had to take valium, but it had no effect on the plane – then when I got on the bus at the other end, I went out like a light.

7 I couldn't breathe, I couldn't swallow, I couldn't get out of my seat. I couldn't even go to the toilet, anything like that.

8 I'm an actor and I used to fly around all over the world, but then I had a bad flight where we nearly crashed and my fear of flying developed from that – it got worse and worse to such a point that it became a total phobia. I couldn't even go to the airport and drop somebody off. I had to stop the car and get out and be physically sick – that's how scared I was. I was petrified. I've been to see psychologists. I've been to see doctors. I've had advice. I've had pills, jabs, everything. Nothing has worked.

Unit 4, Stage one, 9

1 I organised my whole life around this fear.
2 My mother says I loved dolls.
3 My aunt tried to help me …
4 I hear my voice saying …
5 … from my bedroom window …
6 … I wonder how on earth they miss each other.
7 … a little bit of fear …
8 … go to the airport and drop somebody off.

1 You may experience symptoms of your fear anywhere.
2 Many people learn to tackle the problem themselves.
3 If you go to a psychotherapist, you'll be taught techniques to use.
4 These techniques are helpful if you feel an attack coming on.
5 The best treatment for you depends on your symptoms.
6 Most sufferers make complete recoveries.

Unit 5, Stage one, 1

Part 1

Man: We were talking earlier about this other business of somebody dropping a ten-pound note on the floor or whatever.
Woman 1: Yes.
Man: I mean what about that situation? If somebody dropped a ten-pound note on the floor, I mean first of all would you tell … would you tell them?
Woman 1: Yeah, I definitely would.

Part 2

Woman 1: If I thought the person was in the same room as me, I would, yes I would try and find who the person was who'd dropped it. It's always … I've never found a lot of money at any one time but there is always the thought in your mind of what effect keeping the money might have on somebody else. This ten-pound note might have dropped out of the purse of a little old lady who only had this left for this week. And that is sufficient to make me feel awful about keeping the money.

Man: If the person said, 'This is my money,' and you didn't think it was their money, would you think that the only honest thing to do would be to give them the money? Or would you hold the money back?

Woman 1: Well, I think you probably wouldn't be able to hold onto the money because then you would have a confrontation and an argument with a person you didn't know. You can't just confront somebody with that. You can't say, 'This is not true. You're dishonest.' You have no way of proving it.

Woman 2: I think it depends on how upfront you are there, doesn't it? You could say, 'Well, I can't believe it's yours,' but that experience was mine. I saw a ten-pound note. I picked it up immediately. Said to the person standing near it, 'Oh, did you drop this?' and he said yes, immediately took some money out of his pocket and it obviously wasn't his. All his money was used. This was a new ten-pound note so I knew that it wasn't his, but there are … I hesitated to let him know I was doubtful, but you see one thing I couldn't have done was keep it myself because I knew it wasn't mine. I would always try to give money back.

Part 3

Man: Well, like most people, if somebody said to me, 'Are you honest?' I would say yes because I don't think I tell lies … serious lies. I have never robbed anybody but there is one thing that is really dishonest that I do all the time, which is that if I'm in somebody's house and they're not there, I make long-distance telephone calls.

Woman 1: I'm never having you over!

Man: But more particularly in an office. If I'm in someone's office and I can use the phone, I often make a telephone call to Canada or Brazil or anywhere. I say to myself, 'If I'm quick, nobody will notice on the phone bill.'

Woman 1: I admit I have a strange sense of ethics. If it's a corporation, something 'faceless', I usually have no qualms about doing something illegal or dishonest. I remember one place where the … where the ashtrays actually said 'stolen from Brendan's Bar'. But somehow that's all right. It doesn't harm anyone. But if it's a person I know then it's different. I think, 'If I'm not straight with this person, I'll feel bad.'

Woman 2: Sometimes you need to tell someone a white lie to avoid upsetting them. If you always tell the truth, sooner or later you end up hurting someone's feelings. What I mean is that most of us alter the truth a bit where it's too unpleasant or difficult for someone to accept. I really don't see anything immoral about that.

Man: But that's not dishonest, that's being sensitive. You're doing that so as not to hurt somebody's feelings. You're not doing that to be dishonest.

Unit 5, Stage one, 4

If somebody dropped a ten-pound note on the floor …
I've never found a lot of money at any one time.
I picked it up immediately.
He immediately took some money out of his pocket.

1 Is there any salt and pepper?
2 He's an American.
3 The plane's arriving at 1 p.m.
4 She never asked anyone to help her.
5 Take it off at once!
6 If you call us tonight, we'll be in.

Unit 5, Stage one, 5

1 If it's a corporation, I usually have no qualms about doing something illegal or dishonest.
2 If somebody dropped a ten-pound note on the floor, would you tell them?
3 If I'm quick, nobody will notice on the phone bill.
4 If I'm in somebody's house and they're not there, I make long-distance telephone calls.
5 If I thought the person was in the same room as me, I would try and find who the person was who'd dropped it.
6 If I'm not straight with this person, I'll feel bad.

Unit 5, Extension

Announcer: Today we continue our series about famous criminals with the story of the king of conmen, otherwise known as Stanley Lowe.

Journalist: Stanley Lowe was in the great tradition of conmen. He wasn't the first one to sell the Eiffel Tower. In the 1920s it had in fact been sold twice by 'Count' Victor Lustig and Daniel Collings. But shortly after the Second World War Lowe made it three times unlucky for a Texan who paid $25,000 to Lowe for the Tower to use it for scrap. Fortunately for the Texan, the con was discovered and Lowe spent six months in a French prison. In fact, by the time he retired at the age of 50, Lowe had spent more than 16 years in prison for a series of offences, all involving cons of one sort or another. This didn't stop him conning a Japanese tourist out of $10,000 to help restore London's St. Paul's Cathedral. The tourist was partly convinced by the fact that Lowe was dressed as a clergyman.

Lowe claimed he simply couldn't help himself; people everywhere, it seemed, wanted to give him money. His life as a conman at its high point provided him with fast cars, expensive suits, five star hotels and jet-set vacations. Sadly, he ended his life living in a bedsit with all the money and cons just a memory, and possibly reflecting that crime, after all, doesn't pay.

Unit 6, Stage one, 7

Our celebration is different from the Western one. It begins somewhere between the 10th of January and the 19th of February. It's calculated by the appearance of the new moon. In Chinese it's called *Yuan Tan* and it's celebrated in Chinese communities all over the world. The Chinese believe that evil spirits are common at this time and so some of our customs are based on driving them away. So we let off firecrackers to frighten them away and we close the doors and windows so they can't get into the house while the family are having their meal. Also at this time offerings and presents are given to the god of wealth and the god of the house, also to the family's ancestors.

What I like most about the celebrations are the street parades, with dragons which symbolise good luck. They're made of either cloth or paper, and the eyes and mouth are worked by people underneath. The dragons can be very large and heavy too. Sometimes you need as many as fifty people to carry them. Then they run and twist along the streets. It's quite clever. With the dragon there is usually a lion which is also worked by people. It's called *Sze Tsu*, and compared to the dragon it's very funny and very theatrical.

Unit 6, Stage two, 2

Interviewer: How long have you been here now?
James: About three-and-a-half years, almost four years.
Interviewer: And impressions of Mexican characteristics?
James: Um, I think probably the most … the first thing you should mention really is that, um, the Mexicans are much more friendly than the English or the British and that's the first thing you notice when you come here.
Interviewer: In what way? Can you specify?
James: Um, they're much more open. They're much more ready to talk to you, I mean I've, um, got into conversations on the bus, you know in the street, waiting to cross the street. You know there's never a moment when they wouldn't be willing to have a conversation. It doesn't matter who they are … So they tend to be a lot more friendly but having lived here for a while I think you begin to realise that's rather superficial in one way. You know, and after several years you realise that of all the Mexican friends you've got, you've got hundreds of Mexican friends who are workmates, who are people you know fairly well where you're working, but at the weekend or something like that you really don't have a great number of Mexican friends. I think it's hard to get a very close relationship with a Mexican.
Interviewer: What else strikes you as positive maybe?
James: Um, they seem to be much more willing to air their personal feelings in public. I don't know whether that's positive or negative. It seems to work for them. If they're having an argument with their husband or boyfriend or girlfriend or something, it doesn't really matter where they are and to me that seems a lot more healthy than the way we go about these things. Um, so you'll see people in supermarkets having arguments, what seems to be quite personal arguments. And that immediately strikes you as quite odd coming from another culture.
Interviewer: Something a lot of people talk about, I don't know if you agree with it, is the concept of time or the attitude towards time. I don't know whether you've found that.
James: Although they're more relaxed about time, I think this 'mañana' business is probably exaggerated. It doesn't bother me at all. I mean I was like that before I came so I'm in my element here, you know. But I think it depends on the circumstances, and when it comes to business and appointments and so on I haven't, personally haven't, noticed that Mexicans are that bad at keeping appointments.
Interviewer: What about before you came? What was your impression and did that change after you came in terms of what the people were like?
James: I think it probably did. Yes. Um, the stereotype of a Mexican is this sort of, um, man with a big sombrero and pistols wearing a blanket or something. But we don't really have that much information about Mexico living way over the other side of the globe, and so we tend to rely on the stereotype – and then when you come here you realise that, especially in Mexico City – I mean it's a very modern city, it's a very, um, cosmopolitan city, and the metro is ten times better than the London underground, you know. I was quite taken aback.

Unit 6, Stage two, 4

1 They tend to be a lot more friendly …
2 Having lived here for a while …
3 I haven't noticed that Mexicans are that bad at keeping appointments.
4 But I think it depends on the circumstances.
5 A Mexican is this sort of man with a big sombrero.

Unit 6, Stage two, 5

First part

Interviewer: So both of you have lived in Britain. How long were you there?
Patty: I was there about four years.
Interviewer: And you, Conchalupe?
Conchalupe: I was there a year-and-a-half.
Interviewer: And before you went, what was your picture of British people?
Patty: I didn't have a fixed idea. But people told me it was very difficult to get to know British people.
Conchalupe: Yes, I was told that they were cold, distant and very hard to make friends with. That was the stereotype.
Interviewer: When you were there, how far did you change your view? Or did you form a different view of people's characteristics?
Conchalupe: I changed my original idea. Um, I found that while it was true that outwardly they were cold, they were distant, they were quiet and very serious; when you made contact with them they could be open and friendly and could be very close friends.
Interviewer: How about you, Patty?
Patty: Yes, I also changed my ideas. I think they are very kind. I mean even if you ask for information in the street, they take it very seriously.
Conchalupe: You can lose a friend if you are late for an appointment.
Patty: Yes, that's true. As far as time is concerned, they are very rigid. You can really annoy people if you are late for something. It was very difficult to adjust to this in spite of being there several years.
Conchalupe: Yes, for me too.
Patty: I mean if you are invited to a dinner party by an English friend and they say 8 o'clock and you arrive at 9, well it's really terrible, whereas in Mexico it would even be a bit impolite to arrive exactly at 8 o'clock. At 8 o'clock you're in the middle of getting everything ready and if … if someone arrives exactly at 8 o'clock, you are a bit shocked because you expect them to be at least half an hour late. You are socialising.

Second part

Interviewer: What other things would you say are typical?
Patty: They are very good hosts. If you break the ice with

them and they invite you to their house, they make you feel really welcome and if you do break the ice with people, you've got a friend for life. I found that with the few people I got to know. And also they are shy, but if you take the initiative, they sort of open up.

Conchalupe: Yes, they are extremely patient compared to us. Queueing is a good example. They queue patiently for everything and the worst thing you can do is push in front of someone in a queue. I think it's a way of being respectful to others. Also coming back to the question of time, I admire that because it means respect for other people. But, on the other hand, I also feel that the importance of time makes people very tense. You can see this as the British try very hard not to express their emotions or feelings.

Patty: Another thing I remember is that they talk a lot about the weather. If you say hello to someone, they say, 'Nice day, isn't it?' or they say, 'Awful weather. Isn't it cold today?' and that is the way in which you start a conversation.

Conchalupe: Oh yes, I feel that the people there are very strict. For them, rules are rules, and it's very difficult to convince them there is a reason for breaking the rules. For example, once I parked my car on a double yellow line just for five minutes and a traffic warden gave me a ticket. I said, 'But it was only a few minutes. Come on!' She said, 'Either it's illegally parked or it isn't.' Even though I argued with her, I still had to pay a fine.

Unit 7, Stage one, 2

1 **A:** Hmm … I think it's a general … to me it was a fight for freedom, you know, I think that's what being a teenager is all about, isn't it?
   B: And wearing those clothes is part of that …
   A: Just every part of it: you know, what time you can stay out at night and who your friends are and what you wear and what music you listen to …

2 **C:** That's another thing about being a teenager – you're very embarrassed about your parents, they're the biggest bane of your life …
   D: Oh they're so embarrassing!
   C: And if your father says, 'Let's go out,' you think, 'No! I can't be seen out with my dad, people will just laugh at me and …'
   D: That's the thing … parents actually have quite a lot of power especially during the teenage years you're still going to school. You don't have that kind of financial power to buy the clothes you want. You don't have the money. They can literally say, you know, if you say to your parents I want to buy this record or this clothing or …, they can stop you. It's quite a simple power and they can kind of control your life.

3 **Interviewer:** Rob, how do you get on with your parents?
   Rob: I get on very well with my parents, they, I get on well with them. We're very friendly and we don't argue much, about much.
   Interviewer: Is there anything that you do find you differ in opinion with them about?
   Rob: Not really, I tend to accept what they say as what's right, 'cause they're above me and they know what's right. Sometimes I disagree with them about what time I ought to be home when I'm seeing my friends, but I don't really have much that I argue about with them.

Interviewer: If you disagree with them about the time that you should be home, why is it that you disagree? Is it because you think that you are responsible enough to stay out later?
Rob: No, it's just normally that I, well, I suppose so, I think I, it doesn't really matter what time I get back, but, you know, they've got to cook the tea and they like me to be there with them. I think I can look after myself more than they let me sometimes.
Interviewer: So, you do think you're more responsible than they think you are?
Rob: Yeah, I think so.
Interviewer: Can you see trouble coming in the future with that?
Rob: Er, not really, I think, I think they'll sort of let me, er, stay out gradually later and look after myself more, but I can't foresee any trouble, no.

4 **E:** Well I didn't enjoy being a teenager at all.
   F: Why not?
   E: Erm … maybe it's because my mum was very good with very small children, but she didn't have a clue when it came to understanding what goes on in the teenage mind, which was surprising 'cause she'd been a teenager herself, but I felt I was always being criticised … I felt a lot was being expected of me on the one hand and not enough on the other, like I felt that I was expected to behave like an adult in one situation but only given the status of a child in the other … she always used to be telling me to tidy my room, erm, she used to tell me what to wear, which was why I was embarrassed to be a teenager because I could never join in with the fashions because my mother always told me what I looked like, she always told me, 'You look terrible in that' and that sort of thing. 'Don't wear this, don't wear that …'
   G: If I wanted to go out, you know when I was 14 or 15, my dad always sort of asked me where I was going. He had to know if I was going with anyone, what time I'd be back. It was a real bore.
   H: My dad did that until I was about 18. He wanted to know where I was going and who I was going with and he told me to be home by midnight at the latest. And when I got home, he always asked me where I'd been and who I'd met. It was really irritating. Once, he actually grounded me for a whole week.

Unit 7, Stage one, 7

And if your father says, 'Let's go out,' you think, 'No! I can't be seen out with my dad …'

My father walked into this, this party and grabbed me by the hair and nearly dragged me out shouting horrible things: 'You should be in bed by now. You're never going out again!' It was dreadful.

1 He burst through the door and just came out with it. 'I've passed my exam.' It was amazing.
2 … of course I had to stop. I got out and waited by my car. 'Morning, Sir.' He had a really booming voice. 'Did you know you were exceeding the speed limit?'
3 I'd just got into bed when I heard a voice from the garden. 'Are you awake?' So I called back, 'No, I've been asleep for nearly an hour.' That shut him up.

4 With my mother it was always a case of 'Don't do this' and 'Don't do that.'

5 It was always the same old questions, 'Where have you been?' or more often, 'Who have you been with?'

Unit 7, Stage two, 1

1 But, I mean there's a lot of valid concerns that parents have, but one thing that really irritated me about my father in particular was that he used to be concerned about what people would think, you know, if I wore certain clothes or something, and that so annoyed me, you know. What would people think? What would the neighbours think? And er, you know, if he had thought himself that it wasn't right to wear those things … but it wasn't really that, it was only that he would be embarrassed if other people thought it was critical instead of saying, well, you know, we'll decide what our own values are within the family …

2 Yes, now being on the other side I understand my parents' dilemma much better, because you suddenly realise how afraid parents are on behalf of their children, and why they put restrictions on you. Again, one tries not to be too restrictive because you want your children to grow up to be well-balanced and … and independent, but you're also afraid for them. It's a vicious world out there.

Unit 8, Stage one, 9

The people of Miami, which is a famous resort in Florida, thought they had become victims of a science-fiction nightmare when their pleasant residential neighbourhoods were invaded by giant snails. Perhaps 'invaded' is not the right word. The snails, which were as big as a man's hand, were actually brought to Miami by an unsuspecting tourist, who had found them in the tropics. In Florida the giant snails, which have plenty of natural enemies in other parts of the world, found a perfect environment.

Unit 8, Stage two, 3

Diane: … erm, I have cats, I own cats because I live alone and it's nice to have another presence around as such. It's nice to have something you can relate to and something you can feel is living, rather than just the TV, hi-fi, etc., and they are real, they are living. People mock how we say we can relate to animals, but it's not true, you know, they are … people like us!

Louisa: Well, I agree with that, although I haven't got cats. I've got two dogs called Apollo and Zeus, and …

Judith: Oh! What kind of dogs?

Louisa: They're German Shepherds, or Alsatians some people call them, erm, and they're extremely big and they take a lot of looking after, erm … but you know I love my dogs, I think, you know, my home wouldn't be the same, there'd always be a space if they're not there. If I came home and they're not there I'd feel so lost, because they come to greet you and they're just so affectionate, and they've got a lot of human qualities, as I say, you can really feel that they're just another person, and they don't answer you back either!

Unit 8, Stage two, 6

Judith: It's interesting that you've both got two animals. Do you find that they have quite different personalities?

Louisa: Oh definitely, yes. As I say, my two dogs actually come from the same litter and they're brothers, but they look different and they are totally different. One of them is … is a lot more boisterous and a lot more dominant than the other, erm, he eats a lot more and he's a bit bigger, but they're very, very different. Erm, one of them is more of a bodyguard … erm, sort of guard dog, as I say, he looks after the house a lot more than the other one, and the other one doesn't really mind who comes in, you know, he'll sniff them and sort of say hello, but won't … you know that really if it was a burglar they'd probably … he probably wouldn't do anything, but the other one would. He's more defensive and also to the other dog as well. If we go up to a strange dog and the strange dog starts to act a bit … a bit aggressively, then the more dominant dog will actually go and defend him, (yeah), so even though sometimes they have their own rucks at home, but, erm … you know that there's a strong family instinct there and, erm, incredibly different characters when you think about it, because we brought them up exactly the same. We bought them when they were eight weeks old and we … they've done everything together, they've never been apart, and yet they're so totally different.

Unit 9, Stage one, 8

Part 1

Cory: Well, when I was growing up, my father was in the military so we moved around a lot. So I think I changed schools about once every three years or so.

Interviewer: So how many schools did you go to in total?

Cory: Uh, that would have been, I don't know, about six I guess. We lived overseas twice. We lived in Germany first and then later on we lived in Tehran, Iran.

Interviewer: So tell me about the school you remember best, or that you have the clearest memories about.

Cory: That was definitely the school in Iran. And I remember it mostly negatively. I remember the country very positively but the school itself was horrible.

Interviewer: What was the school like, before you get down to likes and dislikes? Physically what kind of facilities did it have?

Cory: Oh, OK. Well, it was a very large school. It had been a hospital and it had students running from first to twelfth grade. That's primary and high school.

Interviewer: How many were there?

Cory: Oh, I don't know. Maybe about 3000.

Interviewer: 3000!

Cory: Maybe.

Interviewer: All American children?

Cory: All American. It was called the American school and it was run by one of the universities. It was a large complex of about three buildings. Had a large gym, a large paved open play area. Across the street was a baseball field. And um, I think it had a library, although I don't remember ever being in it. But it must have. It didn't have very many facilities. It didn't have any extras …

Part 2

Cory: Before we went to Iran I had always done very well in school. I'd gotten all A's, or a few B's but always done very well. And I liked school and I didn't have any problems. And when we got there the students were placed in one of the three groups – A, B or C.

Interviewer: How did they place you?

Cory: Based on your academic record. There was no exam as such. It was your previous record. So I was placed in A. And I did well in all my subjects except I failed completely French. Miserably. And the French teacher was horrible. She … her idea of teaching French was to sit down and make you memorise a paragraph and repeat it, and that was it. I didn't know what I was memorising. What it meant. Nothing. And er, I tried to cheat my way through the course but I failed that, and I just failed it. So that lowered my, er, grade average and they switched me into B.

Interviewer: How old were you then?

Cory: I guess I was in seventh grade which would have been about twelve, I think. And er, well, I felt horrible about that, and my grades just went way down after that. I started making D's and C's.

Interviewer: In everything?

Cory: In everything, yeah, except art.

Unit 9, Stage one, 9

1 My father was in the military.
2 It was called the American school.
3 It was run by one of the universities.

a	the French teacher	e	the teachers
b	the students	f	the hour
c	the oil industry	g	the infants
d	the United States	h	the undergraduates

Unit 10, Stage one, 10

Ladies and gentlemen, before we listen to tonight's concert – Mozart's 40th symphony – let me give you a few biographical details about Wolfgang Amadeus Mozart. He started playing the harpsichord when he was only three, and amazingly enough, only two years later he was already giving concerts and writing his first pieces of music. And by the age of ten he'd performed in half a dozen countries … As you can imagine, the eminent musicians who listened to him play were absolutely baffled by his skills.

The concerts that he and his older sister, Nannerl, gave were really more like circuses than musical events. For instance, Mozart was fond of tricks like playing the harpsichord with a cloth covering the keyboard or playing a difficult piece of music that he'd never seen before. Another thing which amazed people was that he could remember really complicated pieces of music he'd heard only once before and then reproduce them perfectly. He did this with a complicated choral piece once when he was fourteen.

The young Wolfgang had the cleverest manager there was in the 18th century music business: his own father, Leopold. Mozart senior, who was also a fine violinist and composer, realised he had a genius on his hands when he discovered that the four-year-old Wolfgang could be taught pieces from his sister's harpsichord book. Things were difficult for Leopold: it was a time when musicians in Austria were treated like servants. And so with two child prodigies he saw a good way of making money.

Wolfgang made his first foreign trip to Munich when he was five. And from then on his father took him to the most important European cities where he could show off the boy's talent. But travelling was an uncomfortable lifestyle, dirty and unhealthy. Food and sanitation were bad – as a child Wolfgang had smallpox and several other serious ailments as well.

As a child he was given a huge amount of flattery and adulation which led to his very high-spirited – and often plain rude – behaviour in the company of important people. The trouble was, even when he was thirty he was still behaving the same way with patrons whose financial support he depended on.

But on his travels he met and learnt from the finest composers of the age: in Vienna, Joseph Haydn; in London, Johann Christian Bach. When he was sixteen, Mozart was already a master.

Unit 10, Stage two, 4

When I left university I had no idea what I was going to do. I toyed with the idea of doing teaching but finally decided against it. In the end I spent a year in Italy which was terrific. I was living in the north but I travelled around a lot all over the country and picked up some basic Italian, you know, enough to get by with. I was staying with some friends and to earn money I taught English so, ironically, I ended up teaching anyway but I really enjoyed it. The problem was what I was going to do and where I was going to work, and I kept putting it off. Finally I decided to do law, well, I mean start to train as a lawyer. That meant going to law school so I enrolled for a six-month crash course in London. It was completely different from anything I'd ever done. Quite interesting, I suppose, in many ways but it was very, very pressured; we had to learn everything like parrots and every morning we'd take down notes – dictated notes, I mean. And every afternoon we'd learn them by heart in the library. Um, after that I started work in an office as an articled clerk. Sounds very Victorian, doesn't it? I started to do my training to become a solicitor – that's a kind of lawyer. The only problem was I couldn't stand it. I was bored stiff 99% of the time. I thought I was going to be dealing with crimes, the police or interesting cases but it was nothing like that. I think perhaps it was mostly my fault; I should have checked more carefully the kind of firm I was going to work for. Anyway, to cut a long story short, I started to do a course in accountancy, and I decided, 'That's it.' I phoned them up and said I wasn't going back. Naturally it was hard, but they more or less accepted it and I knew I wasn't going to be a success.

Unit 10, Stage two, 6

1 interesting   2 ironically   3 suppose   4 library
5 carefully   6 several   7 secretary   8 police
9 naturally   10 history

Unit 11, Stage one, 1

1 Love is being nice to one another. I love playing with my friend next door because she shares her sweets with me.
2 Love is being kind, and holding hands and getting married.
3 It's needing someone, I think, needing to be with someone, missing someone when you've only been away for a day, something like that.
4 I think being in love is really depending on someone for certain things. I'm always falling in love.
5 There's a big difference between being in love with someone and loving someone or liking someone a lot.
6 Love is when someone keeps on smiling at you. And they give you presents.
7 Love is perfect togetherness, I think.

Unit 11, Stage one, 2

Jeremy: Do you think there is such a thing as love at first sight? Or is it just something we read in the newspapers?
Jenny: I think there's attraction at first sight. I don't think you can actually love someone without knowing them deeply, because it's just silly, you have to learn how they act when they wake up in the morning and things like that; the bad things come with the good things. You can't love someone without knowing them well and without being able to accommodate their horrible habits and things like that, but I think you can definitely fancy someone at first sight … because if they're attractive across the room and they look all sultry, then yes.
Jeremy: Yes, I think this is very true. I once met a woman on a train going to Basingstoke and fell deeply in love with her and never expected to see her again. But I did see her again and we formed a relationship and it was a disaster!
Mike: That's part of the thing about that moment, you know, I suppose being on a train and stuff. Travelling is quite romantic and you form certain links, but … I mean … love at first sight sounds like a nice idea but I don't know.
Margaret: I think as well that people who believe that they fall in love at first sight … I think they fall in love with the idea of love.

Unit 11, Stage one, 4

1 In recent years there has been a steady increase in the divorce rate.
2 You still owe me £20. I refuse to lend you any more money.
3 This year there has been a decrease in the number of marriages.
4 I'm very sorry for what I said. I didn't mean to insult you.
5 Sociologists say they expect the birth rate to increase next year.
6 Modern Valentine cards often contain humorous insults.
7 Marriage is a legal and moral contract between two people.
8 In the winter Britain imports red roses from the Canary Islands.

Unit 12, Stage one, 7

A: In this week's Crimespot we report on some of the crimes that have occurred in the last seven days. If you have any information which may be of use, please contact your local police station. Remember, you needn't give your name, and your call will be treated in the strictest confidence. Our first report tonight is from our Cardiff newsroom.

B: A motorist died after being karate-kicked during an argument with another driver. The incident took place at 11 p.m. last Friday evening in a busy part of Cardiff city centre. Police are looking for a youth in his early twenties. If you were there and saw what happened, please phone your nearest police station.

A: Next, we go over to our East Anglia studio.

C: British Rail have reported that Norwich Station has received a number of hoax bomb warnings during the past fortnight. On each occasion severe disruption was caused to train services and thousands of passengers were delayed. The hoax caller is female, has an American accent and is thought to be in her mid-twenties. Anyone with information should contact the Norwich police.

A: And now, two reports from the North West region.

D: We start with a warning. If you are offered an almost new car at a very low price, insist on seeing all official documents before parting with your money. In the last month a Manchester man in his early thirties has sold five or possibly six hire cars. The conman, who is a master of disguise, has been hiring the cars one evening, changing the number plates and selling them the next morning. On each occasion he has given different names and addresses to the hire companies. Needless to say, all were false.

And our second story concerns two incidents of arson. Liverpool police have issued this description of a man they wish to interview in connection with fires at two churches in the city. He is about 30 years old, of medium height and build, with black swept-back wavy hair and a pale complexion. He has been seen wearing a leather jacket, light blue jeans and pale, but dirty trainers.

A: That's all for this week. Remember, if you saw anything at all, however insignificant it may seem, please contact your local police station. A reward may be given for information which leads to an arrest.

Unit 12, Stage two, 2

Like a lot of people, you're probably worried about walking home late at night. The choices seem limited, don't they? Should you buy yourself a deadly weapon, or just lock yourself in the house and never go out? There are less extreme solutions, though, like self-defence classes or following some simple rules. Let me say straight away, I'd advise you against trying to use physical violence yourself. This really should be a last resort. Here are some of the more basic things you can do to help yourself.

As you probably already know, it is mainly individuals who are attacked, so try to go around in groups of two or more, and avoid badly-lit areas after dark. My advice would be to make sure your parents know where you are going, and what time to expect you back. Whatever you do, don't accept lifts in strangers' cars, and whenever you travel on a bus at night, make sure you sit near the driver.

If you are being followed, I'd advise you to knock on the nearest door and ask the people in the house to call the police. And here's another tip: I suggest you always carry some coins with you to throw in an attacker's face. This could give you enough time to get away.

If you're attacked, scream, shout and generally make as much noise as possible. If all else fails and you have to use force, then don't hold back – bite, scratch and kick as hard as you can and keep making a lot of noise. Run away as soon as you get the chance.

Finally, if an attacker wants your money, then give it to him. The way I see it, no amount of money is worth getting hurt for.

Unit 12, Stage two, 4

1 I'd advise you against trying to use physical violence yourself.
2 This really should be a last resort.
3 Whenever you travel on a bus at night, make sure you sit near the driver.
4 Run away as soon as you get the chance.
5 The way I see it, no amount of money is worth getting hurt for.

Unit 13, Stage one, 9

In almost every house we've been,
We've watched them gaping at the screen,
They loll and slop and lounge about,
And stare until their eyes pop out.
(Last week in someone's place we saw
A dozen eyeballs on the floor.)
They sit and stare and stare and sit
Until they're hypnotized by it.
Until they're absolutely drunk
With all that shocking ghastly junk.
Oh yes we know it keeps them still,
They don't climb out the window sill,
They never fight and kick or punch,
They leave you free to cook the lunch
And wash the dishes in the sink –
But did you ever stop to think,
To wonder just exactly what
This does to your beloved tot?
IT ROTS THE SENSES IN THE HEAD!
IT KILLS IMAGINATION DEAD!
IT CLOGS AND CLUTTERS UP THE MIND!
IT MAKES A CHILD SO DULL AND BLIND
HE CAN NO LONGER UNDERSTAND
A FANTASY, A FAIRYLAND!
HIS BRAIN BECOMES AS SOFT AS CHEESE!
HIS POWERS OF THINKING RUST AND FREEZE!
HE CANNOT THINK – HE ONLY SEES!

Unit 13, Stage two, 5

These days people are living longer. Obviously, as we get older we tend to have more health problems, although with advances in modern medicine many people can keep healthy well into old age.

Another problem is how people cope with retirement – from the psychological point of view, I mean. By the time you retire you will probably have worked for, oh, 45 to 50 years of your life. You'll have been following a routine based mainly on your work. You will probably have made some plans for when you retire; you may have decided to move to another area, to be nearer your children, for example. But you probably won't have sorted out exactly what you're going to do after you stop working. Understandably, many people put off making these decisions, so what frequently happens is that retired people become bored or apathetic. They've always had work to occupy them, and then suddenly they've got all this free time. It's very easy to feel depressed or useless.

On the other hand, retired people have a lot more opportunities available now than in the past. I don't just mean hobbies but education too. Some countries have even set up universities for retired people to study at. Adult education also offers every possible kind of course at a low cost.

If you are coming up to retirement, there are three golden rules to remember. First of all, you must eat healthily; secondly, keep fit by getting plenty of exercise; and thirdly, to go back to what I was saying before, keep your mind active. Healthy eating really means a balanced diet. By exercise I don't mean things like parachuting, but walking, cycling or swimming. Or why not go to keep-fit classes? It's a good way of making new friends. Keeping your mind active means taking up new interests, or doing those things you've always wanted to do, but could never find time for when you were working.

Finally, it's important to consider whether you will have your family near you or not. In some countries, the elderly often live with or very near to their children and grandchildren, which can make a big difference. Perhaps I should also mention that there are countries where people don't retire at all – they just carry on working.

Unit 14, Stage one, 7

Interviewer: How did you become a fashion model?
Model: Well, I was in a fashion show and I liked it so much I decided to join a modelling agency.
Interviewer: Is it a glamorous and highly paid job?
Model: Yes, in some countries. It's not as glamorous as some people think, you know. It's a lot of hard work and you're paid depending on how good you are. If you're good, people ask you to model their clothes.
Interviewer: And what kind of clothes do you model?
Model: All sorts of clothes: swimwear, beachwear, formal and casual clothes, dresses, skirts, jeans …
Interviewer: What kind of qualities do you need to be a successful fashion model?
Model: You have to be able to cope with criticism. You have to feel confident and know that you can do something and always come out on top.

Interviewer: Who criticises you?

Model: The audience. You get some people who just go to fashion shows to criticise, or sometimes you get criticised, you know, by your own colleagues and by your instructor, because you do make mistakes sometimes but you just have to learn to live with it.

Interviewer: What makes modelling hard work?

Model: Because you have, um, five-hour rehearsals and you're in, like, six-inch high heels and there's no time to sit and relax. Or you have a big fashion show with ten or twelve different pieces. It's really hard because you have to change ten or twelve times with all the zips and buttons. You have to get everything lined up and ready, but it's a rush.

Interviewer: What about watching your weight, your figure? Do you have to be careful about what you eat?

Model: Yes, you definitely have to be careful about what you eat. The most you can weigh is 120 lbs – that's about 55 kilos, I think. I watch what I eat a lot because I put on weight very easily. Um, I eat a lot of greens and a lot of fruit. I avoid sweets or snacks except when I'm socialising. But I hardly ever socialise because whenever there's a fashion show I have to look my best. I need to get a lot of sleep so my face doesn't look tired.

Interviewer: Do you have to have your hair done?

Model: Yes, in certain shows everyone needs to have their hair done in the same style. You have to get make-up applied too.

Interviewer: What do you like to wear when you're not modelling?

Model: Jeans and shorts. Not dresses.

Interviewer: What are the advantages and drawbacks of being a model?

Model: The advantages are you get to know a lot of people; you learn a lot more about clothing and how to dress. Um, you also learn a lot about your face, your body in general, how to arrange your hair and about how to apply make-up too. I'm more confident too. Bad things: er, that some people think you're stuck up if you're a model, you're too big for your boots. Long hours and hard work; um, a special diet. But I love it anyway.

Unit 14, Stage one, 9

Part 1: show some model

Part 2: clothes come company confident cope done gold growing know love only other popular socialising soft soles toes wonder

Unit 14, Stage two, 2

I was never really convinced by fortune-tellers or anything like that. But once a friend of mine wanted me to go with her to see a woman who could tell your fortune by reading the coffee stains in a cup. Once I was there I decided I might as well try it. The woman was, well, normal, not exotic-looking, or anything like that. She was middle-aged and I think she was a teacher actually. Anyway, I drank some Turkish coffee, then she told me to turn the cup upside down and let the remains of the coffee drip down onto the saucer. And then she took the cup from me and the stains, the coffee stains, had formed a pattern which is supposed to contain something personal from you, your, er, energy or

personality, something like that. Well she started to talk and told me to ask questions if anything wasn't clear. There was no way she could have known anything about me. She told me my lucky number was five. She also gave me the initials of people who protected me and who were a threat to me. She then told me I had two children, which was correct. But none of this was exactly earth-shattering. Then, out of the blue, she said the most surprising things: she said my husband was far away although we were still together. In fact he was working abroad at that time. She also said I was going to do a test on a date ending in the number five. This was a shock because I had the final exam for my thesis that month on the 25th of October. Then she said she saw a big change coming and we were going to live somewhere else surrounded by water, and she saw us living in a street of houses which were all the same. Incredibly enough we were going to live in Britain, which is an island, and we did live in a small street with identical houses. It was amazing. She didn't charge very much as for these people it's not a business. She didn't talk much about my personality but she knew what things were on my mind. Another thing is that they don't tell you if they see tragedies in your life. By the time she'd finished she was exhausted, so she only does two people at a time for about twenty minutes each. But she definitely had some special ability or power, I'm absolutely convinced.

Unit 15, Stage one, 7

Interviewer: Doctor, you have been accused of pushing your son too hard. How do you react to this?

Dr Rao: I never pushed anybody. It was my duty to assist my sons. It was their destiny. All children have these abilities. The difference is that most children do not have parents who care for them and concentrate on them. Everybody is a genius up to the age of ten. The parents' task is to discover the field in which the child's genius lies.

Interviewer: And are your sons going to succeed?

Dr Rao: I certainly hope so.

Interviewer: You have had arguments with your son's teachers who wanted him to go through the classes in the school in the normal way, like all the other children. Why didn't you accept this?

Dr Rao: I said to them, 'What do you expect him to do? How can you think he should still be doing simple arithmetic when he has already mastered calculus? What are you going to do about this boy? Isn't it your duty to make sure he achieves as much as he can? Isn't it your responsibility to help him rather than to hold him back?'

Interviewer: Don't you think that your interference might turn the school against your son?

Dr Rao: I hope not. If that does happen, I shall simply have to send him to a different school.

Unit 15, Stage two, 2

1 I wish I wasn't an only child. I'd love to have a brother or sister. When I was little I spent all my time with adults.

2 I wish I could afford to travel more. There are so many places in the world I'd like to see.

3 I wish I hadn't changed jobs last year. These days I've got so much to do I never seem to have any time to relax.

4 I wish my parents would stop treating me like a child. It makes me feel really stupid in front of my friends.

5 I wish I'd gone to university. I think I'm a bit too old to start studying again now.

6 I wish I could stop smoking. I know it's bad for me and cigarettes cost a fortune.

7 I wish my parents hadn't got divorced. Our house seems so empty since my father left.

8 I wish I could spend more time with my school friends. The problem is that most of them live too far away.

9 My big problem is my height. I'm so short people never seem to notice me at parties or in meetings, things like that. What I wish most is that I were a bit taller.

10 I've got a Brazilian girlfriend who speaks really good English. That's great, but I often wish I could speak Portuguese so that I could talk to her family and friends.

Unit 15, Stage two, 9

Interview 1

Interviewer: So you got great exam results and all the rest, but is there anything you really regret in your life?

Mick: Well, I regret leaving Spain. I had a wonderful time in Spain.

Interviewer: I didn't know you were there.

Mick: Yes, I went there about six years ago.

Interviewer: Was this for a holiday?

Mick: I lived there for three years (Oh really!) and I, um, had a really fantastic time in Spain. Just the sort of dancing and meeting people and going out. People are very spontaneous, but then I left because I had this burning desire to see the world, but I regret it because I think I was happiest in Spain.

Interviewer: But maybe if you hadn't left, you'd have been unhappy there because you would've wondered what the rest of the world was like.

Mick: Well, that's true.

Interviewer: Always hoping to leave … and never going.

Mick: I never found anything like it. I went to South America hoping that it would be similar to Spain, but it wasn't. The Spanish people are lovely – they always include you in everything that happens. I remember one time …*

Interview 2

Interviewer: So, did you have any burning ambitions as a child then?

Kathryn: Well, when I was little, I mean when I was really little – this was when I was like three or four – I used to want to be a footballer. I used to play football with the kids in the street, but I didn't realise at the time that you had to be male, so my dad had to take me on one side and tell me that …*

Interviewer: You had to be male?

Kathryn: Well … Well, I wanted to play for Liverpool of course, didn't I? Coming from Liverpool that's the ultimate ambition of most children, but it's most, like, most boys, but …*

Interviewer: So were you allowed to play at school?

Kathryn: No, no, we never played football at school – no, it wasn't for girls – we had to play netball or …*

Interviewer: Do you regret not having learnt it really, you know properly?

Kathryn: Well, no. We used to play, we used to play after school anyway, I used to play with my dad, because my dad, there was just me and my sisters, and my dad wanted to have sons, so we used to play football anyway. I mean I was good, but …*

Interviewer: So you wanted to be standing on … in front of the TV cameras with the World Cup above your head?

Kathryn: Well, World Cup, European Cup, you know.

Interview 3

Interviewer: So, what do you hope to be doing in ten years' time then?

Jenny: Well, not what I'm doing now.

Interviewer: Why not?

Jenny: Well, I'm stuck in the house at the moment. I've got three kids. I got married a bit young …*

Interviewer: They're all school age, are they?

Jenny: Yeah. They're sort of, the oldest is ten, the youngest is, what, six now, just six, so they're all at school. So I'm thinking about what I can do in my future.

Interviewer: And what have you come up with? Did you do any higher education or anything like that?

Jenny: Took 'A' levels, so I think maybe I could go back to college. There's nothing really I want to do – but I just want to do something different.

Interviewer: What? You're just lonely, you know, stuck in the house?

Jenny: Well, yes. It's really boring, really boring.

Interviewer: (Is there) any particular job you're going to train for?

Jenny: Well, I'd like something which is, you know, quite exciting. I'd like something where I could travel 'cause I like travelling. When I was younger I wanted to be an air hostess, but I wasn't tall enough, so I couldn't get the job.

Interviewer: Where do you hope to go?

Jenny: Anywhere.

Interviewer: I mean, just work abroad, or have a job that involves travelling?

Jenny: Have a job which involves travelling probably. I couldn't leave the kids for too long, so …*

Interviewer: Oh, of course yeah, you could put them in boarding schools or something.

Jenny: No, I wouldn't do that – no, I think they'd hate that. And I wouldn't feel happy doing that.

Interviewer: I suppose you'd regret it later because you'd missed them growing up.

Jenny: Yeah. I think you miss out a lot if they … if you send them to boarding school – I'd really regret that later I think, and I think they would. I think they'd hold it against me.

Unit 15, Stage two, 11

1 Did you have any burning ambitions as a child then?

2 So were you allowed to play at school?

3 Do you regret not having learnt it really, you know, properly?

4 (Is there) any particular job you're going to train for?

5 Where do you hope to go?

IRREGULAR VERBS

Infinitive	Past Simple	Past Participle	Infinitive	Past Simple	Past Participle
be	was/were	been	lie	lay	lain
beat	beat	beaten	light	lighted, lit	lighted, lit
become	became	become	lose	lost	lost
begin	began	begun	make	made	made
bend	bent	bent	mean	meant	meant
bet	bet, betted	bet, betted	meet	met	met
bite	bit	bitten	pay	paid	paid
blow	blew	blown	put	put	put
break	broke	broken	read	read	read
bring	brought	brought	ride	rode	ridden
build	built	built	ring	rang	rung
burn	burnt, burned	burnt, burned	rise	rose	risen
burst	burst	burst	run	ran	run
buy	bought	bought	say	said	said
catch	caught	caught	see	saw	seen
choose	chose	chosen	sell	sold	sold
come	came	come	send	sent	sent
cost	cost	cost	set	set	set
cut	cut	cut	sew	sewed	sewn, sewed
dig	dug	dug	shake	shook	shaken
do	did	done	shoot	shot	shot
draw	drew	drawn	shine	shone	shone
dream	dreamt, dreamed	dreamt, dreamed	show	showed	shown, showed
drink	drank	drunk	shut	shut	shut
drive	drove	driven	sing	sang	sung
eat	ate	eaten	sink	sank	sunk
fall	fell	fallen	sit	sat	sat
feed	fed	fed	sleep	slept	slept
feel	felt	felt	slide	slid	slid
fight	fought	fought	speak	spoke	spoken
find	found	found	spell	spelt, spelled	spelt, spelled
fly	flew	flown	spend	spent	spent
forget	forgot	forgotten	spill	spilt, spilled	spilt, spilled
freeze	froze	frozen	spring	sprang	sprung
get	got	got	stand	stood	stood
give	gave	given	steal	stole	stolen
go	went	gone	stick	stuck	stuck
grow	grew	grown	sting	stung	stung
hang	hung	hung	sweep	swept	swept
have	had	had	swim	swam	swum
hear	heard	heard	swing	swung	swung
hide	hid	hidden	take	took	taken
hit	hit	hit	teach	taught	taught
hold	held	held	tear	tore	torn
hurt	hurt	hurt	tell	told	told
keep	kept	kept	think	thought	thought
know	knew	known	throw	threw	thrown
lay	laid	laid	understand	understood	understood
lead	led	led	wake	woke	woken
lean	leant, leaned	leant, leaned	wear	wore	worn
learn	learnt, learned	learnt, learned	win	won	won
leave	left	left	write	wrote	written
lend	lent	lent			
let	let	let			

INDEX

The page numbers in **bold** type indicate Language review pages.

Vocabulary

Pronunciation

Thomas Nelson and Sons Ltd
Nelson House   Mayfield Road
Walton-on-Thames   Surrey
KT12 5PL   UK

51 York Place
Edinburgh
EH1 3JD   UK

Thomas Nelson (Hong Kong) Ltd
Toppan Building 10/F
22A Westlands Road
Quarry Bay   Hong Kong

© Simon Haines and Simon Brewster 1992

First published by
Thomas Nelson and Sons Ltd 1992

ISBN 0-17-555925-2

NPN 9 8 7 6 5 4 3 2 1

Printed in Hong Kong

Acknowledgements

*The publishers are grateful to the following for
permission to reproduce copyright material:*

Multi Media for the text (2) from
Sexwatching by Milton Diamond, devised
and produced by Multimedia Publications
(UK) Ltd 1982 (page 5)

The Observer for the texts (3 and 4) from
'Housewife Myths' in *New Internationalist*,
March 88 (page 5), the extract from
'Postmen bite back in vicious dog fight' by
Eileen Macdonald (page 81), the adapted
article 'Guinea-pig villagers google-eyed at
the prospect of 30 TV channels' (page 126),
the text adapted from The Body Report –
Part 7: 'Only Human? Health and our
Future' (page 130) and the adapted article
'Valentine's Day Facts' (page 159)

Ewan Macnaughton Associates for the
article 'Kindred Spirits', © *The Telegraph
Magazine*, 1990 (page 10)

Octopus Publishing Group for the extract
from *Dear Me* by Peter Ustinov, published
by William Heinemann Ltd (page 10) and
for the adapted texts from *The World's
Greatest Blunders* by Sue Blackhall (pages
49, 51)

Faber and Faber Ltd for the extract from
The Story of English edited by R. McCrum,
W. Cran and R. MacNeil (page 16)

Intercontinental Features for the Eureka!
cartoon by Munro Ferguson © Universal
Press Syndicate (page 24)

Times Newspapers Ltd. for the adapted
text 'Thinks Laterally' from *Funday Times
57* of 7.10.90 © Times Newspapers Ltd 1990
(page 31), the adapted article 'Awaiting a
Causeway to Romance' by David Black
from *The Sunday Times*, 21.10.84 © Times
Newspapers Ltd 1984 (page 112) and the
adapted article 'The boy that amazed the
world' by Richard Morrison from The
Sunday Times Magazine, 8.7.90 © Times
Newspapers 1990 (page 147)

The Guardian for the adapted text (2) 'Judge
sheds light on cottage phenomenon' (page
25), the adapted article 'A sigh is just a sigh'
by Darian Stibbe (page 111) and the article
'Misery of an honorary lad' (page 152)

Sport Newspapers for the adapted article
'Cyclops skull found in Sheffield' from
Sunday Sport (page 31)

V.A.G. (United Kingdom) Ltd for the
Volkswagen Golf advertisement (page 39)

News Enterprise Association, Inc. for the
cartoon 'The Born Loser' by Art Sansom
(page 41)

Racal Recorders Ltd for the Callmaster
advertisement (page 41)

NSP Catalogue Holdings plc for the three
advertisements from *The Innovations
Catalogue* (page 42)

Simon and Schuster Young Books for the
texts from *Horrible History* by Tim Wood
(page 54, 137)

Punch Publications for the cartoons
reproduced from *Punch* by Husband (page
44) Myers (page 78) Honeysett (page 87)
Brockbank, Breeze and Artz (page 115)
Matteson (page 126) Heath (page 146)
Burgin (page 148)

Times Books, a division of Random House,
for the extract from *The Russians* by
Hedrick Smith, © Hedrick Smith 1976
(page 61)

Panache Publishing Ltd for the extract
from *Chronicles of the Sixties* (page 64)

W. H. Smith Group plc for the extracts from
A Mother's Fondness by Marion Rachel
Stewart (pages 68, 157)

Harper Collins for the extracts from *The
Trials of Life* by David Attenborough,
published by Collins/BBC (page 74)

Virgin Publishing Ltd for the extract from
The Animal Contract © 1990 Desmond
Morris, published by Virgin Publishing
(page 78)

Company Magazine for the text *Pet Facts*
(page 78)

The People for the extract from 'Noah's Ark
Home', 29.7.90 (page 81)

Oxford University Press for the adapted
extract from *Lark Rise to Candleford* by Flora
Thompson (page 85) and the taped extract
adapted from *The Oxford Merry Christmas
Book* by Rita Winstanley © O.U.P. (page
164)

Thames and Hudson Ltd for the adapted
extract from *Exploring the World of the
Pharaohs* by Christine Hobson © Thames
and Hudson (page 88)

Phaidon Press Ltd for the adapted extract
from *The Story of Art* by E. H. Grombrich
(pages 91, 158)

Express Newspapers plc for the 'Cockney
Classicist' text adapted from an article in
the Sunday Express, 1.4.90 (page 94)

Macmillan Publishing Company for the
extracts from *Daughters of the Earth* by
Caroline Niethammer © 1977 Caroline
Niethammer (page 109)

Hamish Hamilton for the adapted extract
from *Daughter of the East* by Benazir Bhutto
Newsweek for the adapted extract from the
issue of 25.3.91 © 1991 Newseek, Inc. All
rights reserved. Reprinted by permission
(page 125)

Grosset and Dunlap for the text from *The
First Twelve Months of Life* by Frank Caplan
© 1971, 1972, 1973 by Edcom Systems Inc.,
New Jersey (page 133)

A. M. Heath for the extract from *Providence*
by Anita Brookner, published by Jonathan
Cape Ltd (page 141)

George Weidenfeld and Nicholson Ltd for
the taped extract from *Men* by Ana Ford
(page 161)

Minikim Holland B.V. for the taped
adaptations of the 'Love is...' article
published in *The Guardian*, 14.2.90 (page
169)   Love is... cartoon reproduced with
permission, © Minikim Caribbean.

Murray Pollinger for the taped poem from
Charlie and the Chocolate Factory by Roald
Dahl, published by Unwin Hyman Ltd and
Penguin Books Ltd (page 170)

Photographs

A.G.E. Fotostock: p. 7, 55(2), 57, 67; Action
Plus: p. 64; Allsport: p. 66; Aquarius
Picture Library: p. 93(4), 136, 149;
Barnaby's Picture Library: p. 28, 136;
Bridgeman Art Library: p. 30(2), 88(2), 90,
98(3); British Telecom: p. 7; Camera Press:
p. 73; J Allen Cash: p. 4; Bruce Colman: p.
76, 79; E.T. Archive: p. 88; Mary Evans
Picture Library: p. 15, 96, 125(5), 146;
Arlene Gottried: p. 149; Ronald Grant: p.
66, 136; S&R Greenhill: p. 64, 108(2), 131;
Robert Harding: p. 28, 54(3), 55, 109(2);
Derek Hudson/Sygma: p. 73; Hulton
Deutsch: p. 66; Image Bank: p. 14, 28(2), 48,
51, 54; NHPA: p. 75(4), 80(2); National
Medical Slide Bank: p. 140; Nework: p. 18,
64, 108, 142; Panasonic Business: p. 41;
Popperfoto: p. 85; Redferns: p. 94; Rex
Features: p. 10(2), 14, 64(2), 73, 93(3), 94,
101(4), 110, 118, 146(3); C Ridgers
Photography: p. 4, 8(3), 15, 84, 108, 115,
132(2); Peter Sanders: p. 66; Science Photo
Library: p. 4, 64; Tony Stone Worldwide: p.
14(3), 48, 54; Times Newspaper: p. 112;
John Topham Picture Library: p. 4(2), 48,
64, 88, 136

Illustrations

Claire Attridge, Philip Burrows, Jo Dennis,
Terry Thomas, Susan Andre, Josephine
Blake, Bethan Matthews, Jane Cheswright